The Transvaal Rebellion

The Transvaal Rebellion

THE FIRST BOER WAR, 1880–1881

John Laband

PEARSON
Longman

Harlow, England • London • New York • Boston • San Francisco • Toronto • Sydney • Singapore • Hong Kong
Tokyo • Seoul • Taipei • New Delhi • Cape Town • Madrid • Mexico City • Amsterdam • Munich • Paris • Milan

PEARSON EDUCATION LIMITED

Edinburgh Gate
Harlow CM20 2JE
United Kingdom
Tel: +44 (0)1279 623623
Fax: +44 (0)1279 431059
Website: www.pearsoned.co.uk

First edition published in Great Britain in 2005

© Pearson Education Limited 2005

The right of John Laband to be identified as author of this work has been asserted by him in accordance with the Copyright, Designs and Patents Act 1988.

ISBN 0 582 77261 3

British Library Cataloguing in Publication Data
A CIP catalogue record for this book can be obtained from the British Library

Library of Congress Cataloging in Publication Data
Laband, John, 1947–
  The Transvaal Rebellion : the first Boer War, 1880–1881 / John Laband. — 1st ed.
    p. cm.
  Includes bibliographical references (p.) and index.
  ISBN 0–582–77261–3
  1. Transvaal (South Africa)—History—War of 1880–1881. I. Title.

  DT2354.L33 2005
  968.2'046—dc22

                                                    2004063113

10 9 8 7 6 5 4 3 2 1
09 08 07 06 05

Set by 35 in 9/13.5pt Stone Serif
Printed and bound in Great Britain by Biddles Ltd, King's Lynn

The Publishers' policy is to use paper manufactured from sustainable forests.

Contents

List of maps and plates

Acknowledgements

One of the great pleasures of academic life is the collegiality and generosity of one's colleagues and associates. Without their unstinting assistance and hospitality this book, researched and written while shuttling between three continents, would have taken even longer to write than it has.

In South Africa I have especially to thank Dr Bridget Theron-Bushell of the University of South Africa and Dr Jackie Grobler of the University of Pretoria for so readily making their vital doctoral research available to me. Professor John Lambert of the University of South Africa was always bountiful with advice and assistance. Professor Adrian Koopman of the University of KwaZulu-Natal helped me with Zulu terminology. Dr Graham Dominy, National Archivist of South Africa, eased my path through the National Archives in Pretoria, and he and Anne provided me with welcome sustenance, accommodation and company. John Morrison, the Director of the Natal Society Library in Pietermaritzburg, arranged to give me special access to the rare books and newspapers in the collections under his charge. Glenn Cowley in Pietermaritzburg and Margie Murray in Cape Town cheerfully put me up while I was researching in various repositories in those two cities.

In Canada Dr Roger Sarty gave freely of his time and considerable expertise to read through my manuscript and made many astute suggestions and careful corrections. I was able to discuss the book very fruitfully with Professor Ian Beckett while he was at Wilfrid Laurier University for a conference, and he was generous enough to share some of his research material with me.

In England John and Hortense Casson looked after me as lavishly as is customary with them while I was working in the Public Record Office.

Casey Mein and Melanie Carter at Pearson Education have seen this book through all its stages with unflagging encouragement and understanding. Besides them, I also owe a debt of gratitude to Jill Birch, my copy-editor, Fiona Kinnear, who researched the pictures, and to Technical Art Services who made sense of the maps.

I must also thank what was then the University of Natal Research Fund for assistance in the initial stages of my research. I also gratefully acknowledge that financial support for this research was received from a grant partly funded by Wilfrid Laurier University Operating Funds and partly by the SSHRC Institutional Grant awarded to WLU.

In the 25 years I have been writing books Fenella has – and continues – to give me every support and comfort.

Note on measurements

Imperial rather than metric measurements are employed throughout the book since these reflect the practice in the contemporary sources where measurements are, in any case, usually more impressionistic than precise.

Publisher's acknowledgements

We are grateful to the following for permission to reproduce copyright material:

Punch, Ltd. for plate 1; HMSO for plate 2; The National Archives Image Library for plate 3; the South African Museum of Military History for plate 4; *The Illustrated London News* for plates 5, 6, 8 and 9; John Murray, Ltd. for plate 7.

In some instances we have been unable to trace the owners of copyright material, and we would appreciate any information that would enable us to do so.

Abbreviations

AAG	Assistant Adjutant-General
AG	Adjutant-General
AMS	Assistant Military Secretary
BPP	*British Parliamentary Papers*
BV	Argief Boeren Voormannen, papers in the National Archives of South Africa: Pretoria Depot
CTAR, GH	Government House, Cape Colony, papers in the Cape Town Archives Repository
DAAG	Deputy Assistant Adjutant-General
DAG	Deputy Adjutant-General
DAQG	Deputy Assistant Quartermaster-General
DQG	Deputy Quartermaster-General
GH	Government House, Natal, papers in the KwaZulu-Natal Archives
GOC	General Officer Commanding
HQ	Headquarters
JC	P.J. Joubert Collection, National Archives of South Africa: Pretoria Depot
NCO	Non-commissioned officer
NFF	Natal Field Force
NMP	Natal Mounted Police
RA	Royal Artillery
RE	Royal Engineers
SS	Staatsekretaris, Transvaal, papers in the National Archives of South Africa: Pretoria Depot

TS	Sir Theophilus Shepstone Papers, KwaZulu-Natal Archives
WC	Sir Evelyn Wood Collection, KwaZulu-Natal Archives
WO	War Office, papers in the National Archives (Public Record Office)

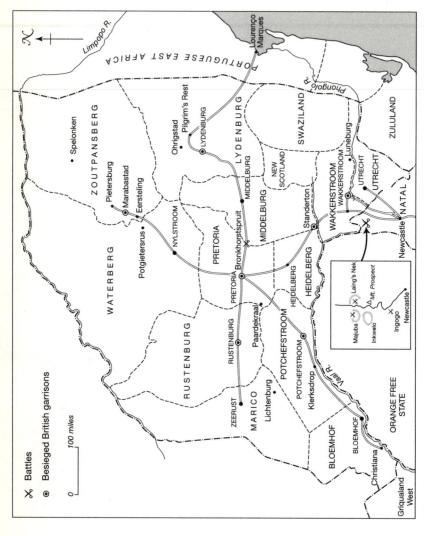

Map of the Transvaal

A clash of military cultures

Two British officers wearing blue patrol jackets and brandishing drawn swords gallop on their foreshortened horses straight out of the canvas at the viewer, whose position is that of their undepicted foes. The black horse of the disconcerted officer on the right is foundering, and his companion turns his head to shout words of encouragement. They are leading infantry in scarlet tunics who are running in extended order, pausing to fire from kneeling or prone positions. The unfurled Queen's Colour is in the background. All the soldiers wear tropical-issue helmets which indicate that this is an incident in one of Queen Victoria's 'little wars' of empire, but this time the enemy is not the typical ill-armed black 'warrior'. For the flat-topped mountain in the distance is Majuba in northern Natal, the painting depicts an episode during the battle of Laing's Nek on 28 January 1881, and the enemy are dismounted Boer irregulars armed with modern rifles, firing with withering effect from behind rocks and other natural defences on the British.

The artist of this oil painting, first exhibited in 1882, was Elizabeth Butler whose fame eclipsed that of any other woman artist of the day in England. Her battle paintings did not seek to glorify British victories and never portrayed hand-to-hand combat, but idealised the courage of the noble soldier undergoing the ultimate test of war. When she made this particular painting she was already beginning to be overtaken by her battle painting rivals who were responding more successfully than she to the growing spirit of popular jingoism, and the associated delight in glorious victories and hard-fought defeats.[1] But Butler was not to be swayed from her habitual purpose by changing fashion, and in her autobiography she explained why she chose the subject and called the picture *Floreat Etona* ['Let Eton Flourish']:

The Boer War [of 1880–1881], with its terrible Majuba Hill disaster, had attracted all our sorrowful attention the year before to South Africa, and I chose the attack on Laing's Nek for my subject. The two Eton boys whom I show, Elwes and Monck, went forward (Elwes to his death)[2] with the cry of 'Floreat Etona' and I gave the picture these words for its title.[3]

Critics in 1882 did not receive the painting favourably, finding its title affected and its treatment sentimental. Moreover, Butler was condemned for commemorating a bungled attack in a disastrous war in which little honour was to be found. It seems this unpopular selection of subject was suggested by Elizabeth Butler's husband, Lieutenant-Colonel William Butler, an intellectual soldier of heterodox views who distrusted Britain's increasingly imperialist intentions. In this case, however, it appears he was more concerned to rehabilitate the reputation of his old comrade-in-arms, Major-General Sir George Pomeroy-Colley, the British commander during the war, whom he believed had been unfairly blamed for the repeated British failures in the campaign, and whose biography he would later write.[4]

In the shadow of the First World War, in a later age which unashamedly exploited patriotic images of imperial derring-do, *Floreat Etona* appeared in *Hutchinson's Story of the British Nation* as an icon of commendable heroism.[5] It most likely was accepted as such by the book's middle-class family readership of 1923. Yet, as Elizabeth Butler had discovered in 1882, what had struck public attention then was not heroism, but military bungling, political duplicity and a disquieting clash of military cultures in which perceived acts of Boer treachery and barbarity would reap a bitter harvest when the struggle against British hegemony in South Africa was renewed in 1899. Quite possibly Butler did not intend it, but her painting was a depiction of war in transition, the clash of an outmoded British military culture and a fading construction of public school masculinity,[6] based on the ethos of 'Play up! play up! and play the game!',[7] in collision with the more appropriate Boer adaptation to the realities of modern warfare. If the battle of Waterloo was won on the playing-fields of Eton, then by the same token the battle of Laing's Nek was lost on the identical location to an opponent who did not abide by the same rules.

John Lynn has recently called for the primacy of the conceptual over the material in the study of war, arguing that the effective adoption and exploitation of new military technologies and practices is an expression of culture. In other words, the contrasting ways in which different armed forces go about things is a matter not simply of how they are armed, but of how a military conceives of war and combat. It is thus a question of how a military develops a discourse that tries to modify reality to resemble more nearly conceptions of how war should ideally be, and which defines types of warfare which fall outside the definition as aberrant and despicable. Of course, military culture is rooted in the cultural assumptions and values of its own wider society, so that choices concerning (say) uniforms, drill, doctrine and weaponry, may depend more upon aesthetic and social preferences rather than upon concrete advantages. What is certain is that military cultures can be sharply alien to each other, and that foes – even if they share the same technology – may fight not only by dissimilar methods, but by mismatched sets of rules.[8]

In the war of 1880–1881 mounted irregulars of the white settler society of the Transvaal were pitted against professional British soldiers. It is true that both sides were similarly armed and shared (at the broad level) many cultural assumptions and practices which set them distinctly apart from the traditional Africans societies of South Africa who represented a common and alien threat. But, more narrowly, their diverging fighting styles and antagonistic political goals were matters of cultural preference within their related societies, and both sides consequently had very different expectations of how a war between them would, and should, be fought. These divergencies will be explored throughout this book.

That does not require, though, that all military operations be described over-minutely. Bill Nasson, in the preface to his *The South African War*, states that he 'does not attempt to reproduce every well-know detail about campaigns, sieges, personalities, regiments and units' because such can be found elsewhere, and because his main purpose is to provide an interpretation.[9] So it is with this work. Close descriptions of operations can be found not only in private, unofficial and official papers (unpublished and published) in various repositories in South Africa and the United Kingdom,[10] but more accessibly in contemporary histories like Thomas Forstescue Carter, *A Narrative of the Boer War* (1882), Charles Norris-Newman, *With the Boers in the Transvaal and Orange Free State* (1882) and Lady Bellairs, *The Transvaal War* (1885),[11] and also in modern books like Oliver Ransford, *The Battle of*

Majuba Hill (1967), Joseph Lehmann, *The First Boer War* (1972), George Duxbury, *David and Goliath* (1981) and Ian Castle's *Majuba 1881* (1996).[12] Studies even more narrowly focused on specific battles, sieges, armaments and military organisations are available in specialist journal articles, especially those in military journals like *Militaria* and the *Military History Journal* published in 1980 and 1981 to coincide with the centenary of the war, in academic theses such as Arthur Davey's 'The Siege of Pretoria' (1956) and D.N. Pitout's 'Die Slag van Amajuba' (1980),[13] and in books like Ian Bennett's detailed coverage of the siege of Potchefstroom in *A Rain of Lead* (2001).[14]

While description and analysis of military operations are obviously integral to this present study, no work which purports to explain the war of 1880–1881 or, indeed, *any* war, can afford to lose sight of the complexity of the interaction between purely military concerns and the social, ideological, economic and political issues which combined to drive forward the Transvaal crisis, to shape how it was played out in armed confrontation, and to determine its termination. This intricacy of factors has led to problems of historical interpretation which have been most obviously reflected in the prevailing uncertainty concerning what the war should actually be called.

From the very beginning the conflict in the Transvaal during 1880–1881 has been known under several different names. Thomas Carter who, as a war correspondent, witnessed some of the military action, wrote a history of the war which first appeared in 1882 and which has remained the classic contemporary account of the campaign. He called the conflict the 'Boer War'.[15] When in 1899 it seemed that a far greater war would soon engulf all of southern Africa, H. Rider Haggard was already calling it the 'last Boer War'.[16] The earlier Boer War was indeed eclipsed and its name usurped by the subsequent and considerably more grim and prolonged war of 1899–1902. That harrowing conflict firmly entered British public consciousness as *the* Boer War, by which name it is still commonly known in the United Kingdom.[17]

Sensibly enough, therefore, when in 1967 Oliver Ransford wrote the first study of the earlier conflict since the nineteenth century, he subtitled it *The First Boer War*, and Joseph Lehmann followed in 1972 when he called his authoritative account simply *The First Boer War*.[18] Soon thereafter, as part of a move by post-colonial historians to invest the names of wars of colonial conquest with something of the sense that they were two-sided struggles in which indigenous peoples resisted the invader, the big – or Second – Boer

War of 1899–1902 came to be known (especially in South Africa) as the Anglo-Boer War. What then to call the limited, previous war fought primarily between the British and the Boers of the Transvaal? Many Afrikaner historians, who had long insisted on a close continuity between the twin wars of rising Afrikaner nationalism against British imperialism, preferred to revere it as 'Die Eerste Vryheidsoorlog' or the First War of Independence.[19] Yet that title has all too sectarian and pre-emptive a ring to be widely accepted, and suggests linkages between the two wars that arguably are not always there. To complicate matters further, the new name for the war of 1899–1902, the 'Anglo-Boer War', was in any case beginning to lose favour as a result of burgeoning academic interest in the considerable part black people played in that so-called 'white man's' war. This awareness led to a growing consensus that the Second Anglo-Boer War should preferably be known as the South African War to reflect the scale and inclusiveness of the struggle – though clumsier variants like the Anglo-South African War have also been canvassed.[20]

The South African War does at present seem to be the officially accepted name of choice for the 'Great' Boer War, even among many British historians in a country where the term 'Boer War' remains generally current.[21] But that leaves the war of 1880–1881 terminologically stranded, for it would be inappropriate to call that relatively small-scale and contained conflict the 'First' South African War. Denis Judd and Keith Surridge have recently written of it as the 'Anglo-Transvaal War'.[22] That seems a sensible solution, for it finds a way out of the dead-end into which modern terminology has worked itself by echoing more closely what contemporaries called the war when they did not refer to it as the 'Boer War'. Colonel William Bellairs was the British brigade commander in the Transvaal in 1880–1881 and kept meticulous notes of unfolding events in Pretoria and other invested British garrison. As a senior serving officer (he was promoted major-general in 1884), the propriety of Bellairs himself turning these notes into a book was questionable, so he published them in 1885 as *The Transvaal War* with his wife, Lady Bellairs (who had never even set foot in the Transvaal) credited as editor.[23] To call the conflict the 'Transvaal War' certainly seems not unapt since, at first glance, it is an admirably non-partisan appellation and reflects the apparently limited scope of the war.

Another possibility is to call it the 'Boer Rebellion', which was Rider Haggard's choice.[24] However, his was hardly a neutral voice, for he had been instrumental in the British annexation of the Transvaal in 1877 against which the Boers were rebelling in 1880–1881. In any case, to refer to a 'rebellion' abandons any pretence of impartiality, for the Boers who took part in the uprising did not acknowledge the legitimacy of British rule in the first place. Furthermore, it is misleading to refer to a *Boer* rebellion. Although the majority of the Boers of the Orange Free State, Cape and Natal might have actively sympathised with their blood-brothers of the Transvaal, very few actually took up arms in their support, and the British government brought the war to a precipitate halt precisely in order to forestall a Boer uprising across all of southern Africa.

Many contemporary British loyalists in South Africa, with whose cause Haggard openly sympathised, instantly dubbed the war the 'Transvaal Rebellion'. Loaded as we have seen this term 'rebellion' to be, it can nevertheless be argued that it is the one which most accurately describes the real nature and extent of the war of 1880–1881. It was indeed technically a rebellion, in that it was an organised armed uprising of the Boers of the Transvaal against established British rule, and had as its stated political objective the reinstatement of the independence they had reluctantly forfeited in 1877. Negotiations before, during and after the uprising were thus an integral, foregrounded feature of the confrontation, and the sieges and armed clashes of the campaign played their instrumental role in determining the decisions reached at the conference table. And, as is typical of rebellions against alien rule, the conflict, precipitated by burgeoning antagonism between an unbending administration and a growing body of organised malcontent, rapidly took on the nature of a civil war, but one that did not simplistically pit the Boer population against their British administrators and supporting military forces. Society in the Transvaal had recently become increasingly complex with a rapid influx of urbanised and commercially-minded 'English' settlers at odds with predominantly rural Boers. Yet contrasts and antagonisms between these two communities were not quite as crude as this dichotomy might imply, with the result that the rebellion in the Transvaal (not unlike the American War of Independence) forced civil society as a whole to divide along lines according to calculations of material interests and ideological preferences. So while most of the English settlers identified themselves as 'loyalists' and sought the maintenance of the authority of the Crown, the Boer community could not altogether escape being fractured into 'rebels', 'loyalists' and 'neutrals'. The rebellion also compelled the indigenous African population, which both the British and the Boers tried to sideline during their struggle, to make a grudging decision between evils and to conclude that their future would be more tolerable under the continuation of British rule. This stated preference would have adverse repercussions when the British withdrew from the Transvaal to the accompaniment of horrified African protests, and vengeful Boers reasserted their control.

Further aspects of the conflict suggest that the term rebellion serves it best. Again, not unlike the American rebels, the Boers only felt free to over-throw British rule because it had succeeded in removing the major threat to their security, in their case the previously unresolved military peril of independent African polities along their borders. And, like the American rebellion, it could not be contained. The actual campaign of 1880–1881, although fought in the Transvaal itself and in the mountain passes from Natal, by its provocative nature as an Afrikaner uprising against British rule sent out shockwaves throughout the subcontinent that would not have been nearly as powerful had this been yet another predictably futile African uprising against colonial rule. The rebellion in the Transvaal most uncom-fortably raised fundamental issues concerning the goals of Afrikaner nation-alism, the prospects for British paramountcy in southern Africa and the fate of African societies under differing forms of white rule. British and Afrikaner communities throughout South Africa were galvanised as never before dur-ing the rebellion into taking stock of their respective identities and were increasingly divided as a result. The British government, once it conceded independence to the rebels, forfeited its ability – except at the risk of another war – of controlling the huge (but still to be discovered) wealth of the Transvaal gold fields and, with it, of maintaining British economic and political preponderance in South Africa.

When viewed in a wider perspective, especially that of the late nineteenth-century British Empire as a whole, the Transvaal Rebellion was indeed a small war, whether in terms of the numbers of troops engaged, civilian hardships, casualties, material damage or immediate political fall-out. Nevertheless, it was fraught with longer-term consequences for South Africa and the Empire that would be played out only eighteen years later in the South African War. More immediately, it was fought at a moment when the British Army was attempting to adapt its military doctrine to the novel realities of modern weaponry and tactics. The military culture of the Boers deviated significantly from that prevailing among the British and, in the clash between the two, that of the British was humiliatingly exposed as having as yet adjusted insufficiently to the new conditions of warfare.

Notes and references

1 P. Usherwood and J. Spencer-Smith, *Lady Butler: Battle Artist 1846–1933* (London, 1989), pp. 15, 72, 167, 173.

2 Elwes died with two bullets in his head (Colley to Lady Colley, 30 January 1881, quoted in Lt-Gen Sir W.F. Butler, *The Life of Sir George Pomeroy-Colley* (London, 1899), p. 292).

3 Lady E. Butler, *Autobiography* (Sevenoaks, 1993; first published 1922), p. 152.

4 See Lt-Gen Sir W. Butler, *Sir William Butler: An Autobiography* (London, 1911), p. 216; Usherwood and Spencer-Smith, *Lady Butler*, pp. 69–72, 84.

5 W. Hutchinson, ed., *Hutchinson's Story of the British Nation. A Connected, Pictorial & Authoritative History of the British Peoples from the Earliest Times to the Present Day* (London, 1923), vol. IV, p. 1843. The emotive description of the illustration read: 'This incident took place at Laing's Nek; a young adjutant from Eton had his horse shot under him, and Elwes, another Etonian, encouraged him shouting: "Come along Monck, 'Floreat Etona,' we must be in the first rank," but was shot dead as the words left his mouth.'

6 See R. Morrell, 'The Times of Change: Men and Masculinity in South Africa' in R. Morell, ed., *Changing Men in Southern Africa* (Pietermaritzburg, 2001), pp. 6–10.

7 Sir Henry Newbolt, 'Vitaï Lampada', *Collected Poems 1897–1907* (London, Edinburgh and New York, n.d.), pp. 131–3.

8 J.A. Lynn, *Battle: A History of Combat and Culture from Ancient Greece to Modern America* (Boulder, CO and Oxford, 2003), pp. xx–xxi, xvi–xviii, 115, 121, 124, 232, 245, 303, 306, 314.

9 B. Nasson, *The South African War 1899–1902* (London, 1999), p. xiv.

10 See Select Bibliography.

11 T.F. Carter, *A Narrative of the Boer War* (Cape Town, Port Elizabeth, Johannesburg and London, 1882; new edition, 1896); C.L. Norris-Newman, *With the Boers in the Transvaal and the Orange Free State in 1880–1* (London, 1882); Lady Bellairs, ed., *The Transvaal War 1880–81* (Edinburgh and London, 1885).

12 O.N. Ransford, *The Battle of Majuba Hill: The First Boer War* (London, 1967); J.H. Lehmann, *The First Boer War* (London, 1972); G.R. Duxbury, *David and Goliath: The First War of Independence, 1880–1881* (Johannesburg, 1981); I. Castle, *Majuba 1881: The Hill of Destiny* (London, 1996).

13 A.M. Davey, 'The Siege of Pretoria 1880–1881' in *Archives Year Book for South African History, Nineteenth Year, Volume 1* (Parow, 1956); D.N. Pitout, 'Die Slag van Amajuba, 27 Februarie 1881' (unpublished MA thesis, University of Pretoria, 1980).

14 I. Bennett, *A Rain of Lead. The Siege and Surrender of the British at Potchefstroom 1880–1881* (London, 2001).

15 Carter, *Boer War*.

16 Sir H. Rider Haggard, *The Last Boer War* (London 1899).

17 See T. Packenham, *The Boer War* (Johannesburg and London, 1979) and still in print; and, more recently, Field Marshal Lord Carver, *The National Army Museum Book of the Boer War* (London, 1999) and J. Gooch, ed., *The Boer War: Direction, Experience and Image* (London and Portland, OR, 2000).

18 Ransford, *Majuba Hill* and Lehmann, *Boer War*.

19 See F.A. van Jaarsveld, A.P.J. van Rensburg and W.A. Stals, eds, *Die Eerste Vryheidsoorlog: Van Verset en Geweld tot Skikking deur Onderhandeling 1877–1884* (Pretoria and Cape Town, 1980) and Duxbury, *David and Goliath*.

20 See P. Warwick, *Black People and the South African War 1899–1902* (Cambridge, 1983); B. Nasson, 'The War One Hundred Years On' (paper delivered at the Rethinking the South African War Conference, UNISA, August 1998); and G. Cuthbertson and A. Jeeves, 'The Many-Sided Struggle for Southern Africa, 1899–1902', *South African Historical Journal*, 41 (Nov. 1999), pp. 2–21.

21 See, for example, I.R. Smith, *The Origins of the South African War 1899–1902* (Harlow, 1996) and D. Lowry, ed., *The South African War Reappraised* (Manchester, 2000). But see also D. Judd and K. Surridge, *The Boer War* (London, 2002).

22 Judd and Surridge, *Boer War*, p. 106.

23 Bellairs, ed., *Transvaal War*.

24 Rider Haggard, *Last Boer War*, chap. v: 'The Boer Rebellion'.

chapter 1

The Imperial factor and the Transvaal

S uccessive British cabinets throughout the nineteenth century debated the merits of formal and informal empire in southern Africa, sometimes seeking to assert political paramountcy over the region, only then to withdraw from direct involvement. The decision in 1899 to go to war with the two Boer republics of the Transvaal and Orange Free State for South African supremacy was thus the culmination of this fluctuating process, and has spawned an on-going debate concerning the motives behind nineteenth-century British imperialism in the sub-continent. Interpretations have waxed and waned in accordance with the dictates of scholarly fashion. The emphasis has swung between economic arguments for empire which have focused on the search for markets, labour and control of mineral resources; through the imperatives of grand strategy and the need to safeguard the route to India; to the contradictory desire to institute imperial administrative and military economies; from the pressure from the humanitarian lobby concerned by the treatment of Africans by Boers and British settlers alike; to the often maverick role of individual local colonial officials and the parochial agendas of white settlers in search of land and economic advantage.[1] Currently, the more monocausal of these explanations have yielded to an integrated, synthetic approach. This is invaluable in unravelling the motives behind the British annexation of the Transvaal in 1877, and in laying out the reasons for the British government's acquiescence in the new colony's humiliating retrocession only four years later after a disastrous, but by no means irretrievable military campaign.[2]

In considering British policy in southern Africa, it is well to remember that cabinets were dependent on the knowledge of the permanent official in the Colonial Office who advised the Colonial Secretary, as well as on imperial officials in South Africa, notably the High Commissioner. The government was also sensitive to public opinion expressed through the press, the clubs and parliament, and through the pressure groups with South African interests like missionary and anti-slavery organisations and commercial and shipping houses. Nor must it be forgotten that the remoteness of South Africa half a world away from Britain, poor communications and the sub-continent's unique problems meant that members of the government were usually ill-informed of its affairs. Consequently, in cabinet a great deal of latitude was allowed by default to the Colonial Secretary who was better informed than most. He, in turn, permitted considerable powers of discretion to his officials in southern Africa. All too often decisions concerning the distant region were simply reactions to events, mere fire-fighting. Yet at other times, when Colonial Secretaries and the local pro-consuls of empire were men of vision and determination, Britain would take the initiative in South Africa.[3]

When Britain formally annexed the Cape of Good Hope from the Dutch in 1814 to secure its sea route to the east, some 27,000 white colonists already lived there. These Cape Dutch were derived from Dutch, Flemish, German and French Huguenot settlers and were already beginning to develop a sense of their own 'Afrikaner' identity. British rule did not sit well with many of them, and by 1836 an organised migration of thousands of farmers, or Boers, was under way north across the Orange River and into the interior of southern Africa. Individual pastoral farmers (or trekboers) in the Cape Colony had long been pushing forward the frontier of white settlement into the interior, but this so-called 'Great Trek' was of another order, and by 1845 perhaps 14,000 Emigrant Farmers (or Voortrekkers) had left the Cape in a series of parties, taking with them not only all their livestock and goods and chattels, but also their black dependants and servants to a number as great as their own.

The Great Trek has naturally been subject ever since to a host of interpretations, though an enduring consensus has held that while it was not unique among the various nineteenth-century migrations of white settlers, it was of enormous import for southern Africa in that it set the historical stage for all that was to follow.[4] Currently, the influential writings of Tim Keegan and Norman Etherington have broken with this more established historiography. In refusing to dignify the Boer exodus with a unique status, Etherington has set out to show that it was but one of many treks during the early nineteenth century by other indigenous peoples of southern Africa, such as the Ndebele, Rolong and Griqua. When all of these migrants set up their new states on the highveld they displaced or incorporated others living there before them and transformed the face of the interior.[5] Keegan is with Etherington in arguing that the Boer emigration was not primarily motivated by some self-conscious sense of national mission as later Afrikaner nationalists might suggest, and that their chief purpose in leaving the Cape was not to establish their republican nationhood as far away as possible from hated aspects of British administration. Keegan prefers to emphasise more positive motives for emigration, primarily an eagerness for new economic possibilities following the extension of the frontier.[6] Having escaped from the authority of the colonial government they replicated their loose-knit, patriarchal and plural society as it had been before the relatively liberal British had interfered with their dominance over the African majority and their well established ideas of proper master–servant relationships. Most emigrants had the skills necessary to maintain their wagons and firearms, but depended on travelling traders (or *smouse*) to supply the vital commodities they could not produce: gunpowder, clothing materials, tea, coffee and sugar. Their hope was always that they could free themselves of the colonial commercial network by gaining access to traders and ports on the east coast of Africa beyond the sphere of British control.[7]

The Great Trek (which the Cape authorities had failed to impede) threatened to create instability and warfare in the interior with likely repercussions on the Cape. But it was difficult to decide how best to assert British control beyond its frontiers. Until German activities in the 1880s, Britain was the only colonial power with an interest in the region, and it seemed that British paramountcy could be exerted without the cost and liabilities of formal rule.[8] One attempt to do just that was the Cape of Good Hope Punishment Act of 1836, passed by Lord Melbourne's Whig government, which proclaimed the extension of British jurisdiction (but not sovereignty) as far north as latitude 25° S. This law became the basis for British involvement during the 1840s and early 1850s in the affairs of trans-Orangia where the emigrant Boers were in constant conflict with the Sotho and Griqua people already living there. Earl Grey, the Colonial Secretary in Lord John Russell's Whig administration, added a further means in 1846 of lending protection to any chief harassed by the Boers through the appointment of Sir Henry Pottinger, the Governor of the Cape, to the new post of High Commissioner for southern Africa. This imperial officer's brief was to exercise an at first extremely vaguely defined authority beyond the Cape's frontiers but, over time, the high commissioner developed into the chief imperial agent in the region and the instrument of British paramountcy.[9]

The British forward engagement with trans-Orangia reached a climax in February 1848 with the assertion of paramountcy and the setting up of the Orange River Sovereignty in the territories between the Orange and Vaal rivers and the Drakensberg Mountains to the east. But difficult military involvements elsewhere along the Cape frontiers and the fractiousness of the new territory caused Russell's government to rethink its troublesome commitment. The first step in the imperial retreat was a settlement with the Boers living north across the Vaal River. From 1838 they had begun to establish a number of widely dispersed settlements (such as Potchefstroom, Heidelberg, Pretoria, Rustenburg and Zeerust) around which they had concentrated, and had set up several volatile and short-lived little republics.[10] These trans-Vaal Boers were in the habit of intervening in the affairs of trans-Oranje, and the British had been forced to cut short their interference in the new Orange River Sovereignty at the battle of Boomplaats on 29 August 1848. But the trans-Vaalers were undeterred, and within only a few years they were again preparing to destabilise the Orange River Sovereignty. To preclude this, the British representatives cut a deal with them. By the Sand River Convention of 17 January 1852, the trans-Vaal Boers stood back from affairs south of the Orange in return for British recognition of their independence. In September 1853 the 'emigrant Boers North of the Vaal River' officially adopted the name Zuid-Afrikaansche Republiek (or South African Republic) for their new state, though it is often referred to as the Transvaal.[11]

The terms of their independence are important for understanding what the Transvaal Boers forfeited in 1877 and hoped to regain in 1881. The British agreed to allow the Boers across the Vaal 'the right to manage their own affairs and govern themselves according to their own laws, without any interference on the part of the British Government'. The British undertook to disclaim all alliances with 'the coloured nations' across the Vaal, in return for which the Transvalers agreed to abolish slavery. They were guaranteed access to supplies of ammunition (so important to their very survival in

30,000 blacks had converged at what had become the Kimberley diamond diggings.[17] Such extensive exploitation of diamonds had all the potential to transform the economy and society of the sub-continent in a 'mineral revolution', and was quickly consolidated by gold-strikes. The finding in 1873 of alluvial gold in the eastern Transvaal at Lydenburg, Pilgrim's Rest and De Kaap started South Africa's first gold rush, though it amounted only to 0.03 per cent of total world production. It was not until the uncovering of the vast seam of gold-bearing ore on the Witwatersrand in 1886 that the Transvaal would develop by the 1890s into the world's single biggest gold producer.[18] Concurrent with the mineral revolution, philanthropist agitation for British intervention was growing as a consequence of repeated reports of Transvaal slave-raiding and ownership in contravention of the Sand River Convention.

Meanwhile, Wodehouse actively intervened to bring an end to the Orange Free State's interminable wars with the Sotho by annexing the mountain kingdom in 1868. He also put the brakes on the Transvaal's attempts to expand west across the traders' route to the north, as well as east towards Delagoa Bay, Zululand and a seaport which would reduce the landlocked republic's economic dependency on British controlled territory. Such active imperial intervention north of the Orange provoked Boer resentment because it was not incorrectly seen as tacitly subverting the British commitment to non-interference central to the Sand River and Bloemfontein Conventions. But Wodehouse, in the interests of bringing order and justice to the sub-continent, began to push the old plan for federation under Britain. Lord Derby's and then Disraeli's Tory administrations of 1866–1868, though interested, took no positive steps in support, however. Only with the formation of Gladstone's first Liberal government in 1868 did a new policy begin to take shape, and was implemented when Sir Henry Barkly arrived as High Commissioner in December 1870. Cape Colony, the largest, richest and most populous settler state in southern Africa with 237,000 whites (more than twice the number of the three other states put together),[19] was seen as the key to any confederation since it would inevitably have to shoulder the chief burden. To this end, a devolution of power to the Cape was necessary to relieve Britain of its administrative and defence commitments. Barkly consequently persuaded the Cape in 1871 to take over Basutoland from the imperial government, and in 1872 to accept responsible government.[20]

To effect federation required accumulating all the necessary pieces and fitting them together. The diamond fields, southern Africa's first industrial community, proved an immediate challenge, for they were situated on territory between the Cape and the two Boer republics.[21] On the face of it, that argued for closer cooperation between the three polities, especially since the republics lay between the diamond fields and the sources of African labour necessary to work them in Basutoland, the eastern Transvaal and Portugeuse Mozambique. Instead, the Orange Free State, the Transvaal and the local communities who lived in the area put in their rival claims. Arbitration was required, and the doctrine of British paramountcy required that this must be British. The Keate Award of October 1871 assigned the territory, to be known as Griqualand West, to the Tlhaping people. They immediately made it over to the Crown. Barkly tried to induce the Cape to assume responsibility for it, but Basutoland was proving difficult enough to digest, and the incorporation of Griqualand West could only sour relations with the Boer republics. So the Cape passed, and Britain had a new colony. Yet, however one looked at it, this latest imperial advance violated the terms of the Sand River and Bloemfontein Conventions. The post-1854 era of informal paramountcy British in southern Africa was clearly drawing to an end.[22]

In the years between imperial retreat in the early 1850s and the end of Gladstone's first ministry in 1874, both Tory and Liberal administrations had (as we have seen) never ceased to toy with the possibilities of South African confederation. Crucially, though, they had done so with an eye to the limitation, rather than the extension, of imperial involvement, and this encompassed the Cape's taking greater financial responsibility for its own administration. During Disraeli's second administration, formed in February 1874, the Colonial Secretary, the Earl of Carnarvon, adopted a much more aggressive approach to confederation. This shift of policy has attracted considerable debate. Explanations for the change have ranged widely, from the view it reflected nothing more than Carnarvon's personal quirk, to the Marxist inspired argument that it was the inevitable result of the impersonal economic forces being unleashed in South Africa by the mineral revolution.[23] As is customary in historical debate, narrow or determinist explanations such as these have been melded together to form a more broadly based synthesis.

Imperial planners in the 1870s were still seeking to consolidate, rather than expand, the British Empire.[24] Even though southern Africa's economy was at the threshold of being transformed by the burgeoning mineral revolution, it was still India that remained central to British commercial interests and her status as an imperial power. India's security depended on the Royal

Navy's control of the sea routes to India through the Suez Canal and around the Cape, which in turn meant possession of sufficient ports and coaling-stations for steam-driven naval vessels. Southern Africa's primary import-ance, therefore, lay in her strategic position on the way to India, and it was consequently essential to remain the paramount power there, as it was in Egypt. Yet, as successive British governments had understood since the 1830s, the difficulty in maintaining British dominance in southern Africa lay not so much in the ambitions of rival colonial powers, as was the case in Egypt, as with the unstable political and economic fragmentation of the region. Besides the British colonies, there were the shakily based Boer republics of the interior as well as surviving independent African polities, some of which, like the Sotho, Zulu, Swazi and Pedi kingdoms, were military powers to be reckoned with. The boundaries between white settlers and these and other African states were still ill-defined and, in many cases, hotly contested. The consequence was endemic and debilitating conflict. Nevertheless, for Carnarvon, the developing economic viability of southern Africa suggested how a comprehensive political structure might be erected from a confederation of the white-governed states that would enable the region to shoulder its imperial strategic role. Because such a confederation would create a settled environment for greater economic integration and progress, it would be able to bear the costs of its own centralised and streamlined administration. And since internal conflict would be all but eliminated, the confederation need only maintain its own small, affordable armed forces, and not have to rely as previously on a large and expensive imperial garrison for its security. The strength and self-reliance of such a confederation would not only fulfil its prime purpose as an unassailable link in the British route to India, but would provide the base for future British economic and political expansion into the African interior.

However, there were several major obstacles in the way of Carnarvon's idealised confederation. Not only would the two Boer republics have to be persuaded to join, but the continued existence of independent African king-doms posed a security risk to the settler states, both through the likelihood of frontier conflicts and on account of their capacity to foment unrest among Africans already under white rule. For confederation to succeed, therefore, it was necessary to assume some form of British supremacy over all the indigenous peoples of southern Africa. What made the fulfilment of this requirement particularly pressing was the reluctance of the Cape Colony (which was the largest and – until the discovery of gold in the

Transvaal – the most economically viable element in the structure) to commit itself to confederation until it could be assured that this would not entail fresh and costly wars with neighbouring African states.

Thus it was that the Transvaal's unsuccessful struggle between May 1876 and February 1877 against the Sotho-speaking Pedi of the north-eastern Transvaal under their paramount, Sekhukhune woaSekwati,[25] to secure land, labour and tribute precipitated direct imperial intervention. Despite his determination to push through confederation, Carnarvon had been finding it a frustrating business even getting the representatives of the various white states to sit around the same table, let alone to agree on some form of union. So word that in August 1876 the Pedi had inflicted severe reverses on the inept forces of the anarchic and bankrupt Boer republic gave him the excuse to take the dramatic decision to promote confederation through the annexation of the South African Republic. The republic's mismanaged and unresolved war with the Pedi was precisely the sort of conflict which the Cape so strongly wished to see concluded before consenting to confederation. The understanding was that with annexation British troops would swiftly succeed against the Pedi where Boer commandos had failed, and so reassure the Cape. Besides which, the Transvaal had obvious potential as a source of considerable mineral wealth and, standing as it did across the road to the African interior with its fabled, untapped riches, its annexation was essential to secure the northern component of confederation. Alarmingly, the Transvaal was currently trying to raise money to build a railway line east to Delagoa Bay, which was confirmed as Portuguese territory in 1875. At last a nearby port outside British control was available which would release the Transvaal from dependence on its outlet to the sea through Durban in British Natal to the south, thus loosening its commercial links with the British colonies and undermining the economic motives for federation. Carnarvon had also been encouraged to believe that annexation would even be welcomed by a significant element of the white population. In the intelligence report which Colonel George Pomeroy-Colley had compiled the previous year, he had indicated that the influence of English settled in the Transvaal was 'likely before long to become dominant'.[26] Emboldened, in December 1876 Carnarvon instructed the Colonial Office to draft enabling legislation – the Permissive Federation Bill – very similar to the British North America Act of 1867 which provided for the federation of Canada.[27]

Armed with Carnarvon's secret instructions to annex the Transvaal with or without popular consent (and in blatant violation of the Sand River

Convention), Sir Theophilus Shepstone entered the republic in January 1877 as Special Commissioner with a small force of 25 Natal Mounted Police and a small staff, including H. Rider Haggard. The English-speaking community was eager for him to take over the government, while the Volksraad (or parliament) was sullen rather than hostile, and divided between the factions of President the Reverend T.F. Burgers and his vice-president and political rival, Paul Kruger. The burghers were unwilling to pay the emergency taxes levied by the Volksraad, the public debt was £192,399, and concern about the threat apparently posed by a resurgent Zulu kingdom in alliance with the Pedi was much played up by Shepstone. Thus, when Shepstone proclaimed the Transvaal a British colony at 11h00 on 12 April 1877 and ran up the Union Flag in Church Square in Pretoria, opposition was muted. The Volksraad resolved to send a delegation abroad to make objections to annexation widely known, and meanwhile appealed to citizens to refrain from violence so as not to prejudice their mission.[28]

Carnarvon determined to entrust his accelerating plans for South African confederation to a statesman capable of carrying them into effect. The instrument he selected was the great Indian administrator, Sir Bartle Frere, who departed for Cape Town in March 1877 as Governor of the Cape and High Commissioner. His intention was to complete the stumbling process of confederation and then to stay on as the first governor-general of the new South African dominion, an architect of empire in the mould of a Lord Durham.[29] When Frere arrived in South Africa in March 1877, Shepstone was on the verge of consummating the annexation of the Transvaal, thus securing the northern component of confederation and putting pressure on the isolated Orange Free State. However, the Cape Parliament had rejected the Permissive Federation Bill before he arrived, and the Orange Free State would do likewise in May. Frere thus had to work to create conditions that would make confederation more acceptable. So he turned his attention to closing the festering Cape eastern frontier, and during the course of the Ninth Frontier War of 1877–1878 against the Ngqika-Gcaleka Xhosa fitted the Transkei into the developing confederation structure. His annexation of Walvis Bay in March 1878 and Port St John's in September 1878 secured the best potential ports in southern Africa not yet under British control. However, some portions of the frontier remained obstinately open. The Mpondo continued to be a source of unresolved difficulty on the Cape eastern frontier, as did the Griqua of Griqualand East. In Griqualand West many of the Tlhaping joined an abortive uprising in April–May 1878 against

British rule. As a result of these disturbances the Cape continued to be chary of confederation. To add to the Cape's disquiet, the Pedi were proving much more difficult to overcome than had been anticipated, and their resistance posed a real threat to Shepstone's Transvaal administration and to confederation as a whole. The untamed and apparently truculent Zulu kingdom seemed to pose an even greater threat than the Pedi. Carnarvon, Frere's patron, resigned in February 1878, but the High Commissioner stayed on, determined to see confederation through, especially since the Permissive Federation Bill had received the royal assent on 10 August 1877 as the South Africa Act of 1877. The new Colonial Secretary, Sir Michael Hicks Beach, engrossed in Balkan and Afghan crises, was inclined to leave the experienced Frere to his own devices. Frere was convinced that the key to continuing disaffection in the Transvaal, which was undermining the consummation of confederation, was the 'native question'. Until the Zulu had been humbled and Sekhukhune brought to his senses, this could never be solved and the Boers would never be mollified.[30]

Indeed, British rule in the Transvaal was not going down well after some initial optimism. The parlous financial state of the new British territory was not rescued by the paltry grant-in-aid of £100,000 made by the British parliament, nor helped by Shepstone's own inept economic management.[31] The delegation of disaffected Transvalers mandated by the defunct Volksraad, and consisting of former Vice-President Paul Kruger, E.J.P. Jorissen, a civil servant, and Edouard Bok as secretary, visited London in July 1877 to request a plebiscite to test the popularity of British sovereignty. Carnarvon received them graciously but turned them down flat, and the delegation reported back on 7 January 1878 to an indignant mass-gathering in Pretoria. Since Carnarvon had refused the request for a plebiscite on Transvaal independence, the decision was taken at a second meeting on 28 January at Naauwpoort near Potchefstroom to appoint a committee under M.W. Pretorius, Kruger and M.F. Viljoen to collect signatures against annexation. The Signatures Committee, or *Volkskomitee* [People's Committee] as it became known, tried to keep a curb on manifestations of outright sedition, for Shepstone was itching to take action against the protesters, but the meeting held on 4 April 1878 at the farm Doornfontein near Pretoria proved stormy. It was announced that 6,591 signatures were against annexation and only 587 for, which, even if the considerable duress brought to bear upon signatories is taken into account, was a sharp slap in the face for Shepstone's administration. The meeting elected P.J. Joubert and Kruger, accompanied by Edouard Bok as secretary, to go to London to present the figures to the Colonial Secretary. This second delegation found Hicks Beach, who had recently replaced Carnarvon, as unbending as his predecessor concerning Transvaal independence, and as insistent on the new colony's place within the confederation. The delegation expressed its deep disappointment and reported back to a public meeting on 10 January 1879 at Wonderfontein. The meeting vented its deep collective anger with British oppression. It authorised the Volkskomitee to remain in being with sub-committees to assist in politicisation, and to create a structure that was in fact a state within a state.[32] It also decided on a policy of non-cooperation without independence, and set March 1879 for 'an assembly of the people' to which Frere was invited.[33]

It was in this context that Shepstone and Frere tried to win over those Boers unreconciled to their loss of independence by a demonstration of the advantages of British paramountcy. Ever since 1848 the Transvaal Boers and the Zulu had been involved in a smouldering border dispute as Boer farmers encroached ever deeper into Zulu territory. Open conflict in 1876 had only been averted when the Boers backed down. Shepstone intervened openly in October 1877 to support Boer claims. As the border crisis mounted, Frere was drawn into a situation where the future of confederation seemed to hinge on the breaking of Zulu power which he increasingly saw as the centre of a 'black conspiracy' aiming to overthrow white power in the sub-continent. Frere believed as a consequence that it was impossible 'to decline the contest',[34] even though he marched to war against the express wishes of his government. Such wilful insubordination might have been condoned had the war Frere forced on the Zulu been swift, decisive and cheap, and successfully consummated confederation. Instead, initial humiliating military disaster at Isandlwana on 22 January 1879 which threw the British invasion of Zululand back on its heels, and the consequent prolongation of the costly conflict until September, not only failed to settle the regional problems of southern Africa, but revealed the imperial colossus to have feet of clay.[35]

For the Transvalers, British military setbacks against the Zulu only confirmed the inept British record against the Pedi in their aborted campaign of February–October 1878,[36] and encouraged the belief that it would be far from impossible to overthrow their rule. The mass meeting summoned by the Volkskomitee met as arranged in March at Kleinfontein outside Pretoria, and gradually moved camp ever closer to the town while it waited for Frere to arrive. That thousands of burghers (or citizens) had proved willing to travel often hundreds of miles to attend the meeting publicised the new political message of Boer unity and obedience to emerging nationalist leadership. Since this was also a protest under arms, with reviews and sham fights, it also demonstrated that an armed uprising was far from impossible. When on 12 April 1879 Frere finally met the Transvaal leaders in their camp at Erasmus's farm, Hennopsrivier, it was in the wake of Colonel Evelyn Wood's crushing victory at Khambula on 29 March which had finally tipped the Zulu campaign in the British favour. Nevertheless, Frere was hardly in a strong position to push confederation. He offered self-government within the framework of a watered-down confederation, but the Boers were accepting nothing short of independence, and Kruger warned him that he would not for much longer be able to restrain his people from open resistance.[37] Frere reported to London on 23 April after a third and final meeting that he had failed to reconcile the Boers to British rule, and his only recourse was to force them to endure it. This was easier said than done, for it required more troops than were available simply to enforce the laws and to break down the widespread refusal to pay taxes.[38] Frere's stock was now disastrously low with his government, who sidelined him on 28 May 1879 by dividing the high commissionership and leaving him only as Governor of the Cape. General Sir Garnet Wolseley was sent to South Africa on special service to replace him as High Commissioner in South Eastern Africa, Governor of Natal and the Transvaal, and Commander-in-Chief of the Forces in charge of the Zulu, Natal and Transvaal hot-spots.[39]

Yet Wolseley, for all his success in winding up the Anglo-Zulu War in September 1879 and ending the Zulu military threat by breaking the former kingdom into thirteen toothless petty chiefdoms – and then in going on to defeat the Pedi by December 1879 after a brutal campaign[40] – was no more successful than Frere in winning over the Boers or easing the way to confederation.[41] In fact, his double success in eliminating the longstanding Zulu and Pedi threats to Boer security had an effect the reverse of that intended, for by removing the Boers' most pressing security problems it allowed the republican leaders to apply all their energies to anti-British agitation. In this the consequences were not dissimilar from those in the Thirteen Colonies before the American Revolution, when British victory in the Seven Years' War removed the spectre of French invasion. Wolseley had, in any case, little room to manoeuvre, even though he came rapidly to believe that the Boers were irreconcilable, and that the annexation of the Transvaal had been 'a great political blunder'.[42] It remained his commission to make it as clear as could be that the Transvaal would remain British, come what may, and he issued a proclamation to that effect on 29 September 1879.[43] He nevertheless attempted to make the Transvaal administration, where Colonel Sir Owen Lanyon (who had previously been the Administrator of Griqualand West) had replaced Shepstone as Administrator on 4 March 1879,[44] more acceptable to the Boers. In October 1879 he expanded the machinery of government so that, in standard Crown Colony style (as followed in neighbouring Natal) a limited representative element was added.[45] However, many Boers were offended by such limited representation, no Boer of any standing proved willing to serve, and the structure never gained any real credibility in Boer eyes. To make matters worse, Wolseley offended the Boers by making all too widely known his personal contempt for them. There was disaffection throughout the country, in October 1879 troops had to compel compliance with the laws in Middelburg,[46] and there was open talk of rebellion to follow the next mass meeting of burghers. This was held at Wonderfontein from 10 to 15 December 1879, during which there was much angry rhetoric and assertions of willingness to die for the *Vierkleur*, the ex-republic's flag. Kruger, who already enjoyed a considerable reputation as a brave and resourceful military commander, and was a prominent (if controversial) political figure,[47] emerged as the dominant figure during the meeting. Soon afterwards he exercised his influence when he successfully counselled against premature armed rebellion when, in January 1880, Wolseley provocatively arrested some of the Boer leaders of the Wonderfontein meeting. Yet Wolseley was correct to see that Wonderfontein presented a genuine challenge to British rule. The Queen's sovereignty had been publicly denounced, it had been agreed to boycott all things English in the Transvaal. Paradoxically, British occupation seemed to be fomenting a sense of national consciousness in the Transvaal which years of fractious independence had failed to elicit.[48]

The Afrikaner nationalist historian, F.A. van Jaarsveld, has argued that a sense of Afrikaner nationalism, which had not been much evident before 1877, was a reaction to the mounting challenge of British imperialism in South Africa during that decade.[49] He singled out the Transvaal Rebellion as a crucial stage in this process of national self-awakening for, without that crisis, he believed that Afrikaners would have gradually become absorbed into an English-speaking South Africa. His thesis is, of course, debatable, and it is quite possible that the wave of Afrikaner nationalist sentiment that accompanied the Transvaal crisis was only a momentary emotion, what Derek Schreuder has called 'the *chimera* of a nationalist revolt, nothing but the illusion of Afrikaner unity'.[50] Yet what counts is that the British at the time came to believe firmly in the reality of a pan-Afrikaner danger – just as they had fallen in the late 1870s for a non-existent 'black conspiracy' master-minded by the Zulu – and framed their policies in 1880–1881 accordingly.

Piet Joubert, one of the Transvaal's most prominent leaders, succinctly expressed his people's case in November 1880 when he wrote: 'Our forefathers – the Voortrekkers – emigrants because of oppression, wrested the land from the wilderness and the barbarians in order to live here as a free nation with their own government.'[51] And it certainly does seem that the Emigrant Farmers of the Great Trek had developed a group consciousness born out of their wanderings and sufferings. Yet the way of life they believed in and were willing to defend had at its core the primary freedom of a family (or, at a wider level, the regional group) to regulate its own affairs.[52] Left to themselves (as we have seen) during the 1850s and 1860s in their remote republics, the political inexperience and deep-seated individualism of the thinly scattered Boer communities led to factionalism, lawlessness and political anarchy. Nor was there much contact with the increasingly anglicised Afrikaners of the British colonies of the Cape and Natal, and little or no sense of national solidarity, or even of a common language. Most of the educated clergy clung to Dutch and looked down on Afrikaans as a dialect, while most Afrikaners could neither understand English nor speak Dutch correctly. But they all did have a common historical background, for almost all were descended from the burghers of the late seventeenth-century Cape, and resented being looked down upon by those of British stock.

This situation began to change in about 1868 with renewed British interest in the interior. The British annexations of Basutoland and then Griqualand West both seemed to threaten the independence and viability of the Orange Free State and drew the Boers living there together as never before. The empathy of the Boers both in the Transvaal and in the Cape was stimulated by these 'wrongs', and a sense of 'brotherhood' under oppression began to form. The British annexation of the Transvaal in 1877 was a huge shock to the fractious Boers of the north, for once again they were being ruled by 'strangers'. The Free Staters found themselves an island in a British sea and looked outside their border to their 'fellow-countrymen' for support. As for the Transvalers, a consciousness of themselves as a people began to grow out of their gathering resistance to foreign British rule. In the Cape an Afrikaner cultural and political revival began in the mid-1870s both in inflamed response to the apparently increasing danger that Dutch would disappear from public discourse as a result of British pressure, and in reaction to British bullying of the Boers of the interior. Stephanus du Toit and several associates founded *Die Genootskap van Regte Afrikaners* [The Fellowship of True Afrikaners] in August 1875, and published *Die Afrikaanse Patriot*, the first newspaper in Afrikaans, to further the nationalist cause. The position they hammered home was that Afrikaners were a distinct nation, occupying a distinct fatherland, which was South Africa, speaking their God-given language and enjoying the God-given right to rule South Africa and civilise its heathen Africans. The paper struggled until revivified by the annexation of the Transvaal in 1877 when its call on the Boers to drive out the British by force of arms, and its advocacy of the coordination of Afrikaner organisations in the Cape, Transvaal and elsewhere led to a leap in circulation. Du Toit built on his journalistic success by founding the first branches of *Die Afrikaner Bond* [Afrikaner League] in 1879 to consolidate existing nationalist groups in the Cape. The *Bond* strongly attacked the spread of English influence at the expense of traditional Afrikaner ways and adopted a rigorous neo-Calvinism as a defence against the culture of 'liquor, lucre and redcoats' which symbolised British rule. The *Bond* also aimed to encourage Afrikaner commercialism and to penetrate this area so dominated by the British. It can be argued that this brand of nationalism was directed more against imperial rule than against English-speaking colonials, though this was not always at all apparent to contemporaries.

Central to developing Afrikaner nationalism was the ingrained Calvinist theological assumption that they were the elect, the chosen people of God, whose hand was visible in the history of the nation.[53] This was a theology based almost exclusively on the Old Testament to the exclusion of the Christology of the New, and emphasised a re-enactment of episodes in the story of the children of Israel, notably the making of the covenant with God, the exodus from Egypt and the conquest of Canaan. Like the children of Israel entering the land of Canaan, the Boers had been called to open up the interior for civilisation and Christianity and to live as one people free from British rule in the new Zion. Thus history became vital to the sense of nation, for the heroes of the past, their persecution, courage and sacrifices gave meaning to the nation's mission and showed the way to the future. The pious speeches of Boer leaders were filled with biblical allusions and injunctions which identified their righteous cause with that of God, and encouraged the faithful in their preordained victory over the forces of evil.

Not that the Transvaal was free from doctrinal divisions. In 1853 the Nederduits Hervormde Kerk was formed in Rustenburg and broke away from the more liberal Nederduits Gereformeerde Kerk ruled by the Cape Colonial Synod. Then in 1859 the Nederduits Hervormde Kerk, served by *predikants* [ministers] brought in from the Netherlands, split in turn with the formation of the Gereformeerde Kerk van Suid Afrika which followed a fundamentalist biblical literalism based on a movement originating in the Netherlands in the 1830s, and objected both to hymns and church organs. The Doppers, as its followers were known, interpreted their covenant with God as their promise to do His will in their national as well as their personal life. To fail God's will was to lay oneself and one's nation open to divine punishment, and such failure included not strenuously opposing changes to a God-given combination of religious forms, conservative cultural traditions and reactionary political policy. Doppers, like Paul Kruger, the Transvaal vice-president, saw themselves as closer to God than other groups since they possessed a special understanding of God's purpose. Their manner of dress was unique. The women always wore hoods with their hair behind their ears, and the men short jackets and broad-brimmed hats on their closely cropped heads with rather wide trousers pinched up at the back, with an opening at the side in which they carried a kind of bowie knife, for use chiefly to cut up their food.[54] Outside their own circles, the term 'Dopper' was synonymous with extreme conservatism and uncouth manners.

As Boer political consciousness increased in the late 1870s, and as bitterness filled their souls and indignation made their blood boil under the hated English yoke (to appropriate the rhetoric of the rallies and the newspapers) a resistance movement began to evolve with all burghers expected to join under pain of being otherwise branded a despicable traitor to their blood brothers, a 'British Afrikaner' rather than a 'true' one. Neutrality was regarded in the same adverse light as collaboration, and a sharp division began to appear in Afrikaner ranks.[55] To the dismay of colonial officials, the Afrikaner press in both the Cape and the Orange Free State came out in virulent solidarity with the Afrikaners of the Transvaal. In the Orange Free State strong public pressure began to mount for the government to abandon its official policy of strict neutrality and to go to the aid of its sister republic in restoring its independence. Encouraged by this wave of sympathy, in April 1880 Paul Kruger and Piet Joubert began an extensive speaking and fundraising tour of the Cape and Orange Free State to mobilise Afrikaner opinion against confederation. So successful were they that in June the Cape parliament rejected a motion for confederation without even going to a division. To appalled British officials, the agitation among Afrikaners the length and breadth of South Africa not only spelled the rejection of confederation, but raised the unwelcome spectre of a general Boer uprising against British hegemony.[56]

Agitation died down in the Transvaal during the autumn of 1880 as this was the season when the Boers began moving their stock to the lowveld for the winter grazing. Besides, political developments in Britain seemed more promising for their cause. In April 1880 the Liberals won the election in Britain. Since W.E. Gladstone, the new prime minister, had virulently attacked Tory confederation policy in South Africa in his Midlothian election campaign, and since other Liberal leaders seemed of the same mind, the Boers paused to see if the new administration would live up to its rhetoric. It did not, for this was a fractious administration only kept together by Gladstone's political legerdemain, and it was anxious to avoid potential bones of contention like the Transvaal in favour of concentrating on the more immediately demanding issues of Ireland and the Afghan crisis. Gladstone himself, with more radical cabinet members like John Bright and Joseph Chamberlain, sympathised with the Boer demand for self-determination, but humanitarians like W.E. Forster favoured the retention of British rule to protect the Africans from Boer excesses. The Earl of Kimberley who, as Colonial Secretary, was directly responsible for the Transvaal, urged a strong hand to uphold the imperial image in southern Africa. It seemed fewer apple-carts would be upset if the status quo were maintained, so on 12 May 1880 the new cabinet decided it had to uphold the policy of confederation. On 8 June Gladstone wrote to Kruger and Joubert to confirm he would not let the Transvaal go, citing his government's obligation to the British settlers in the Transvaal and its duties to the Africans.[57]

Nevertheless, despite paying lip-service to confederation, the Liberals had actually come round to believing that they were pursuing a mirage. Frere, confederation's discredited champion who was lingering on in living reproach as Governor of the Cape, had to go, and on 1 August 1880 he was finally recalled.[58] Gladstone replaced him as High Commissioner for South Africa and Governor of the Cape with the experienced technocrat, Sir Hercules Robinson. Sir George Strahan was to act for Robinson until he arrived from New Zealand in January 1881. In the Cape any lingering enthusiasm for confederation died soon after Frere's ignominious recall. The 'Gun War', which broke out in Basutoland in September 1880 when the Cape authorities attempt to disarm the Sotho provoked resistance that lasted a full year, cost the Cape £3 million to suppress and led to a retreat from commitments in the interior.[59]

The drive to South African federation was clearly out of steam once again (or at least for as long as the Liberals remained in power), but the problems it had created in its wake lay unresolved and ready to trip up an unwary administration. In 1880 the attention of Gladstone and his cabinet was grimly focused on the hugely intractable Irish question, so the Transvaal problem was allowed to drift. Gladstone felt able to let it go for the moment because Major-General Sir George Pomeroy-Colley, who had succeeded Wolseley in July 1880 as High Commissioner of South Eastern Africa and Governor of Natal with military command of Natal and the Transvaal, and Lanyon, the Administrator of the Transvaal,[60] both sent in reassuring but hopelessly myopic reports about the mellowing mood among the Transvaal Boers who, in reality, were reaching breaking point.[61] Bitterly disappointed with the uncompromising position maintained by Gladstone's government, Kruger and his close associates came to the conclusion that further meetings and protests were useless, and that the 'best course appeared to be to set quietly to work and to prepare for the worst by the purchase of arms and ammunition.'[62]

Notes and references

1 T.R.H. Davenport and C. Saunders, *South Africa: A Modern History* (Basingstoke and New York, 5th edn, 2000), pp. 194–5. Note that the quality of maps and illustrations is far superior in the 4th edition of 1991, but that the later edition has the advantage of taking the story up to 1999 and incorporating more recent historiography. See also N. Worden, *The Making of Modern South Africa* (Oxford, 3rd edn, 2000), pp. 22–3.

2 See, for example, R. Cope, *Ploughshare of War: The Origins of the Anglo-Zulu War of 1879* (Pietermaritzburg, 1999), in which these explanations are thoroughly canvassed and woven into a much broader based interpretation of imperial policy in southern Africa in the late 1870s.

3 L. Thompson, 'Great Britain and the Afrikaner Republics, 1879–1899' in M. Wilson and L. Thompson, eds, *The Oxford History of South Africa* (Oxford, 1971), vol. II, pp. 289–90.

4 This discussion of the Great Trek is based on M. Legassik, 'The Great Treks: The Evidence'; C. Saunders, 'Great Treks?'; and N. Parsons, 'Reviving the Trek Debates' in the Book Feature on Norman Etherington's *The Great Treks*, *South African Historical Journal*, 46 (May 2002), pp. 282–311.

5 N. Etherington, *The Great Treks: The Transformation of South Africa, 1815–1854* (Great Britain: Harlow, 2001), pp. xix–xxv, 1–9.

6 T.J. Keegan, *Colonial South Africa and the Origins of the Racial Order* (Cape Town, Charlottesville, VA and London, 1996), pp. 184–96.

7 L. Thompson, 'Co-operation and Conflict: the High Veld' in Wilson and Thompson, eds, *South Africa*, vol. I, pp. 405–8.

8 C. Saunders and I.R. Smith, 'Southern Africa, 1795–1910' in A. Porter, ed., *The Oxford History of the British Empire. Volume III: The Nineteenth Century* (Oxford, 2001), p. 602.

9 See J. Benyon, *Proconsul and Paramountcy in South Africa: The High Commission, British Supremacy and the Sub-Continent 1806–1910* (Pietermaritzburg, 1980), especially chap. 1.

10 Thompson, 'High Veld' in Wilson and Thompson, eds, *South Africa*, vol. I, pp. 412–13.

11 D.H. Heydenrych, 'The Boer Republics, 1852–1881' in T. Cameron and S.B. Spies, eds, *An Illustrated History of South Africa* (Johannesburg, 1986), p. 150.

12 See G.W. Eybers, ed., *Select Constitutional Documents Illustrating South African History 1795–1910* (London, 1918), pp. 358–9 for the text of the Sand River Convention.

13 See Eybers, ed., *Select Constitutional Documents*, pp. 282–5 for the text of the Bloemfontein Convention.

14 Davenport and Saunders, *South Africa*, pp. 195–9.

15 R. Dalziel, 'Southern Islands: New Zealand and Polynesia' in Porter, ed., *British Empire*, vol. III, pp. 581–5.

16 Thompson, 'High Veld' in Wilson and Thompson, eds, *South Africa*, vol. I, pp. 424–35.

17 L. Thompson, *A History of South Africa* (New Haven, CT and London, 1990), p. 115.

18 A.M. Grundlingh, 'Prelude to the Anglo-Boer War, 1881–1899' in Cameron and Spies, eds, *South Africa*, p. 184.

19 Saunders and Smith, 'Southern Africa' in Porter, ed., *British Empire*, vol. III, p. 605.

20 Davenport and Saunders, *South Africa*, pp. 199–202.

21 For the diamond fields and their impact, see A.S. MacKinnon, *The Making of South Africa: Culture and Politics* (Upper Saddle River, NJ, 2004), pp. 131–8;

H. Houghton, 'Economic Development, 1865–1965' in Wilson and Thompson, eds, *South Africa*, vol. II, pp. 10–12.

22 Davenport and Saunders, *South Africa*, pp. 202–3.

23 J. Laband, *Kingdom in Crisis: The Zulu Response to the British Invasion of 1879* (Manchester, 1992), pp. 4–6; Cope, *Ploughshare of War*, pp. 2–8.

24 The following discussion on the impulses behind Carnarvon's confederation scheme is based on Cope, *Ploughshare of War*, pp. 257–64 and J. Laband and P. Thompson, *The Illustrated Guide to the Anglo-Zulu War* (Pietermaritzburg, 2nd edn, 2004), pp. 3–5.

25 See P. Delius, *The Land Belongs to Us: The Pedi Polity, the Boers and the British in the Nineteenth-Century Transvaal* (Johannesburg, 1983), chap. 8.

26 Quoted in Davenport and Saunders, *South Africa*, p. 206.

27 Sir L. Woodward, *The Age of Reform 1815–1870* (Oxford, 2nd edn, 1962), pp. 383–4; Thompson, *South Africa*, p. 133.

28 Davenport and Saunders, *South Africa*, p. 206; Heydenrych, 'Boer Republics' in Cameron and Spies, eds, *South Africa*, p. 157.

29 Benyon, *Proconsul and Paramountcy*, pp. 144–8.

30 Laband, *Kingdom in Crisis*, pp. 6–9.

31 For a recent assessment of Shepstone's lack-lustre administration of the Transvaal, see B. Theron, 'Theophilus Shepstone and the Transvaal Colony, 1877–1879', *Kleio*, 34 (2002), pp. 104–27.

32 See L. Scott, 'Die Volkskomitee: 'n "Staat" binne 'n Staat' in Van Jaarsveld, Van Rensburg and Stals, eds, *Eerste Vryheidsoorlog*, pp. 15–27.

33 G.H.L. Le May, *The Afrikaners: An Historical Interpretation* (Oxford, 1995), pp. 67–72; F.A. van Jaarsveld, tr. F.R. Metrowich, *The Awakening of Afrikaner Nationalism 1868–1881* (Cape Town, 1961), pp. 158–9; J. Alton Templin, *Ideology on a Frontier: The Theological Foundations of Afrikaner Nationalism, 1652–1910* (Westport, CT and London, 1984), pp. 163–5.

34 J. Martineau, *The Life and Correspondence of the Right Hon. Sir Bartle Frere, Bart.* (London, 1895), vol. II, p. 253: Frere to Hicks Beach, 8 December 1878.

35 Laband, *Kingdom in Crisis*, pp. 9–14.

36 For the official account of the 1878 operations against the Pedi, see Great Britain, War Office Intelligence Department, *Narrative of Field Operations Connected with the Zulu War of 1879* (London, 1881), pp. 1–10. See also Delius, *Pedi Polity*, pp. 225–39.

37 P. Kruger, *The Memoirs of Paul Kruger, Four Times President of the South African Republic, Told by Himself* (London, 1902), pp. 156–9. For Frere in the Transvaal and his three meetings with the Boer leaders, see B. Worsfold, *Sir Bartle Frere. A Footnote to the History of the British Empire* (London, 1923), pp. 213–25.

38 Le May, *Afrikaners*, pp. 73–8.

39 J. Laband, ' "The Danger of Divided Command": British Civil and Military Disputes over the Conduct of the Zululand Campaigns of 1879 and 1888', *Journal of the Society for Army Historical Research*, 81, 328 (2003), p. 347.

40 Delius, *Pedi Polity*, pp. 239–46.

41 The most recent analysis of Wolseley in the Transvaal can be found in B.M. Theron-Bushell, 'Puppet on an Imperial String: Owen Lanyon in South Africa, 1875–1881' (unpublished D.Litt. et Phil. thesis, University of South Africa, 2002), chapters V and VI.

42 Wolseley to Hicks Beach, 29 October 1879, quoted in Theron-Bushell, 'Lanyon', p. 224.

43 Theron-Bushell, 'Lanyon', p. 212.

44 Lanyon was only appointed permanent Administrator of the Transvaal on 4 June 1880 after having held the appointment for fifteen months in a temporary capacity. See Theron-Bushell, 'Lanyon', p. 135, n. 1.

45 The Letters Patent sanctioning the new constitution arrived in Pretoria on 1 January 1881.

46 Theron-Bushell, 'Lanyon', pp. 222–3.

47 'Stephanus Johannes Paulus Kruger' in W.J. de Kock, ed., *Dictionary of South African Biography* (Cape Town, 1968), vol. I, pp. 444–8.

48 Theron-Bushell, 'Lanyon', pp. 228–30; Le May, *Afrikaners*, pp. 78–82; Van Jaarsveld, *Afrikaner Nationalism*, p. 159; Templin, *Ideology on a Frontier*, pp. 167–70.

49 Van Jaarsveld, *Afrikaner Nationalism*, in particular Section III. The term 'Afrikaners' for the Dutch-speaking settlers of southern Africa was already current by the 1870s and the Afrikaans language was becoming distinct from Dutch. Paul Kruger referred to his people as 'Afrikaners', a term also used by the British at that time. See D.M. Schreuder, *Gladstone and Kruger. Liberal Government and Colonial 'Home Rule' 1880–85* (London and Toronto, 1969), p. 3, n. 1.

50 Schreuder, *Gladstone and Kruger*, pp. 33–4.

51 P. Joubert in the *Volksstem*, 16 November 1880, quoted in van Jaarsveld, *Afrikaner Nationalism*, p. 161.

52 Thompson, 'High Veld' in Wilson and Thompson, eds, *South Africa*, vol. I, p. 427.

53 For the following discussion see Templin, *Ideology on a Frontier*, especially chapters V and IX.

54 For the Doppers, see Templin, *Ideology on a Frontier*, pp. 149–52, 183 n. 23.

55 Van Jaarsveld, *Afrikaner Nationalism*, pp. 155–6.

56 Heydenrych, 'Boer Republics' in Cameron and Spies, eds, *South Africa*, pp. 158–9; C. Saunders, ed., *Reader's Digest Illustrated History of South Africa: The Real Story* (Cape Town, 3rd edn, 1994), pp. 194–5; Templin, *Ideology on a Frontier*, pp. 170–2.

57 *BPP* (C. 2676), enc. 2 in no. 24a: W.E. Gladstone to S.T. Kruger and T.C. Joubert, 8 June 1880. See Schreuder, *Gladstone and Kruger*, pp. 81–5.

58 C.F. Goodfellow, *Great Britain and South African Confederation 1870–1881* (Cape Town, 1966), pp. 193–5.

59 Saunders, ed., *South Africa*, p. 193; P.J. Haythornthwaite, *The Colonial Wars Source Book* (London, 2000), p. 193.

60 Lanyon was made a KCMG in May 1880.

61 Theron-Bushell, 'Lanyon', pp. 239–44; Davenport and Saunders, *South Africa*, p. 208.

62 Kruger, *Memoirs*, p. 166.

chapter 2

The situation in the Transvaal Territory in 1880 and the outbreak of rebellion

The British officials in the Transvaal made little effort to fathom the reasons for swelling Boer antagonism towards their rule; nor did they attempt to disguise their contempt for the Boers themselves.[1] Sir Garnet Wolseley was a man of acute observation, though he could never be described as unprejudiced, and in his private journal he gave his waspish and uncharitable sentiments the freest of rein. On the road through the Transvaal in October 1879 to Pretoria where he intended to take the territory's tottering government in hand, he jotted down his reflections concerning the Boer inhabitants in the most unflattering of terms:

A Boer's idea of life is, that he should pay no taxes of any sort or kind, that he should be amenable to no sort of law he disliked, that there should be no police to keep order, that he should be allowed to kill or punish the Natives as he thought fit, that no progress towards civilization should be attempted, that all foreigners should be kept out of the country & that he should be surrounded by a waste of land many miles of extent each way which he called his farm, in fact that he should have no neighbours as the smoke of another man's fire was an abomination to him. These Transvaal Boers are the only white race I know of that has steadily been going back towards barbarism. They seem to be influenced by some savage instinct which causes them to fly from civilization . . . Altogether I regard them as the lowest in the scale of white men & to be also the very most uninteresting people I have ever known or studied.[2]

The outward and visible sign of this declension from civilisation was the unhygienic state of Boers' homes as fastidiously observed by Wolseley, many of them wretched and filthy, the children unwashed and the ground surrounding the houses 'a mass of refuse, bones, old pieces of sheep skins, dinner refuse, fowl-dirt &c'.[3] Added to these multiple failings (which apparently included a notorious propensity for petty theft from English storekeepers)[4] was the besetting sin of female ugliness:

The women are all prematurely old in appearance; very ugly with complexions like mutton-fat: their figures are detestable: the use of stays is little resorted to: if they have breasts, they must hang down inside their gowns for externally their bodies are as flat about the chest as mine is. Bottoms they have none, but they run largely to stomach. I hear that this last named phenomenon is owning to the quantity of coffee they drink daily at all hours. They are an ill-favoured race certainly.[5]

Lest Wolseley's notorious disparagements seem beyond the acceptable bounds even of British prejudice towards the Transvaal Boers, it is instructive to turn to Henry Rider Haggard who had first entered the territory in April 1877 on the staff of Sir Theophilus Shepstone. Writing in 1899 on the eve of the South African War, Haggard also emphasised the Boer lack of honesty and 'absence of regard for the truth'. He seconded Wolseley's description of the Boer person, characterising the Boers as 'fine men, but as a rule ugly. Their women-folk are good-looking early in life, but very stout as they grow older.' The Boer home he remembered as 'too frequently squalid and filthy to an extraordinary degree', and the Boer as uneducated, xenophobic, resistant to government control and taxes, and always ready to move on if civilisation began to impinge too closely. He emphasised that their brand of Christianity was based on 'the darkest portions of the Old Testament' and that, like the Israelites, 'they think they are entrusted by the Almighty with the task of exterminating the heathen native tribes around them, and are always ready with scriptural precedent for slaughter and robbery.' In fine, Haggard contemptuously concluded, the Transvaal Boer resembled 'no other white man in the world'.[6]

On the other side of the spectrum, the Boers had British apologists. Addressing the Royal Colonial Institute in June 1869 on the social and domestic life of the Boers, H.J. Barrett declared that, like 'the patriarchs of old' they had 'one grand and glorious object before them, which is, to subdue the wilderness, rescue it from heathen desolation, and utilise it for the

adherence to Roman-Dutch law which gave them an absolute right to the ownership or alienation of land. Part of the Transvaal was consequently roughly surveyed into 10,500 farms, though large tracts of land, especially in the north, remained unsurveyed. Two of these 6,000 acre farms, the second being for winter grazing, were given as of right to each claimant before 1870. Roman-Dutch inheritance law required sub-division among heirs, but Boer notables successfully compensated for the fragmentation of their holdings through constant land speculation, strategic marriages and government patronage. Population on these farms was very sparse and un-even. The highveld was avoided by the majority of farmers since it lacked wood and water, and suffered from frost in winter. Large areas of the lowveld were equally unpopular because, being infested with tsetse fly, it was unsuitable for horses and other livestock. However, in these fertile east-ern districts more enterprising farmers were beginning to grow cash crops like tobacco, while it was the temperate south-western zone which was earl-iest the most adequately cultivated. Land with mineral deposits was begin-ning to become a source of wealth to some lucky owners. Even though the land holdings of the prosperous were too large and often inaccessible to be farmed effectively or even occupied (only about 5,000 farms were actually inhabited), existing ownership of these under-utilised lands meant that farmland was becoming unobtainable by 1880. Less successful Boers who abandoned or sold their holdings, and who could not make ends meet through alternatives like transport, riding or hunting, were reduced to eking out a living on other men's farms as sharecropping clients, or *bijwoners*.[13]

The Boer frontier had traditionally expanded through the accretion of stock, the space needed to accommodate large flocks of sheep and herds of cattle, and the skilled labour to manage them. Dutch settlement was sustained through the export of stock, stock products, and the proceeds of the hunt.[14] Because hunting seemed so much more profitable (and exciting) than farming, many burghers sold or abandoned their farms to pursue it as a living. Commercial hunting, mainly for ivory and animal skins, intro-duced arms and ammunition on a large scale. The monopoly in arms and ammunition gave the Boers an economic as well as military advantage over the other peoples of the interior. It is certainly a caricature to portray the Boers as never undertaking mercantile activities in their own right (which they did, particularly in the sphere of land speculation), but their way of life and external factors certainly limited their commercial activities. Commerce was largely in the hands of the coastal merchants of the British colonies and their inland agents, and it was they who determined credit, rates of exchange and the commodities which they would exchange for hunting products. The profits of this 'Overberg trade' over the Drakensberg Mountains onto the highveld were very considerable for Natal merchants.[15]

The very extent of Boer land holdings and execrable roads (wagons made their own tracks through the veld, only converging at drifts and passes) ensured that the Boers in the countryside lived relatively isolated, self-sufficient lives, cut off from many social amenities. A small group of trees, generally weeping willows, would mark a farmstead in the otherwise treeless veld. Round the house or to one side would be between six to a dozen acres of ploughed land for growing mealies [maize], with a small orchard and usually a kitchen garden. There might also be some ditching and draining and irrigation furrows, but almost no enclosures at all, whether of arable land or pasturage. Except among better-off farmers, houses were simply (if comfortably) built of strongly-built clay walls roofed with thatch. In place of windows were louvred shutters which were closed at night. Walls were white-washed inside and out, and the uneven clay floors smeared every five or six days with cow-dung and water to keep down the dust. Thirty or forty yards away from the house would be a large, outside oven. Furniture in the two main rooms was simple. In the living room would be a fireplace, a clock, two solid deal tables, cutlery and china, several benches with lockers under them, a chair or two and small stools. The bedroom featured a large bedstead, feather bed and counterpane. Small rooms would be added to the outside of the house as further sleeping apartments.

Apart from a few of the richer farmers who could afford to maintain their own schoolmaster for their children, country Boers often could secure no schooling whatever unless they sent their children to town. They generally considered it education enough if their children could read the Bible and understand the precepts of their Calvinist faith well enough to pass the examination necessary for confirmation, without which it was not permitted to marry. The rustic Boer's greatest contempt and suspicion was reserved for the educated and arrogant immigrants from the Netherlands whom the Transvaal government employed as preachers, teachers and government officials.

Religion was the great cement of Boer society, and ministers of religion the most influential individuals in society. The Boers, as we have seen, were strict Calvinists with a fundamentalist faith in the Word of the Bible, though fractious in their faith in a way common to many Protestant sects.

Distance from the nearest village with its church meant that the Boers partook of Communion, or *Nachtmaal*, only once every three months. Then the whole community gathered together in their wagons, and the religious observances were made the occasion not only for merrymaking, the holding of fairs and trade, horse racing and shooting competitions, but also for energetic discussions of topical events, both religious and secular, expressed in their colloquial language, a form of Low Dutch full of loan words and expressions from German, French, English and African tongues which was already in the process of transforming itself from High Dutch into Afrikaans. Typically of many another self-reliant and independently minded frontier community, the Boers had no great respect for authority and, as the War Office report noted, were certainly politically aware. They were not cut out to be docile and uncritical subjects to British authority.

Boer occupation of the Transvaal had been a slow and haphazard process with (as we have seen) most farmers concentrated in the southern half of their republic and much land either unoccupied or still in the hand of the indigenous African population. The Voortrekkers believed they had acquired the land by conquest, and so had the right to demand tribute and labour from the people on it, but many chiefs around the periphery repudiated that claim and insisted on their independence. The 'closing of the frontier' which the Great Trek had initiated in the interior was therefore far from complete in the Transvaal Territory, and it would not be so until the suppression of Mphephu's resistance in Vendaland in 1898, on the very eve of the South African War.[16] Meanwhile, the frontier remained fluid and volatile along a great horseshoe of African occupation encircling the south-cental core of white settlement.

The Sotho-speaking Pedi people of the north-eastern Transvaal, who by the end of the eighteenth century had formed a unified political structure under a paramount chief, had posed the most organised threat to the Boers.[17] From the 1850s the Boers made increasingly heavy demands on them for tribute and labour and encroached on their lands. The Pedi were in a better position to resist such intrusions than many another African polity because migrant workers had earlier come under missionary influence in other parts of South Africa, where they had gone to acquire cattle and guns, particularly from the Diamond Fields. Thus armed and educated, they were dangerous and determined fighters whom, as we have seen, the Boers failed to overcome in their war of 1876–1877. Wolseley himself had to take command of the campaign of November–December 1879 which finally

overcame their resistance and subjected their territory to the British administration in Pretoria.

Situated diagonally across the Transvaal from the Pedi, in the south-
west, were the petty Tswana chiefdoms, such as the Kwena, Ngwato,
Ngwaketse, Hurutshe, Tlhaping and the four branches of the Rolong, all of
whom enjoyed much cultural but little political homogeneity.[18] Perhaps
it was the Tswana sense of vulnerability which made them particularly
receptive both to early missionary influence and also to traders who supplied them with horses and guns. The Boers asserted their sovereignty over
them and interpreted the Sand River Convention to mean that the British
had left them free to fix their western boundary at the Tswana's expense.
Through steady encroachment, labour demands and exploitation of divisions within Tswana society, the Boers brought increasing turbulence to their
south-western frontier. The discovery of diamonds increased pressure on the
Tswana, for some were herded into locations in British Griqualand West as
their former lands were surveyed into farms, while the Boers continued to
encroach on those who remained outside. The Griqua rebellion of 1878
brought further divisions, for while Chief Botlasitse of the Tlhaping joined
the uprising, many – notably Mankurwane and his followers – along with
the Rolong chief, Montshiwa, actively helped the British in suppressing
it. The troubled south-western boundaries of the Transvaal thus remained
uncertainly under British rule, and these 'loyal' chiefs looked to Britain to
protect them from further Boer depredations.

The Venda, who had strong historical links with the Shona people to the
north across the Limpopo River, had been settled for centuries in the fertile
Soutpansberg mountains in the far north of the Transvaal, protected by
their mountain strongholds and by the tsetse fly and mosquito which
deterred the Boers from settling on their lands since their horses and cattle
could not survive.[19] Gradually, like the Pedi and Tswana, the Venda were
drawn into the Boer orbit as labourers, traders, hunters and porters, though
they allowed no missionaries. In the 1860s the Boers became disastrously
embroiled in Venda dynastic disputes which culminated in the Boers abandoning their settlements in the north to the Venda, though they continued
to claim jurisdiction as far north as the Limpopo. The British administration
maintained this claim, but had no means (or particular desire) to enforce it.

During the mid-nineteenth century King Mswati had firmly established
the Swazi state, which was closely related to the neighbouring Zulu kingdom to its south.[20] However, he and his successors had to cope with the

expansive tendencies of the Transvaal Boers across his western and northern borders, and over the years made territorial concession. In 1866 the Swazi agreed to a demarcated boundary with the Boers, but in 1868 and again in 1875 the Transvaal asserted its sovereignty over Swaziland, but lacked the means to put this into effect. Concession-hunters began to show a special interest in Swaziland after the discovery of gold in the eastern Transvaal in 1873. Prospectors flocked into the country in search of gold, and the king granted away numerous hunting, grazing and wood-cutting concessions. The greatest of these was the grazing concession of 36,000 acres King Mbandzeni granted Joachim Ferreira and Ignatius Maritz in southern Swaziland. After the British annexed the Transvaal they appointed a commission in 1879 to delimit the Transvaal–Swaziland border, for they believed it was imperative to regularise their standing with the Swazi whom Wolseley considered the key to future relations with adjacent African polities. Wolseley had deployed Swazi levies during the later stages of the Anglo-Zulu War, and they proved crucial in his defeat of Sekhukhune. The British in the Transvaal therefore felt they owed the Swazi a great debt of gratitude and continued to view them as their chief African collaborators in the region.

Areas where Africans were effectively still autonomous shaded off into those occupied by the Boers where the African inhabitants were required to perform tribute labour (*opgaaf*) for the proprietor of the farm. They were subjected to Transvaal law, which forbade Africans to possess firearms, ammunition or horses (the means of war), and required they carry a pass signed by their employer or an official which effectively held them to their farm. *Opgaaf* was vital for the Boer rural economy since it provided labour for agriculture, domestic help for the household and bearers for the great hunts. Yet, in a sense, the system worked for Africans too. Since farms were so large, labour tenants were allowed to graze considerable cattle and other stock and grow crops on a fairly large scale. This allowed them to remain relatively economically independent, and to retain their homes and families and the support of their kinship groups.[21]

As Administrator of the Transvaal, Lanyon believed the British administration should make its impact on African policy. From 15 June to 13 August 1880 he visited the Pedi chiefs Wolseley had overcome the previous year and promised them the advantages of the Crown's protection in return for paying the statutory hut tax of 10 shillings, accepting British rule and more comprehensive pass laws. Lanyon also envisaged a system of native locations, such as he had instituted in Griqualand West, to serve as labour reservoirs. Indeed, in taking and planning these measures, Lanyon never disguised that they were aimed at facilitating the provision of labour to the diamond mines, controlling land use and securing revenues for the Transvaal administration.[22] Moreover, Lanyon's custodianship over the Africans also in effect condoned longstanding Boer slavery practices.

It is only recently that historians have accepted that slavery remained an established feature of Boer society long after its official abolition.[23] Frontier slavery began at the Cape, the Voortrekkers continued its practice in the interior, and it persisted along the open frontier of the Transvaal until the 1870s. The Boers were aided in their slaving raids by African allies (though they also traded with slave-raiding African societies).[24] Since slavery was forbidden under the Sand River Convention, republican law deliberately created a facade which technically forbade it, but permitted the seizure of children who were deemed to be orphans (and slave raiding often ensured that they indeed were) and had to be registered as such. These *inboekelinge* (or 'apprentices' in the British documentation) were required to serve their masters until the age of 25, if male, and 21 if female, though there is no evidence of their ever being emancipated. They grew to adulthood as deracinated and then acculturated labourers known as *oorlamse kaffers* (civilised or sophisticated blacks) skilled in agricultural, pastoral, artisanal and domestic activities. They were socialised into Boer culture and taught to cultivate their sense of superiority over, and alienation from, surrounding Africans. Some even read the Bible to their masters and were used on military expeditions against other Africans, rather like the military slaves in the Muslim states of north and west Africa. Yet they remained a racially inferior social caste in Boer society, their children would remain in the household, and although the law forbade their sale, 'compensation' would be paid if they were passed on to new masters. The British attitude to *inboekstelsel* in the Transvaal was ambivalent. Despite the strength of the abolitionist cause in Britain, research does show that colonial officials tended to tolerate slavery in Africa wherever slave owners were needed to control colonial subjects and generate capital to cover the costs of the administration. The Transvaal seems to have been no exception. The anti-slavery furore in the British parliament in the late 1860s had little practical effect on *inboekstelsel*, and the British administration of 1877–1881 made no determined impact on the institution either.[25] But the lingering stench of Transvaal slavery would not dissipate. Humanitarian groups periodically fanned the embers and no administration, especially a Liberal one, could ignore the potential plight of Africans if surrendered once more to full Boer control.[26]

Rider Haggard who, as a member of Shepstone's staff, had run up the Union Jack in Pretoria in what he later recalled as 'one of the proudest moments' of his life,[27] was one of those who had absolutely no doubts as to the benefits of British annexation accruing to the bankrupt South African Republic. He would write in 1882 of annexation's 'perfectly magical' effects: 'Credit and commerce were at once restored; the railway bonds that were down to nothing in Holland rose with one bound to par, and the value of landed property nearly doubled.'[28] However, Haggard was quite certain that it was not merely the act of annexation which effected the conjuring trick, but the influence it had in attracting hard-working and enterprising emigrants, mainly of British stock, to invest, live and prosper in the new Transvaal Territory. Moreover, these people, Haggard insisted, were not mere adventurers, but were intensely conscious of being British:

People in England seem to fancy that when men go to the colonies they lose all sense of pride in their country, and think of nothing but their own advantage. I do not think this is the case; indeed, I believe that, individual for individual, there exists a greater sense of loyalty, and a deeper pride in their nationality, and in the proud name of England, among colonists, than among Englishmen proper.[29]

Echoing Haggard over a century later, Marjory Harper drew attention in 1999 to the way in which late nineteenth-century dismissive views of the overriding self-interest of British migrants jostled with portrayals of settlers' 'umbilical attachment to their flag'.[30] Such dichotomous perceptions feed into current examinations of the cultures of imperialism. In particular, they are relevant to the way in which colonisers attempted to construct new cultures through which they defined themselves and others in varied colonial sites.[31] Certainly, for John Mackenzie the possession of empire helped forge a sense of distinct 'Britishness' and a popular imperial culture which was a 'potent mixture' – among other ingredients – of patriotism, the military virtues, reverence for the monarchy and a 'self-referencing approach to other peoples'.[32] Naturally, this last led to a sense of racial superiority and the concomitant belief in the right to rule which, from the mid-nineteenth century, was taken increasingly for granted across the British Empire and endowed it with its distinct identity (though in the late 1870s the 'scientific racism' of Social Darwinism had not yet fully permeated the more culturally based discourse of race).

Until very recently, there has been little historiographical attention paid to the evolution of an English-speaking identity in South Africa comparable to the work being undertaken in other Commonwealth countries, notably Britain, Australia and Canada. What pioneering research has been undertaken by John Lambert and others, shows that English-speaking South Africans have always been marked by multiple identities but, until the advent of the Republic in 1961, they were united by strong feelings of Britishness and loyalty to the Crown, symbolised by the fervent flying of the Union Jack and expressed through the continuation of British cultural norms and practices in an alien environment. In return for such loyalty, it was the axiomatic settler assumption that they could always depend upon Britain to protect them from those who would overthrow the British way of life.[33]

It was no easy task for the British in the Transvaal Territory between 1877 and 1881 even to begin to create a new colonial identity for themselves especially since, in James Morris's memorable phrase, the Transvaal was 'the high retreat of everything most doggedly Boer'.[34] The 5,000 or so 'Non-Dutch' emigrants constituted only a small minority of about 11 per cent of the total number of whites living in the Transvaal. The majority of these 'Outsiders' (two-thirds of whom lived in the small towns) were of British stock, though there were other 'foreign adventurers' – Irish, Jews, Americans, Hollanders, Germans, Belgians and Portuguese – whom the British liked to deprecate as 'rarely men of high character and disinterested aims'.[35]

This small 'English' segment of the settler population was, nevertheless, disproportionately influential. In the towns, in the mining districts of Lydenburg and Zoutpansberg, in the inns along the roads, in the country trading stores, wherever there was a field for enterprise, the British predominated commercially. And though the rural settler population was mainly Boer, scattered over their isolated farms, even there individual British farmers were beginning to gain ground. In the fertile Lydenburg District in particular, which bordered on Swaziland and encompassed the Gold Fields around Pilgrim's Rest opened in 1871, farmers from the Cape Colony were increasingly purchasing up land, their farms distinguishable from those of the Boers on account of their 'general air of neatness & cleanliness'.[36] Commercial companies were buying up hundreds of square miles of farms in the same district as an investment.[37] The Glasgow Company, for example, held 100 farms of 6,000 acres each.[38]

Under the British administration, headed by an Executive Council consisting of the Administrator, four more officials and three appointed members,[39] the influence of the British in the civil establishment was also making itself increasingly felt, and not only at the higher levels of the heads of department, judicial officials, landdrosts and commissioners, but lower down with the postal officials, field cornets, clerks, native commissioners and schoolmasters. These officials divided themselves by nationality into 80 'Dutch Afrikanders', 41 'English Afrikanders' (natives of South Africa, mainly the Cape Colony), 68 Englishmen, 35 Hollanders, 28 Germans, 1 Dane and 1 Swede.[40] The Hollanders, Germans and other Europeans had entered the administration of the South African Republic to aid in its executive work prior to British annexation. However, the influx of English-speakers which ensued provided the administration with a preponderance of officials upon which it believed it could rely, and alienated the existing officials who saw their previous political power being whittled away.[41] In the Legislative Assembly, which came into operation on 10 March 1880 and comprised the Executive Council and six additional members nominated by the Administrator (not one of whom was a representative of the Boer opposition),[42] a considerable programme of legislation was enacted in its opening sessions despite its business being conducted in both Dutch and English, which doubled the work[43] – and pointed up the deep differences between many of its members.

Inevitably, the bedrock of the British administration was the garrison of British troops with their headquarters in Pretoria. In November 1880 the 1,800 regulars under the command of Colonel William Bellairs were distributed across the Transvaal. The Pretoria garrison consisted of five companies and a mounted troop of the 2nd Battalion, 21st Regiment (Royal Scots Fusiliers), a battery of artillery and a detachment of Royal Engineers. Two further companies of the Fusiliers were deployed in Rustenburg. Two companies of the 94th Regiment were stationed in Lydenburg, with two more companies of the same regiment in Marabastad, a company at Standerton, and another company and a mounted troop in Wakkerstroom.[44] Trollope commented that when entertained in the officers' mess in Pretoria surrounded by officers in their uniforms, 'it seemed as though a little block of England had been cut out and transported to the centre of South Africa'.[45]

The economic and social effects of the presence of these garrisons on the little towns where they were stationed was considerable – with every soldier purchasing as much as a whole Boer family[46] – for these scattered settlements normally ranged (with the exceptions of Pretoria and Potchefs-troom, the two largest towns) from only a hundred dwellings to less than ten. They always had a court house, church and a central market place, for towns had begun under the Boers as administrative centres for the manage-ment of the land and entrepots for the sale of its produce, and as conveni-ently central situations where farmers could drive in to attend *Nachtmaal*, or send their children to the school (if the place had one). There were at first no hotels because the idea of paying for food or entertainment was prepos-terous to the Boers.[47] Only very recently had traders and speculators moved in, and shops and public hotels, inns and private houses of accommoda-tion sprung up to cater for new customers such as British bureaucrats, soldiers and (in the Gold Fields) prospectors.[48] Travellers, like Trollope, found accommodation in establishments kept by Englishmen decent, clean and up to their standards, not only in the larger towns like Potchefstroom, but even in tiny places like Klerksdorp, which had but half-a-dozen houses.[49] Yet even Lydenburg, considered a lively place since the working of the Gold Fields began, and where property values were rising considerably, was described by Mrs Mary Long, the wife of the Old Etonian Second Lieutenant Walter Long of the garrison, as lacking 'buildings of any con-sequence' and unable to 'boast of a hospital, much less of a town-hall'.[50] A few places, like Pretoria, the seat of the administration, began to develop in tandem as commercial centres, and by 1880 were predominantly English-speaking. Yet even Pretoria, though the fastest growing town in the Transvaal, catering to British administrative, military and commercial inter-ests with its barracks, officers' quarters, court-house, hospital, schools, gov-ernment offices, banks and insurance companies, general stores, churches and rows of new houses, had a civil population of around only 2,250.[51]

The identity of the British settlers in the Transvaal at the time of the Transvaal Rebellion was consequently an ambivalent and vulnerable one, for they were simultaneously the mainstay of the British administration and the economy, yet were seen as distrusted *Uitlanders* (Outsiders) among the Boer settler majority. In such precarious circumstances, the obvious alternative to fashioning an unlikely new colonial identity for themselves was to assert their Britishness and to cling to the tried and secure alternative of an exaggerated loyalty to the Crown and flag, for their future security and prosperity depended upon the maintenance of British rule.

Their insecurity induced the British in the Transvaal – as elsewhere in similar circumstances – to participate in cultural and social activities which class differences and social habits would otherwise have constrained in Britain itself, and to sink often antagonist British regional identities in a show of solidarity.[52] Cultural aloofness was encouraged by the failure to transmit ideas, customs, fashions and games to a suspicious and unreceptive Boer host society. Those hallmarks of British male and commercial solidarity in the colonies, Friendly Societies, were thoroughly established by 1880 in the more markedly British towns of the Transvaal, with four Masonic and five Good Templar Lodges distributed between Pretoria, Potchefstroom and Rustenburg.[53] Confessional affiliation was a significant identifier, and Protestantism (especially of the evangelical variety) was a crucial marker of 'Britishness',[54] though it differed in many essentials from the fundamentalist Calvinism of various of the Dutch Reformed sects to which the Boers overwhelmingly belonged. British and other foreigners were members of the Anglican, Roman Catholic, Wesleyan and Lutheran churches with a combined membership in 1879 of 3,299 with 914 communicants. Significantly, the Anglicans of the Established Church formed the largest of these congregations with a bishop in Pretoria and vicars at Potchefstroom, Rustenburg, Heidelberg, Standerton, Wakkerstroom, Marico and Lydenburg.[55]

There were two classes of school in the Transvaal, namely Government and Aided (or private). The pupils at the former were over 70 per cent Dutch Reformed and instruction was in both Dutch and English. The British preferred their children not to be subjected to this regimen, and this accounted for the trebling between 1878 and 1879 of Aided Schools where the children of non-Boers could be educated in English and in their own religion.[56] No lunatic asylum existed in the Transvaal, but if the British were missing that ubiquitous symbol of settled civic responsibility, they possessed that vital organ of public opinion and free speech, an English newspaper. The *Transvaal Argus* was brought out three times a week in Pretoria; while *De Volksstem* appeared in English on Fridays and in Dutch on Tuesdays. Two further English-medium newspapers, the *Transvaal Advocate* in Potchefstroom, and the *Gold Fields Mercury* of Pilgrim's Rest, ceased publication during 1878.[57] Public facilities for adult education, such as the public reading room in the newly laid out town of Zeerust (which went with an English church and school) attested to the desire – even in the remote Marico District – for the British to establish 'the comforts of civilized life', as they understood them.[58]

In terms of landscape and architecture, the British were determined to create an environment in which they felt at home. Not for Mary Long in

Lydenburg the square houses of the Boers built 'on the bare veldt', with the 'only thing approaching a garden' a vegetable plot nearly half a mile away. Her choice of dwelling was a 'pretty little cottage' in the town, 'buried' under the spreading branches of trees, and her deepest approbation was reserved for the 'charming' English parsonage bordered by hedges and surrounded by 'a perfect wilderness of roses'.[59] Wolseley also commented admiringly on the Lydenburg rose hedges and compared them to those which also proliferated around the houses of the English in Pretoria, with every street 'like a grassy English lane'.[60] Trollope reported exactly the same of Potchefstroom,[61] which also testified to the English talent for creating their preferred landscape wherever they settled. There was an exception, however. Standerton, with its stone and corrugated iron single-story houses, was unusual in its general absence of trees, fruit gardens and hedges.[62]

While he was in the Transvaal, Wolseley noted in his journal the extent to which exotic British sports, entertainments and social occasions were fostered. He mentioned playing lawn tennis, attending cricket matches in Pretoria with cocoanut matting spread between the wickets over the bare ground,[63] and enjoying the regular concerts of the military band at Government House and the Town Square – which angered many Boers when they had gathered to attend *Nachtmaal* the following day.[64] He graced a ball given in his honour at the Masonic Hall with the supper laid out in a tent, and himself held a levee and several receptions at Government House, where the kilted Highland pipers 'astonished the Afrikanders'. Wolseley did not enjoy these occasions – he believed 'an hour or so on a lively treadmill' would have been preferable – but they were an essential assertion of the official British presence.[65]

Nor did Wolseley find the colonial women of Pretoria the least attractive. He privately sniggered at their social airs and 'meretricious finery' when he knew that shortly before they had been busy with menial domestic chores since African domestic servants, though much cheaper than servants in England, were untrained, migratory and often alarming in dress and habits to English eyes.[66] He genuinely pitied what 'the woman brought up as a lady in England must undergo here', thus drawing attention to the inevitable paradox of colonial life where the social graces and aspirations of 'home' collided with the rougher 'hardness of their position'.[67] If, however, a family were prepared to conform with the more relaxed social customs of the colonial world, Trollope believed it could live comfortably and for considerably less than in England. He noticed that Pretoria, like any colonial city struggling into birth, struck the visitor with its untidiness and the sight of brandy bottles, sardine boxes, old boots, paper collars and other rubbish everywhere, while the small houses produced an 'air of meanness'. Nevertheless, on being entertained in a number of these lowly cottages, Trollope 'found internal prettiness' and that his English hosts had 'managed to gather round them within a very small space all the comforts of civilized life'.[68]

C.E. Carrington has written of the pioneers of the nineteenth century that prominent among their numbers were the traders, prospectors and missionaries[69] who blazed the trail for colonisation.[70] Such indeed were the British who first settled in the Transvaal before annexation, but those who came in during the period of British rule were predominantly artisans and working men (carpenters, blacksmiths, bricklayers, bakers, tailors, saddlers and so on) who could demand good wages on account of the skilled labour shortage.[71] Clerical workers found that they could get far better salaries in offices or stores than in government employ, because the professional or mercantile communities were becoming increasingly dominant in the Transvaal economy.[72] Such people were not truly pioneers opening up a wilderness, but immigrants bringing modern skills, urban habits and commercial practices to a society dominated by Boer farmers still resolutely pre-industrial in outlook and preference.

The very fact, though, of a large influx of 'English' capital and immigrants into the Transvaal, and their claims to own a third of the saleable property in the state, to pay more than half the land-tax, and to control almost all mercantile and commercial business,[73] only exacerbated relations with the Boers. As Trollope pointed out, 'Let an Englishman be where he may be about the surface of the globe, he always thinks himself superior to other men around him . . . He expects to be "boss".'[74] In the Transvaal, this instinctive feeling of ascendancy naturally produced something akin to contempt of the rustic Boers, particularly among the more cosmopolitan miners and town-dwellers, who, secure in their belief in the protection of the British garrison, scoffed at the rising Boer discontent with British rule.[75] Though, as Trollope queried, why should the British taxpayer be obliged to go on financing a large military force in the Transvaal to procure the safety of 'the English who have settled themselves among the Boers'?[76]

The Transvaal British, however, were confident that British military protection would continue. The unequivocal and repeated assurances by those in power, such as Wolseley and Gladstone, encouraged many Englishmen to settle in the Transvaal, and persuaded those already there to invest fully in the country confident that they would not lose their property through its being made over to the Boers.[77] But it was Wolseley who saw most clearly the implications for the British settlers in the Transvaal if the British withdrew:

[A]lmost all the trade and commerce of the country is in the hands of Englishmen who welcomed the advent of British Government with rejoicing, and who have incurred much ill-will by the open and patriotic avowal of their support of our policy. . . . [T]he position of insecurity in which we should leave this loyal and important section of the community by exposing them to the certain retaliation of the Boers, would constitute, in my opinion, an insuperable obstacle to retrogression.[78]

The appointment in March 1879 of Lanyon as Administrator had indicated a tough new approach to the recalcitrant Boers of the Transvaal. Lanyon saw himself fundamentally as a military man, and his style of administration (as he had previously exercised it in Griqualand West) was unbending and authoritarian. It pleased him when, with Wolseley's departure from the Transvaal in April 1880, he was able to exercise practically unfettered authority since a distracted Colonial Office tended to leave him practically alone, and Colley in Pietermaritzburg (whom he disdained as his junior in experience) could exert little supervision over him. Lanyon understood very well that the necessary key to effective government and a prosperous territory was the implementation of a workable tax-collection system. With commendable focus he strove to create one, and did indeed greatly improve the Transvaal revenues. Yet this success came with considerable political debits. The Boers had never submitted to taxation, not even when they ruled themselves, and to pay taxes to the British symbolised their submission to alien rule.[79] It was unfortunate that Lanyon, like Wolseley, held the Boers in unconcealed contempt, and they responded in kind. Although Lanyon was in fact Irish, he was apparently of swarthy complexion and the Boers spread the unfounded slur that he was of mixed blood.[80] To be ruled by a black man was not to be endured, so insult was added to the injury of British rule and enforced taxation.

The Transvaal Rebellion, like any other with its long train of causes, was set alight by a specific spark which, in this case, was provided by Lanyon's determination to root out tax evaders. And, as Captain Edmund Verney, RN, Chairman of the Transvaal Independence Committee, expressed it: 'It is very usual to find the crisis of discontent brought on by a tax-gatherer.'[81]

The Potchefstroom District was proving particularly recalcitrant, and the landdrost, A.M. Goetz, began issuing summonses for payment. P.L. (Piet) Bezuidenhout refused to pay a tax demand of £27 5s for his farms (about £14 more than he believed he owed), and after a long wrangle with Goetz provocatively offered to pay £13 5s on condition that it be put aside for the coffers of a future Boer republic. Lanyon could not countenance this, and to make an example of Bezuidenhout, he was taken to court, and though he won his case, he refused to pay the £8 in costs. Goetz confiscated his wagon in execution and put it up for auction in Potchefstroom on 11 November 1880. On the day of the auction P.A. (Piet) Cronjé, a well-known activist in the district,[82] rode into town with as many as a hundred armed companions, seized the wagon to return to Bezuidenhout and then provocatively encamped outside the town. Convinced he could not condone such an act of insubordination, Lanyon ordered the ringleaders of the Potchefstroom fracas arrested. The local special constables were prevented from exercising their duty by Cronjé's armed bodyguards, so Lanyon ordered up troops who entrenched themselves outside Potchefstroom and manned various strong-points in the town itself. The Boers were not to be intimidated, and a stand-off ensued.[83]

As it happened, Piet Bezuidenhout was the son of Frederik Bezuidenhout, one of the 'martyrs' of the Slagters' Nek revolt of 1815 which broke out when the British in the Cape sought to punish him for mistreating his black servant. Here, the cry went up, was a repetition of British tyranny against the son, as against the father.[84] Seeing the political potential of this affair and the inability of the British garrison to assert itself, the Boer Volkskomitee brought forward a public gathering scheduled for 8 January 1881 to 8 December 1880. Meanwhile 111 burghers of the Wakkerstroom District declared that they would only pay taxes under protest: another direct challenge to the British administration.[85] Lanyon, however, breezily refused to accept that the despised Boers could ever really mean business and delayed making appropriate troop dispositions to forestall a crisis, or to call in time for reinforcements.[86] What few actions he adopted to meet the situation were inflammatory, especially his notice in the Government Gazette of 6 December 1880 warning those intending to attend the meeting on 8 December that they would be punished for sedition.[87]

About 5,000 burghers turned up at Paardekraal,[88] near present-day Krugersdorp, for an emotion-charged and decisive rally which lasted until 15 December. The Volkskomitee conferred between 9 and 11 December, and after suspending its deliberations on the Sabbath, put its ideas to a mass meeting on Monday, 13 December. The determined gathering resolved to reconstitute the old *Volksraad*, and in the absence of former President T.F. Burgers (who had left the Transvaal on annexation to live in retirement in the Cape), Paul Kruger resumed his vice-presidency of the South African Republic. Like a latter-day Luther, Kruger addressed the overwrought throng:

I stand here before your face, chosen by the people; in the voice of the people I hear the word of God, the King of all people, and I am obedient . . . After the annexation [the people] protested, have resisted and suffered, and would have attempted every other peaceful means had not English authority in Pretoria made this impossible. The rights of the people are on our side; and although we are very weak, God is a just God. My friends! May the Lord bless your activities and protect our Fatherland.[89]

At Kruger's urging the reconstituted Volksraad elected a triumvirate to lead it consisting of himself, former president Marthinus Wessel Pretorius, and Piet Joubert who had acted as president in 1875–1876. They were joined in an Executive Council by J.P. Maré, W.E. Bok (the State Secretary) and E.J.P. Jorissen (the State Attorney). The revived republican government approved a proclamation announcing the restoration of the republic which was described as being in a state of siege and under the rule of martial law.[90] The assembled burghers next gathered around a flagpole where the *Vierkleur* (the old republican flag with its red, white and blue horizontal stripes and green perpendicular stripe next to the pole[91]) was unfurled and, exhorted by Piet Joubert, erected a cairn around it, each stone a symbol that the burghers had sworn loyalty to each other to fight to the death in the republic's defence.[92]

To keep such an oath required military organisation. Already, on 10 December, field cornets (officers) had been elected for several districts, and Piet Cronjé appointed as commandant over them. On Kruger's motion the assembled burghers elected Piet Joubert Commandant-General on 13 December, even though he protested he was no general and not suited to the job.[93] Nevertheless, he took energetic action and, in terms of the proclaimed martial law, sent out far and wide to appoint further military commanders and to mobilise the Boer forces. These, J.E.H. Grobler has calculated, consisted of approximately 7,000 mounted burghers.[94] The Boers knew they must move rapidly, and on 14 December they resolved to send a commando of 400 men under Piet Cronjé to Potchefstroom to force the printer, J.P. Borrius (the only other printer in the Transvaal was in Pretoria), to print the proclamation of the republic. On 15 December Cronjé's commando cut the telegraph wires, ending communication between Lanyon in Pretoria and Colley in Pietermaritzburg,[95] and rode into Potchefstroom. British officials attempted to prevent the printing, but the Boers seized the printing press and set it to work.[96]

That same day the Boers still gathered at Paardekraal resolved that the restored republic required a temporary capital since Pretoria was firmly in the hand of the British. They chose the little town Heidelberg between Pretoria and Standerton, strategically situated on the wagon road south to Natal by which route British reinforcements must march. No British garrison was stationed there and, nestled in a ring of rocky hills, it would be easy to defend. To forestall a possible British sortie by the Pretoria garrison, Field Cornet D.J.E. Erasmus set off in that direction with a commando of 200 men. The members of the provisional government, followed by a commando of 800 men, set off for Heidelberg on 16 December where the British officials had no choice but to surrender, and the Boers offered no violence to the townspeople.[97] To the accompaniment of great rejoicing the *Vierkleur* was hoisted that evening, which was the potent anniversary of the battle of Blood River (when in 1838 God's hand was believed to have been manifest in His chosen people's rout of the Zulu army), and the proclamation of the restoration of the South African Republic read out. The Triumvirate sent at once to Lanyon enclosing a copy of their proclamation and explaining their uprising in diplomatic terms.[98] Their representative, Hendrik Schoeman, handed it to Lanyon on 17 December. While stressing they had no desire for war, they warned him that they would fight if he did not hand the administration of the Transvaal over to them 'within twice 24 hours'.[99] Lanyon's response to what he saw unequivocally as a rebellion was swift and straightforward. On 18 December he issued a proclamation calling on Colonel Bellairs, the commander of the imperial garrison, 'to vindicate the authority of Her Majesty's Government, and to put down insurrection wherever it may be found to exist'.[100]

But events had already slipped Lanyon's control. On 16 December the Boers had not only proclaimed their republic, but on the same day in Potchefstroom, where the British troops had been facing down the Boer forces in the town, shots had been exchanged and casualties suffered. Both sides held the other responsible for firing first. It is not entirely certain who the first person was to be shot.[101] However, as far as the Boers were concerned, Frans Robertse of Wijsfontein Farm in the Rustenburg District, who was wounded in the arm, was the first heroic victim in the struggle for independence.[102] Force of arms would now decide the issue, and the success of the Boer uprising would hinge on the effectiveness of the British military response.

Notes and references

1 Theron-Bushell, 'Lanyon', p. 221.

2 A. Preston, ed., *Sir Garnet Wolseley's South African Journal 1879–80: Zululand/Transvaal: Military Campaigns/Cetywayo/Sekukhuni/Negotiations with Boer Committee* (Cape Town, 1973), p. 139: 18 October 1879.

3 Preston, ed., *Wolseley's Journal*, p. 218: 22 January 1880.

4 Preston, ed., *Wolseley's Journal*, p. 254: 14 March 1880.

5 Preston, ed., *Wolseley's Journal*, pp. 218–19: 22 January 1880.

6 Haggard, *Last Boer War*, pp. 10–14. For another example of unalloyed British prejudice against the primitive and treacherous Boers contemporary with Haggard, see L. Creswicke, *South Africa and the Transvaal War* (Edinburgh, 1900), vol. I, pp. 15–23.

7 H.J. Barrett, 'Social and Domestic Life of the Dutch Boers of South Africa', Ordinary General Meeting of the Society, 14 June 1869, *Proceedings of the Royal Colonial Institute 1869* (London, 1870), vol. I, pp. 178, 181, 194, 206.

8 See The Transvaal Independence Committee, *Deputation to Lord Kimberley and Mr. Grant Duff* (London, 1881).

9 See, for example, C.F. Davison, *The Case of the Boers in the Transvaal* (London, 1881) and G.B. Clark, *Our Future Policy in the Transvaal: A Defence of the Boers* (London, 1881).

10 A. Trollope, *South Africa* (1878; reprint with introduction and notes by J.H. Davidson, Cape Town, 1973), pp. 258–9.

11 Great Britain, War Office Intelligence Department, *Précis of Information Concerning South Africa. The Transvaal Territory* (London, 1878), pp. 50–2; Trollope, *South Africa*, pp. 260, 263–6, 275, 293, 307, 322. For a more recent synthesis of descriptions of Boer life in the 1870s, see A.F. Hattersley, *An Illustrated Social History of South Africa* (Cape Town, 1973), pp. 225–33. General descriptions below of Boer life are based on these works.

12 See *Blue Book for the Transvaal Province 1879* (Pretoria, 1879), pp. 8–9; War Office, *Transvaal*, pp. 50–3. BPP (C. 2950), Appendix II: Sketch Map of the Transvaal Territory, published in March 1880 by the British Intelligence Branch of the Quartermaster-General's Department, gives the unrealistically precise population figures of 33,739 'Dutch', 5,316 'Non-Dutch' and 774,930 'Kaffirs'.

13 S. Trapido, 'Aspects in the Transition from Slavery to Serfdom: the South African Republic 1842–1902' in *University of London Institute of Commonwealth Studies Collected Seminar Papers No. 20: The Societies of Southern Africa in the 19th and 20th Centuries, Volume 6* (London, 1976), p. 28.

14 F. Morton, 'Slavery in South Africa' in E.A. Eldredge and F. Morton, eds, *Slavery in South Africa: Captive Labour on the Dutch Frontier* (Boulder, CO, San Francisco, CA, Oxford and Pietermaritzburg, 1994), p. 258.

15 Trapido, 'Slavery to Serfdom', pp. 24–6.

16 H. Giliomee, 'Processes in Development of the South African Frontier' and C. Saunders, 'Political Processes in the Southern African Frontier Zones' in H. Lamar and L. Thompson, eds, *The Frontier in History: North America and Southern Africa Compared* (New Haven, CT and London, 1981), pp. 102–3, 164–6.

17 For the Pedi, see Delius, *Pedi Polity*, chapter 9; P. Maylam, *A History of the African People of South Africa: From the Early Iron Age to the 1970s* (Claremont, 1986), pp. 127–30.

18 For the Tswana, see Maylam, *African People*, pp. 119–24.

19 For the Venda, see Maylam, *African People*, pp. 52–3, 130–1.

20 For the Swazi, see P. Bonner, *Kings, Commoners and Concessionaires: The Evolution and Dissolution of the Nineteenth-Century Swazi State* (Johannesburg, 1983), pp. 109–44, 155–7; Maylam, *African People*, pp. 92–5.

21 Trapido, 'Slavery to Serfdom', pp. 25–6; Morton, 'Slavery', p. 260.

22 Theron-Bushell, 'Lanyon', pp. 249–53, 257.

23 Morton, 'Slavery', p. 262.

24 F. Morton, 'Slavery and South African Historiography' in Eldredge and Morton, eds, *Slavery in South Africa*, pp. 1–2.

25 Morton, 'Slavery', p. 267.

26 See *BPP* (C. 2866), no. 8: The Committee of the British and Foreign Anti-Slavery Society to Kimberley, 3 February 1881.

27 Haggard, *Last Boer War*, pp. 88–9.

28 Haggard, *Last Boer War*, p. 88.

29 Haggard, *Last Boer War*, pp. 165–6.

30 M. Harper, 'British Migration and the Peopling of Empire' in Porter, ed., *British Empire*, vol. III, p. 75.

31 See C. Hall, 'Introduction: Thinking the Postcolonial, Thinking the Empire' in C. Hall, ed., *Cultures of Empire: Colonizers in Britain and the Empire in the Nineteenth and Twentieth Centuries: A Reader* (New York, 2000), pp. 1–33, *passim.*

32 J.M. Mackenzie, 'Empire and Metropolitan Cultures' in Porter, ed., *British Empire*, vol. III, pp. 273, 290–1.

33 J. Lambert, 'South African British? Or Dominion South Africans? The Evolution of an Identity in the 1910s and 1920s', *South African Historical Journal*, 43 (November 2000), pp. 197–8, 220.

34 J. Morris, *Heaven's Command: An Imperial Progress* (Harmondsworth, 1979), p. 423.

35 Sir Bartle Frere, quoted in W.E. Garrett Fisher, *The Transvaal and the Boers: A Short History of the South African Republic, with a Chapter on the Orange Free State* (London, 1900), p. 179.

36 Preston, ed., *Wolseley's Journal*, p. 140: 20 October 1879.

37 War Office, *Transvaal*, pp. 45, 50; *Blue Book 1879*, p. 15.

38 *BPP* (C. 3219), Transvaal Royal Commission Report, Part II: Report of Evidence given by Sir Morrison Barlow, Bart., and by Captain Dahl, 28 May 1881.

39 The Executive Council, which replaced the entirely unrepresentative administration Shepstone had put in place, met for the first time on 23 February 1880 (*BPP* (C. 2584), no. 87: Lanyon to Wolseley, 5 March 1880). Its functions were to advise the administrator with whom all the final responsibility rested. See also Theron-Bushell, 'Lanyon', pp. 245–7.

40 *Blue Book 1879*, p. 7; see. pp. 104–19 for lists of officials in the various government departments.

41 Preston, ed., *Wolseley's Journal*, p. 212: 17 January 1880.

42 Theron-Bushell, 'Lanyon', pp. 247–8.

43 *BPP* (C. 2676), no. 26: Lanyon to Kimberley, 12 June 1880.

44 Bellairs, ed., *Transvaal War*, p. 43.

45 Trollope, *South Africa*, p. 305. In Pretoria, the young Haggard found the rumbustious and opinionated Trollope 'obstinate as a pig'. Quoted in V. Glendinning, *Trollope* (London, 1993), p. 455.

46 Trollope, *South Africa*, p. 298.

47 Barrett, 'Dutch Boers', pp. 184–5.

48 War Office, *Transvaal*, pp. 23–6.

49 Trollope, *South Africa*, pp. 327, 330.

50 Mrs W.H.C. Long, *Peace and War in the Transvaal. An Account of the Defence of Fort Mary, Lydenburg* (London, 1882), p. 6.

51 Davey, 'Siege of Pretoria', pp. 271–2.

52 K. Robbins, *Great Britain: Identities, Institutions and the Idea of Britishness* (London and New York, 1998), pp. 213–14.

53 *Blue Book 1879*, pp. 9–10, 146.

54 Mackenzie, 'Empire and Metropolitan Cultures', pp. 274–5.

55 *Blue Book 1879*, pp. 10, 148–9.

56 *Blue Book 1879*, pp. 11–12; War Office, *Transvaal*, p. 23.

57 *Blue Book 1879*, pp. 13, 17.

58 War Office, *Transvaal*, p. 26.

59 Long, *Fort Mary*, pp. 4–7.

60 Preston, *Wolseley's Journal*, pp. 124, 128, 158: 27 September; 5 October; 4 November 1879.

61 Trollope, *South Africa*, pp. 328–9.

62 Bellairs, ed., *Transvaal War*, p. 327.

63 Preston, ed., *Wolseley's Journal*, pp. 126, 129, 207: 1 October, 7 October 1879; 14 January 1880.

64 Preston, ed., *Wolseley's Journal*, pp. 124, 128: 27 September; 4 October 1879.

65 Preston, ed., *Wolseley's Journal*, pp. 129, 132–3, 197: 6 October, 10 October, 29 December 1879.

66 Trollope, *South Africa*, pp. 299, 303–4.

67 Preston, ed., *Wolseley's Journal*, pp. 129–30: 7 October 1879.

68 Trollope, *South Africa*, pp. 299–301, 304.

69 The most active missionary societies in the Transvaal were the Berlin, Hermannsburg and Cape Dutch Reformed Church. However, the Mackenzie Anglican Mission was active in the Lydenburg District, and the Wesleyan Mission in the Potchefstroom and Marico districts. See *Blue Book 1879*, pp. 1–11, 150–1.

70 C.E. Carrington, *The British Overseas. Exploits of a Nation of Shopkeepers* (Cambridge, 1950), p. 495.

71 War Office, *Transvaal*, p. 47. For the average wages of such labourers, see *Blue Book 1879*, p. 167; Trollope, *South Africa*, pp. 304–5.

72 *BPP* (C. 2866), enc. 2 in no. 1: D.M. Kisch, Acting Auditor-General to the Commissioner, Finance and Revenue Transvaal, 30 November 1880.

73 *BPP* (C. 2950), enc. 1 in no. 49: C.K. White and Martin J. Farrell to W.E. Gladstone, n.d. [c. 7 April 1881]; Haggard, *Last Boer War*, p. 118.

74 Trollope, *South Africa*, p. 263.

75 Garrett Fisher, *Transvaal and the Boers*, pp. 192, 199.

76 Trollope, *South Africa*, p. 294.

77 Haggard, *Last Boer War*, pp. 111–16; *BPP* (C. 2676), enc. 2 in no. 24a: Gladstone to Kruger and Joubert, 8 June 1880.

78 *BPP* (C. 2866), Appendix: Wolseley to Hicks Beach, 29 October 1879.

79 Theron-Bushell, 'Lanyon', pp. 258–9, 299–302.

80 Bellairs, ed., *Transvaal War*, p. 9, n. 1; Davey, 'Siege of Pretoria', p. 272, n. 6. Wolseley, it should be noted, accepted that Lanyon had a 'taint of black blood' (Preston, ed., *Wolseley's Journal*, p. 265: 2 April 1880).

81 Captain E.H. Verney, *Four Years of Protest in the Transvaal* (London, 1881), p. 55.

82 Cronjé was born near Colesberg in the Cape and accompanied his parents on the Great Trek. He was later in command of the commando that forced the surrender of the Jameson raiders in 1896, and in the South African War was given command of the western front when he failed to capture Mafeking and finally surrendered at Paardeburg in February 1900. See Cmdt C.J. Nöthling, 'Military Commanders of the War (1880–1881)', *Militaria*, 1, 11 (1981), pp. 77–8.

83 *BPP* (C. 2740), enc. 1 in no. 60: Goetz to Hudson, 11 November 1880; no. 61: Lanyon to Kimberley, 14 November 1880; enc. 2 in no. 61: Lanyon to Bellairs, 14 November 1881; enc. 3 in no. 61: Morcom to Public Prosecutor, Potchefstroom, 13 November 1880 and Hudson to Goetz, 14 November 1880; (C. 2783), enc. in no. 12: report by P.A. Cronjé; Bellairs, ed., *Transvaal War*, pp. 46–8; Bennett, *Rain of Lead*, pp. 43–8.

84 Templin, *Ideology on a Frontier*, p. 172.

85 *BPP* (C. 2740), enc. in no. 68: Declaration by Wakkerstroom burghers, 16 November 1880.

86 Theron-Bushell, 'Lanyon', pp. 268–73. See Chapter 4.

87 *Transvaal Government Gazette Extraordinary*, 6 December 1880: Government Notice 257 of 1880.

88 Though conflicting estimates ranged from 4,000 to 10,000, the tally is complicated by late arrivals. See Theron-Bushell, 'Lanyon', pp. 274–5, n. 68.

89 BV 5, p. 6: Aanspraak van S.J.P. Kruger, 13 December 1880; translation in Templin, *Ideology on a Frontier*, p. 173.

90 *BPP* (C. 2838), enc. 7: Proclamation, South African Republic, 16 December 1880.

91 The Vierkleur was hoisted for the first time on 6 January 1857 at Potchefstroom at the inauguration of the first President of the South African Republic, M.W. Pretorius, and subsequently approved by the Volksraad on 13 February 1858. See D. Conradie, 'The Vierkleur and the Union Jack in the 1880–1881

War between the Zuid-Afrikaansche Republiek and Britain', *Militaria*, 1, 11 (1981), p. 58.

92 J.E.H. Grobler, 'Paardekraal: Eensydige Herstel van die Onafhanklikheid' in Van Jaarsveld, Van Rensburg and Stals, eds, *Eerste Vryheidsoorlog*, pp. 104–6; Van Jaarsveld, *Afrikaner Nationalism*, p. 171.

93 J. Meintjes, *The Commandant-General: The Life and Times of Petrus Jacobus Joubert of the South African Republic 1831–1900* (Cape Town, 1971), p. 74.

94 Grobler, 'Paardekraal', pp. 106, 108.

95 *BPP* (C. 2783), enc. 2 in no. 49: Bellairs to DAG, Pietermaritzburg, 17 December 1880.

96 Grobler, 'Paardekraal', pp. 105, 107–8.

97 See *BPP* (C. 2959), enc. 4 in no. 4: Report of Acting Landdrost of Heidelberg, 16 December 1880.

98 Grobler, 'Paardekraal', p. 106; Templin, *Ideology on a Frontier*, pp. 173–4; Heydenrych, 'Boer Republics' in Cameron and Spies, eds, *South Africa*, p. 159; Saunders, ed., *History of South Africa*, pp. 196, 199; Le May, *Afrikaners*, p. 86.

99 *BPP* (C. 2838), enc. 7: Kruger, *et al.* to Lanyon, 16 December 1880.

100 WO 32/7812, enc. 2 in no. 079/3975: Proclamation by Lanyon, 18 December 1880.

101 See Bennett, *Rain of Lead*, pp. 71–5.

102 Kruger, *Memoirs*, p. 172.

chapter 3

The Boer and British military systems

The Transvaal war was fought by contrasting military systems in a militarily complex and transitional period which provided a devastating demonstration of the effects of modern fire and movement tactics, as successfully practised by the Boers, against the less agile approaches which the British tactical manuals laid down.

The British thought they understood the Boer military system and its apparent shortcomings.[1] Prior to 1880 they had faced the Boers in battle on a number of occasions. True, the Boers had worsted the British in a night skirmish at Congella in 1842 during the struggle to control Natal, but the British had soon retrieved the situation and the Boers had capitulated.[2] More recently, the supposed superiority of British regulars over Boer irregulars had been confirmed in the skirmishes at Zwartkopjes in 1845 and Boomplaats in 1848 which had temporarily established British control over the territory north of the Orange River.[3] During the course of the nineteenth century British forces had fought side-by-side with Boer soldier-settlers in no less than seven of the nine Frontier Wars in the Eastern Cape. However, any notion of the effectiveness of the Boer military system had been somewhat vitiated by the fluctuating successes of the Boers of the Orange Free State against the Basotho kingdom in the wars of 1858, 1865–1866 and 1868.[4] Then, most recently, the British had witnessed the poor Boer morale, disorganisation and abject military failure in their war of 1876 against Sekhukhune and the Pedi people in the north-eastern Transvaal,[5] a reverse that had helped precipitate British annexation in 1877. For the British – and most English-speaking settlers likewise – the 1876 Boer military debacle only served to confirm an ingrained contempt for their military qualities; a contempt based on racial and cosmopolitan prejudice against country bumpkins in disreputable civilian clothes who could not even cope militarily with African savages, and who certainly could never be expected to prevail against British regulars.

It was to take a series of humiliating British defeats at Boer hands before Major-General Sir Archibald Alison, the Deputy Quartermaster-General for Intelligence at the War Office, would concede in February 1881 that the Boers were 'probably the most perfect Mounted Infantry in the world'.[6] Of course, old colonial hands like Felix Schermbrucker, who had commanded irregular mounted troops in the Anglo-Zulu War and was entirely familiar with Boer fighting methods, early advised the British that the Boers were 'most splendidly mounted, and every one of them a crack shot, armed with the best firearms available'. He warned that with their intimate knowledge of the terrain and a 'system of spies and scouts' they would be able to ambush and pick off advancing British columns at will.[7] Still, it would only be with chastened hindsight that a military theorist like Colonel C.E. Callwell – whose famous treatise, Small Wars, became the British army's official handbook on how best to fight irregular soldiers – would appreciate the virtues of the Boers as determined men with excellent firearms who were commanded with great skill.[8]

It is true that the Boer republics lacked conventional military forces or standing armies, which were alien to their supposedly egalitarian culture. Their forces were a militia in which no structured military training or parade-ground drill took place, and Boers were never inclined blindly to obey orders. The outspokenness and informality of the men and their stout refusal automatically to concede the authority of their officers led the British in 1880–1881 to believe they were entirely undisciplined – a misconception the British would repeat in their impression of Australian or Canadian troops in the two World Wars. Not that it can be denied that officers in the Boer military system usually had to struggle to exert command and control over their men, even when they had earned their respect through military merit. All too often the lax discipline of burghers during action did indeed adversely affect the outcome of operations. Certainly, the practice of holding a krijgsraad, or council of war, before going into action was always a potential weakness because battle plans were freely discussed by all present, though only officers had the vote. Those whose preferred plan was not adopted often lost heart and, indeed, took a sour satisfaction if the preferred strategy went awry. Then they had no compunction in packing up in protest and leaving the *kommando* [commando] to its misguided devices. In general, burghers thought little of simply absenting themselves and riding home for a while, because they knew that if they decided to come back there was no machinery for punishing them for desertion.

It was easy to deride such failings and so to discount Boer military capabilities. But it was also a matter of military culture. The Boers possessed a military structure and combat skills which were suited to their environment and reflected their notions of a citizen's obligations to the community. If properly motivated – as they were in 1880–1881, but had not been in 1876 – the Boers were capable of mounting a determined and skilful campaign which would tellingly probe the manifest weaknesses in the British military system.

The commando system was the organisational basis of the Boer military system. It had first been formalised in 1715 on the Cape frontier when the Dutch East India Company, whose urban-based Burgher Militia and garrison of soldiers were designed to repel a sea-borne attack on Cape Town by European foes, looked to an alternative and more mobile mode of border defence against African raiding. The commando system became a central feature of burgher society, and continued in the Cape after 1806 when British rule was established. As both a military and an economic institution it – together with the Calvinism of the burghers – created a web of social relations essential in holding together and ensuring the survival of the community. It is no surprise, therefore, that the emigrant Boers, or Voortrekkers, perpetuated the commando system when they left the Cape in the mid-1830s for the interior, and institutionalised it once they established their republics on the highveld.

With certain exceptions, every able-bodied free burgher between sixteen and sixty was required to serve without pay in time of need as part of his civil responsibility. In 1876 the official statement of the number of burghers in the Transvaal capable of bearing arms listed 7,326.[9] Young men under eighteen, however, and men over fifty, were only called out in an emergency. Members of the volksraad, officials, clergymen and school-teachers were exempt from service, but had to contribute financially towards the cost of the war. Owners of land residing outside the Transvaal had to find a substitute, or pay a fine.

By the 1870s the Transvaal burgher was expected to provide himself with a rifle and 50 rounds of ammunition. Requiring his firearm for hunting and defence, the Boer farmer bought the best weapon he could obtain. In 1880 a variety of breech-loading, falling block or bolt action rifles and carbines of American, British or Swiss manufacture were available for purchase in southern Africa. The most popular firearm was the British-made .450 calibre Westley Richards falling block, single action breech-loading rifle firing the no. 1 or no. 2 musket cartridge, and which was very accurate up to 600 yards. This was a weapon very similar in manufacture, sighting, calibre, weight and ammunition to the Martini-Henry Mark II carried by the British troops, the standard infantry weapon of the time. Boer officers, along with their rifle, often carried a revolver.[10]

Besides his weapon, the burgher was expected to provide his own horse and saddlery. Boer ponies were trained to stand without being held, which allowed every rifle to be put into the firing line. The Boers were easy on their ponies, not usually pushing them more than six miles an hour, and rode light, not carrying much more than a blanket, saddlebag, tin mug and haversack. On being called out, burghers were supposed to carry eight days' rations. After that, they relied on what supplies the commando carried in its wagons, or lived off the countryside. Their horses and the draft animals were put out to graze, herded by *oorlamse kaffers* serving with the commando.

These black servants carried out all the other behind-the-line services as well, including driving the wagons and managing the teams of oxen, grooming horses, slaughtering livestock, collecting firewood, cooking, guarding ammunition, digging trenches and emplacements for the burghers and helping with the sick and wounded, for there were no ambulance or hospital services to speak of. Known as *agterryers* ('after-riders' or lackeys who accompanied their masters on horseback on a journey, a hunting expedition or to war), they had been an inseparable part of the commando system since its inception in the Cape, and the institution had moved inland with the Boers during the Great Trek. Before the British annexation of 1877 *agterryers* had taken part in the campaigns of the South African Republic, performing both their customary menial tasks and sometimes taking a direct military role, as in the campaigns against the Pedi. Unfortunately, because their presence on campaign was so much taken for granted, there is little specific reference to *agterryers* in the sources. Thus their familiar presence on the battlefields of 1880–1881 must be largely inferred, and it must be presumed that their participation was almost entirely confined to a support role (unlike the war of 1899–1902, where on occasion they became directly involved militarily), and that they took little part in the actual fighting.[11]

Unlike the British soldiers, the burghers had no uniforms and wore their ordinary clothes on campaign, though these were often adapted to special purposes with ammunition pockets and pouches sewn or otherwise attached to shirts, waistcoats and jackets. Nor were these clothes as formal in the field as in the stilted, posed photographs of the men about to leave for war, when they wore their best for the record of posterity. The wide-brimmed felt hat was ubiquitous on campaign, as were comfortable cor-duroy trousers.

An oft-cited potential weakness of the commando system (already referred to above) was the selection of officers by popular vote, which made them excessively accessible and answerable to ordinary burghers. Yet, contrary to popular myth concerning the lack of social distinction in an egalitarianism military system, from its earliest days the commando system reflected the dominance of the rich frontier farmer who, as *kommandant* (or commandant), lorded it over his band of armed retainers. The ballot for military office was not secret, and the notables could exert considerable pressure on burghers dependent on their good offices. The Great Trek leaders were drawn from the class of the wealthiest migrants supported by their clientage, and thus the relationships of power and property that had existed in the Cape Colony were reproduced in the new republics.

The most important official was the *veldkornet* (or field cornet), invari-ably elected from a family of local notables. In the Transvaal in 1880, in each of the thirteen districts into which the territory was divided for elect-oral and administrative purposes, there were between two and six *veldkornette* depending on the number of wards.[12] Every *veldkornet* was responsible in his duties to the *landdrost*, or magistrate, and through him to the Krijgsraad, or state war council. His primary tasks were to ensure that the burghers in his ward were combat-ready, and in wartime to muster them within 48 hours into the district commando under its *kommandant*, whom the *veldkornette* had previously chosen. The right was also vested in *veldkornette* to com-mandeer wagons, trek oxen, slaughter cattle, horses and whatever else was necessary to supply the commando. Discretion of choice was with the *veldkornet*, and demands inevitably lay heaviest on those whom he did not favour.[13] Besides these wide-ranging powers, the *veldkornet* was also respons-ible for tax assessment, the registration of farms and the administration of Africans. He was thus in a fine position to accumulate landed property and the labour to work it. The office of *landdrost*, superior to that of *veldkornet*, was the ideal stepping-stone to higher elected office in the state, such as that of *kommandant-generaal*, or commandant general. The latter was one of the most influential in the Transvaal, for the position was more than simply a military one. The *kommandant-generaal* fixed the price of all commodities, acted as a general broker in relation to the valuable sale of ivory, and controlled the distribution of arms and ammunition, normally procured through Cape, Natal and Portuguese traders. Thus the commando system and its officers, drawn from an oligarchic class interconnected through ties of kinship, political alliances and economic interest based on the control of land, labour and trade, dominated the rest of Transvaal Boer society which (as we have seen) consisted mainly of lesser farmers with a few professionals, ministers of religion and government officials thrown in.

The election of all military officers on the basis of wealth, influence and sometimes even popularity naturally did not guarantee effective command or militarily sophisticated leadership. Too much depended on family credentials and the spurious wisdom associated with the wearing of a long, white beard. In 1880–1881 Boer officers were familiar with fighting only Africans, and had little training in strategy and tactics as the British would have understood them, though good sense and experience with local conditions did much to compensate. In practice, and especially on campaign, forceful and efficient men who had the confidence of their companions usually came more to the fore, but generally not at the higher levels of command which remained in the hands of the oligarchs.

Boers lived to fight another day, and the merits of dying in a glorious last stand were entirely discounted. As members of a citizen militia made up from a very small male population with few or no reserves available, they were most unwilling to take unnecessary casualties. Hand-to-hand fighting meant sharp losses, and made no sense to marksmen. Burghers raised on farms grew up with a rifle in their hands and with an ability to judge distance accurately, which resulted in accurate individual fire.[14] Habitual hunters by the age of ten or so, who had learned not to waste expensive and not easily obtained ammunition, they mastered the ability to stalk their prey and developed a fine sense of bushcraft. Indeed, the commando system called for initiative and self-reliance, essential in irregular warfare when men were widely scattered and not in close communication with their leaders. These qualities – when allied to superior marksmanship and field-craft, practised horsemanship and a sense of how best to use terrain, and when combined with a toughness bred from eking a living from a harsh and unforgiving environment, in constant danger from attack by wild animals or hostile Africans – made for individually excellent fighting-men.

There were three interconnected elements to Boer effectiveness on campaign. Horses gave mounted men the advantages of mobility and surprise, and permitted swift tactical withdrawals; small-arms, expertly handled, laid down a devastatingly heavy and accurate fire; and the ox-wagon, when drawn up in an all-round defensive position, allowed Boers to maximise their firepower and avoid being outflanked. This combination made the Boer military machine almost unbeatable against Africans armed with traditional sharp-edged weapons or clubs, especially when they persisted in mass attacks in the open. As a rule, the preferred Boer tactic was to ride to within range of the normally fairly dense formation of African warriors, dismount and fire in almost one movement, remount, retire behind the next rank of mounted men and reload.[15] In this way they would draw the African forces onto their entrenched wagon laagers where the attack was stalled by concentrated firepower, and then broken up by a mounted sortie.[16]

These tactics, so successful in the 1830s in pitched battles against Ndebele and Zulu warriors, soon required adjustments as enemies and technologies changed. In their subsequent wars against African polities such as the Sotho, Pedi or Swazi, Boers found themselves having to storm mountain strongholds determinedly held by warriors armed with modern rifles which were becoming increasingly available to them from the 1860s. Africans such as the Sotho also adopted the pony and became as mobile as any Boer commando. Wagon laagers might still act as effective strongholds against enemies with small-arms, but once the British entered the field with artillery, laagers lost their usefulness except as base camps, and the Boers had to learn how to dig in and create systems of trenches.

By the late 1850s Boers in the interior were operating like mounted infantry, for to storm a defended position on high ground meant leaving horses in the rear and employing coordinated infantry fire and movement tactics. Well-aimed covering fire by selected marksmen made it difficult for the defenders to show themselves to fire back at their assailants, as the British were to discover on Majuba. With the introduction of the fast-firing breech-loader, which supplanted the muzzle-loading rifle, the carefully aimed barrage was replaced on occasion by an intense volume of less carefully aimed suppressing fire. This 'hose-pipe' method could be both effectively daunting and demoralising for opposing troops, and was the Boer riposte whenever they realised the British were contemplating a bayonet charge and hand-to-hand combat.

By the time the Boers faced the British in 1880–1881 the normal commando formation for driving home an attack was a loose swarm intent on outflanking their opponents. Boer forward scouting was efficient. Once the enemy was located, the commando would approach under cover of dead ground (even if this meant a wide detour) in order to bring the striking force unseen to within effective rifle range. Then the men, who would have been riding in a solid column, would shake themselves out into line, gallop into the nearest dead ground, dismount and open fire as described. These effective manoeuvres were employed at the battles of both Bronkhorstspruit and Ingogo (or Schuinshoogte). Whatever the circumstances, the essential Boer tactics were speed in concentration and attack, and a readiness to withdraw to a more favourable position before they became too decisively engaged in a fire-fight that was going against them.

These commando methods were at their most effective in wars of movement which, for the Boers, were to have their apotheosis in the guerrilla phase of the South African War of 1899–1902. Though handicapped by lack of discipline, such tactics were adequate (when morale was up) even for storming African mountain strongholds – and the British atop Majuba. Burghers showed at the battle of Laing's Nek that, when properly deployed behind natural defences, they could work together well in comparatively large bodies, accept battle and stolidly hold their positions even under heavy bombardment. But commando fighting style and rudimentary discipline were not best suited to the static, attritional and often demoralising tactics of siege warfare which formed such a large part of the fighting in 1880–1881 when the Boers invested the British garrisons in the Transvaal. Nor were the Boer forces suitably equipped for siege warfare. Those burghers who volunteered to work what few artillery pieces they possessed had never undergone any formal training in handling them.[17] There had been no standing artillery force in the Transvaal until 1874, when President Burgers visited Europe and acquired four 4-pounder Krupp guns and a Mitrailleuse. The British took over these modern weapons when they annexed the Transvaal, which left the Boers in 1880 with a strange collection: two old muzzle-loading ship's guns; two carronades (or short-barrelled ship's guns intended for close work); 'Ou Griet', a revered muzzle-loader which had seen service on the Great Trek and which the Boers had buried in 1877 to keep out of British hands; and three amateur muzzle-loaders constructed by Marthinus Ras, a blacksmith who lived near Rustenburg. Only one of these Ras guns would ever see service. In 1880–1881 all this makeshift artillery was employed in siege work, where its effectiveness was limited. None of it was used in field battle.[18]

The Stanhope Memorandum of 8 December 1888 defined the purposes for which the British Army existed and placed them in an order of priority which had not previously been officially stated. Even so, the first three of these priorities had applied to the army at the time of the war of 1880–1881, that is, to aid the civil power in the United Kingdom, to provide reinforcing drafts for India, and to provide garrisons for colonies and coaling stations.[19] It is a truism, but empires are based on power. Traditionally reluctant to finance a large standing army, the British put their faith in the navy to maintain their overseas supremacy. But naval bases also needed to be garrisoned, and colonies required the army to help defend them from internal revolt or attack. Yet without the familiarising effects of conscription, the general public in Britain continued to view the small and professional British army with considerable disparagement and suspicion.[20] The army was indeed a self-contained and authoritarian institution in which the forces of conservatism were deeply entrenched. Nevertheless, it played an essential role in imperial defence, and during the nineteenth century the British government, rather than downgrading the army, made various attempts to improve its effectiveness.

Since the 1840s British governments had been attempting to make the colonies militarily more self-reliant. Sheltered by imperial garrisons, they were all too irresponsible in provoking wars to extend their frontiers. In 1862 Lord Palmerston decreed that colonies should bear more of the cost of their own defence and ease the need for large garrisons of British troops by raising and training volunteer units from the local settlers, supported by auxiliaries drawn from the indigenous population. This was easier to decide than enforce, however, and colonies persisted in believing that it was the obligation of the British garrisons overseas to defend them. Overseas garrisons continued to be used as a reserve force to be rushed to emergencies wherever they might detonate about the Empire, the Transvaal Rebellion being a case in point.

The army reforms carried out under Edward Cardwell, Secretary of State for War in Gladstone's first cabinet (1868–1874), must be understood as a determined attempt to remedy this situation. Troops would be withdrawn from colonies of white settlement and garrisons scaled down elsewhere, except for India. The introduction of short service in 1870 – whereby recruits spent six years in the regular army and six more in the reserve – was designed to create a large pool of trained reservists, reduce unhealthy service abroad and save money. The Localisation Bill of 1872 established 66 territorial districts in Britain with two linked battalions attached to each brigade depot. The intention was that the battalions would alternate in recruiting at home and serving abroad, so ensuring that the Empire would by guarded only by seasoned troops. However, mounting demands for imperial defence, of which the Anglo-Zulu War of 1879 was a notable instance, required a stronger presence overseas than Cardwell had envisaged. Since the reserve was not to be called out except in the event of a national emergency, minor colonial campaigns could only be provided for by calling upon regular and reserve units for volunteers, and by draining standing garrisons, as became necessary in South Africa in 1880–1881. This demand upset the balance between battalions stationed at home and those serving overseas, and resulted all too often in imperfectly trained battalions being posted to the colonies. To maintain establishments and meet the larger turnover of men caused by short-term enlistment, the army had to lower physical standards. Furthermore, as experienced soldiers now left the ranks earlier, the proportion of young men rose to such an extent that the efficiency of regiments on active service was undermined.

Cardwell's territorial brigade districts usually conformed to existing counties in Britain, for it was his intention to tie infantry battalions to particular geographical regions in order to foster local loyalties and community ties, and to encourage recruitment.[21] Unlike the infantry, cavalry regiments had no 'county' recruiting grounds, but were recruited from the whole country. Hugh Childers, Secretary of State for War between 1880 and 1882, took Cardwell's plan to its logical conclusion in 1881 by permanently linking regular battalions within specific geographical areas. On the recommendation of the Ellice Committee on the Formation of Territorial Regiments, the first 25 numbered line regiments were each given two battalions, while the remainder of the line regiments were amalgamated in pairs to form the two battalions of the new regiments. The old regimental numbers and county affiliations, which had previously characterised individual battalions, were changed to territorial titles. This reform took effect very soon after the conclusion of the Transvaal Rebellion, with the consequence that contemporary commentators and later historians have often used the new territorial titles to describe battalions involved in the war, rather than the numbers they still bore. Thus, for example, the 2nd Battalion, 21st Regiment (Royal Scots Fusiliers) became the Royal Scots Fusiliers, the 58th (Rutlandshire) Regiment the 2nd Battalion, Northamptonshire Regiment, the 92nd Regiment (Gordon Highlanders) became the 2nd Battalion, Gordon Highlanders and the 94th Regiment the 2nd Battalion, The Connaught Rangers.

The Cardwell reforms failed to raise either the quantity or quality of recruits.[22] Economising governments neglected to make pay competitive with urban rates, and the conditions of service life (though improved) remained harsh. The men received a shilling a day and unvarying and unpalatable staple rations of bread and meat. Over half their meagre pay was deducted for extra food, laundry services and so on. Discipline was rigid and punishment by flogging, though abolished in 1872 in time of peace, was permitted for wartime service until 1881. Service life, when not on campaign, was a monotonous round of drill, parades, fatigues and gymnastic exercises, with recreational activity centred on regimental canteens and local brothels, so that the widespread incidence of venereal disease posed a real problem. When their time in the ranks was up, soldiers re-entered civilian life with few of the necessary skills, and all too often ended up as unemployable vagrants. On the other hand, certain aspects of service life had been improved by the reforms of the 1870s. New barracks were built, cook houses provided and temperance and education facilities provided to help men pass their off-duty time less harmfully and more usefully. Many late-Victorian officers, who associated the ingrained concept of a gentleman with the Christian, evangelical virtues of unselfishness, thoughtfulness and a sense of noblesse oblige, adopted a more conspicuous recognition of an officer's paternalistic responsibilities towards other ranks. They showed concern about their men's conditions, some attempting to stamp out drunkenness and encouraging alternatives like team sports and further study. Indeed, soldiers had to attend school for five hours each week, and promotion to non-commissioned officer required a basic certificate of education. It is reasonable to estimate that by the 1870s about half the NCOs and private soldiers were literate, and were writing expressive (and uncensored) letters home while on active service about the Empire, presenting a perspective of common experience under the stress of campaign hardships and enemy fire.[23] Recruits, if no longer entirely drawn from the flotsam of criminals, bankrupts, run-aways and the least respectable elements of the working class, nevertheless still came from the poorest sectors of society. The great trade depression of the 1870s brought an influx of the urban and rural destitute from the British mainland which replaced the large number of recruits previously raised from impoverished Ireland. In all, the status of soldiers in society improved somewhat in the late Victorian era in recognition of their greater respectability and role as guardians of Empire, but civilians still remained wary of them, and many families felt deeply disgraced if one of their members enlisted.

Although the purchase of commissions had been abolished in 1871 and promotion opened to merit to encourage the development of a professional officer corps, the social composition of the officer corps remained homogeneous and resistant to change.[24] Low rates of pay and expensive uniforms and regimental traditions meant the necessity of a private income in all except the technical arms. The Household Cavalry and the Foot Guards remained the preserve of aristocratic officers, but in other regiments most officers still came mainly from the younger sons of the gentry, clergy and the professional middle classes, and were increasingly products of the burgeoning public schools. A public school education, with its emphasis on order, authority, discipline and loyalty was intended to inculcate qualities necessary in an officer. The training of body and spirit through the cult of team games was intended to develop health, strength, coordination and quickness of eye, as well as moral virtues like self-discipline and team spirit. And officers from public schools tended to cleave to an honorific and gentlemanly code of values, which included calm resolve under fire and a predisposition to fight as chivalrously as possible. They also freely indulged their passion for sports, especially field sports. With the end of purchase and a required higher level of military education, a good number also passed through either the Royal Military Academy, Woolwich, founded in 1741 to train gentleman cadets for the Royal Artillery and Royal Engineers, or the Royal Military College, Sandhurst, founded in 1799 to train gentleman cadets for the cavalry and infantry.[25] A tiny minority also passed through the Staff College established in 1858 at Camberley to turn out officers better prepared than previously for strategic intelligence and other staff duties; the Staff College was allowed to languish on account of the hostility to a Prussian-style professionalism at odds with the pervasive but amateurish gentleman-ideal among many officers.[26] It is true that the curricula at the military colleges and Camberley were undemanding, yet military periodicals and works on strategy and tactics were increasingly available – though it is hard to judge to what extent they were read or disseminated. Consequently, it would be wrong entirely to endorse the persistent image of the Victorian army as an anti-intellectual, static institution resistant to embracing any change.

Undoubtedly, it was still difficult to advance in the profession without either money or connections, and the only alternative way to gain promotion was distinguished service in the field – which in itself often required influence in order to gain a posting where laurels could be won. Prejudice against intellectuals and bookworms certainly persisted in the service, though all too often the preferred exhibition of 'pluck' coincided with military ineptitude. Some officers gained promotion from the ranks, but there is ample evidence that the rank and file preferred their officers to be gentlemen born, preferably from a family with a long tradition of military service. That said, there were still many reforming officers who prized intellect over athletic prowess. They saw that for the army to perform its duties effectively in the far-flung Empire required the whole-hearted embrace of new technologies such as the submarine telegraph cable, the constant adoption of new armaments and the reassessment of tactics.[27]

The late Victorian army was engaged primarily in colonial campaigns against irregulars inferior in armaments, organisation and discipline, and employing varied and unpredictable tactics and levels of military skill. Colonel C.E. Callwell famously defined such campaigns as 'small wars'.[28] These were a specialised form of combat that did not demand of British officers the same degree of technical knowledge and complex managerial expertise necessary for officers of the great continental armies. The latter were trained to cope with the problems of mass movement and organisation which characterised warfare between the industrialised powers of Europe and North America. Rather, what was required for successfully conducting small wars was frequent experience under fire which inculcated disciplined solidarity among the men, and honed tactical adaptability, initiative and flair among officers. Some career officers saw these requirements as a call to improve the effectiveness of the British army in the field. On the other hand, untaxing colonial campaigns could lead only too easily to complacency in an insular and imperial tradition. To make matters worse, the army was weakened by antagonistic schools of military thought which prevented the emergence of a common military doctrine.

Between 1856 and 1895 the Field Marshal Commanding-in-Chief at the Horse Guards, who held office at the pleasure of the Crown, and who implemented the military decisions of the government, was the Queen's militarily conservative cousin, H.R.H. the Duke of Cambridge, Wolseley's 'poor bloated bag of Royalty'.[29] While conceding that the supreme control of the army rested with the Secretary of State for War, Cambridge nevertheless doggedly maintained his grip on matters of command, discipline, appointments and promotions. He was extremely jealous of these prerogatives and furiously resisted the interference of civilians – including cabinet members – in military affairs. Conservative military circles, who deplored reform and advanced military ideas as epitomised by Cardwell's reforms,[30] gravitated around the reactionary Duke and encouraged him in his propensity to judge the army's efficiency in terms of spit-and-polish, parades and field days rather than on effectiveness on campaign. Sir Evelyn Wood, though a reforming soldier, was also a determinedly ambitious one, and knew how best to please the Duke. In the aftermath of the Transvaal Rebellion he made sure when he wrote privately to Cambridge that he assured him how pleased he would have been to have seen the 2/60th Regiment looking 'magnificent' in Pietermaritzburg where 'they were in tunics and the morning being bright they showed to great advantage'; while the 15th Hussars sauntered about the town with 'belts, gloves etc as clean as if they were at Hounslow'.[31] No matter that only a few months before they had ignominiously lost a war.

Sir Garnet Wolseley was the most influential reforming soldier of his time, firmly supporting the Cardwell reforms. He was convinced that although the Duke and his cronies could no longer resist the inauguration of the new system, they would nevertheless do their best to undermine it.[32] He therefore saw it as his mission to make the reforms work, and believed he could overcome their shortcomings by relying in his expeditions on elite formations, properly prepared and equipped for war. He creamed volunteers from other units, and in assembling his staffs, relied primarily upon a 'ring' of officers, first formed for the Ashanti expedition of 1873–1874,[33] who were either decorated veterans of distinguished service, or Staff College graduates who showed promise. They, in turn, benefited from their successful service with Wolseley which helped them gain public recognition and rapid promotion. Certainly, the 'Ashanti Ring' (or 'Mutual Admiration Society', as it was known to its detractors) proved a pragmatic adaptation to the demands of small wars, providing staff continuity and cohesion. Nevertheless, the Duke was probably correct in his disapproving concern that it depressed morale elsewhere and failed to bring on new officers of promise. It also encouraged emulation, and Sir Frederick Roberts's rival ring in India formed a similar coterie of favoured officers grouped around a charismatic commander. These rings naturally accentuated the inevitable divisions and rivalries within the service which were played out in command selection. This had always been a matter of immensely complex internal manoeuvring between various military factions, but it was made particularly acute in the 1870s and 1880s by the deep divisions between the Duke's conservative circle and the reformist 'Ashanti Ring', of which Colley was a prominent member.[34] These politics of command were (as we shall see) inevitably played out in South Africa during 1880–1881.

The British soldiers who were stationed in South Africa in 1880–1881 were very different in their coloured uniforms from their drably apparelled Boer opponents. No tropical uniform was issued to the British soldier. The standard overseas field dress remained the undress uniforms of a single-breasted five-buttoned unlined serge frock which was scarlet for infantry and Engineers, and blue for all others except the Rifles, who wore dark green. Officers wore either scarlet tunics or (the preferred option in the field) the dark blue patrol jacket introduced in 1866. The various regiments still wore their traditional facing colours on cuffs and collar (blue for the 21st, black for the 58th, scarlet for the 60th, yellow for the 91st and 92nd, Lincoln green for the 94th, sky blue for the 97th), though these would be swept away with the organisational changes of 1881 discussed above. Trousers were dark blue with a red welt down the seam for infantry and a wide red stripe for artillery; they were tucked into black leather boots – all too often of poor quality. Highland regiments wore tartan kilts instead of trousers. The 92nd Highlanders, who came to South Africa from service in the Second Afghan War, wore khaki tunics instead of scarlet ones, the first unit in South Africa to do so. The widespread use of mud-coloured uniforms began in India in the 1840s, though the use of khaki (from Urdu *khak*, or dust) by British regiments serving in India was not adopted until during the Indian Mutiny of 1857–1858. The adoption thereafter of khaki throughout the army was slow and often reluctant. On 18 February 1881 the Secretary of State for War was asked in parliament whether the reinforcements being sent out to South Africa would be dressed in their 'present conspicuous uniforms and accoutrements, and thus enable the Boers to shoot them down without danger to themselves?' Hugh Childers' response was that it did not seem 'desirable' to alter the uniforms in any way.[35] Scarlet as a battledress was only officially discredited by the Colour Committee of

1883.[36] It was last worn on campaign in Zululand in 1888, when the moral effect of wearing scarlet (presumably etched on the Zulu mind as a consequence of the Anglo-Zulu War of 1879) was thought to outweigh the negligible danger from indifferent Zulu marksmen. In 1897 khaki was finally adopted as service wear on all overseas postings.

The Royal Artillery wore dark blue tunics with scarlet facings, and blue trousers with the scarlet welt. Sailors of the Naval Brigade were dressed in an assortment of styles of blue uniform, which officers sometimes varied with a white jacket and white canvas leggings or trousers. Headgear was blue (or white and blue), though the broad-brimmed straw sennet was often adopted. Mounted infantry wore their regimental frocks with dark buff corduroy trousers tucked into their boots and carried ammunition in leather bandoliers like the Boers. Accoutrements for the rest of the infantry, including ammunition pouches, were of the Valise pattern equipment, introduced in 1871. It consisted of a black waterproofed canvas sack, or valise, supported in the small of the back by shoulder straps. The straps were attached to a waist belt to which were fitted three ammunition pouches holding 70 rounds. The rolled greatcoat and mess-tin were secured above the valise and the wooden water bottle attached to the belt. Headgear was the light cork sun helmet, adopted for overseas service in 1877. The brass shako-plate badge was usually removed on active service, and the white helmet stained light brown with coffee or mud, as were the white equipment straps and pouches.

Uniforms on active serve were seldom replaced, and a regiment like the 94th, which had gone through both the Anglo-Zulu War and the Sekhukhune campaign, was wearing a tattered assortment of garments by 1880, some of them civilian clothes, and everything patched and worn, including their accoutrements (which were missing straps and other elements). Their helmets were misshapen from having been slept in throughout months of campaign.[37] By the end of the 1881 campaign the clothes of the Natal Mounted Police (whose pristine uniform was a smart black tunic and breeches with a white helmet) were so dilapidated that scarcely two men were dressed alike. Half of them still wore battered helmets, while the rest sported forage caps or smasher hats.[38] Scarlet frocks faded to the colour of brick-dust. Officers in the field tended in any case to adopt an idiosyncratic assortment of non-regulation dress. Many of the officers and men also sported beards on campaign, completing their wild appearance which would doubtless have dismayed the Duke of Cambridge.

The organisation of the Victorian army was clear-cut, on paper at any rate. The standard infantry tactical unit was the battalion. On service, the battalion was made up of a headquarters and eight companies, with a nominal complement of three officers and 110 ranks in each, or about 900 men. In the 1880s a cavalry regiment on overseas service normally consisted of eight troops grouped into four squadrons. The cavalry troop, which was the standard tactical unit, nominally consisted of 75 men of all ranks, including a farrier and a trumpeter, so that a cavalry regiment's strength hovered around 600 men. A battery of Royal Field artillery was made up of six guns and 174 men. Each gun had its own limber, ammunition-wagon and crew. The battery was the usual tactical unit, but was often broken up if necessary into three divisions of two guns each. Artillery was often in short supply, and had to be supplemented by naval landing-parties and ordnance brought ashore from ships. Colonial warfare, combined with the experiences of the American Civil War and the Franco-Prussian War, had taught the British of the need to combine the speed of cavalry with the infantry's firepower for scouting and fighting, a combination basic to the Boer commando. The first experiments with mounted infantry were in New South Wales in 1825, and in 1827 the first dedicated mounted rifle unit was raised in the Cape. Mounted infantry were thereafter regularly raised from volunteers among the infantry battalions, and it was accepted even by conservative soldiers that their mobility and ability to make use of natural cover were particularly suited to colonial warfare.[39] A squadron of mounted infantry usually consisted of three officers and 110 men. Royal naval crews were trained in the use of small arms and light artillery to enable them to serve in landing-parties. In times of crisis it was often more convenient to employ naval personnel than await the arrival of soldiers, for the navy was always at hand for immediate service in coastal areas.

Campaigning in Africa generally took place across great distances along rudimentary tracks, in difficult terrain with an unforgiving climate. The war of 1880–1881 was no exception. The theatre of operations was partly the flat or undulating tableland of the Transvaal highveld, between 3,000 and 6,000 feet above sea level and dotted with solitary rounded hills (koppies). Most of the heavy fighting took place in the passes over the escarpment which marks the generally abrupt transition between the highveld and coastal plains of Natal, and which in summer is often shrouded in cloud and rain. The veld experiences extremes of temperature between winter and summer and, being a region of summer rainfall, there is a contrast between the good grazing and plentiful water of the summer months, and the dearth of the winter period. These contrasts were not of major importance during the Transvaal War, which was fought during the summer months. On the other hand, the poor roads were critical. The campaign (as we shall see) hinged on the British successfully advancing from the port of Durban to the Transvaal highveld up steeply rising gradients along few and poorly maintained roads. Dependence on animal-drawn transport for supplies (the railway ended in Pietermaritzburg, only 60 miles from the coast)[40] further severely limited their manoeuvrability.[41]

The essential supply and transport of troops, which was consequently always in danger of breaking down, were in the hands of the understaffed and overworked personnel of the Commissariat and Transport Department (formed in 1875) which provided the officer establishment, and the Army Service Corps (created in 1870) which provided the NCOs and other ranks. Partly as a result of the problems Colley encountered in 1880 in purchasing local transport to supply his troops, the Commissariat was overhauled again in 1880–1881, the Commissariat and Transport Department being re-designated the Commissariat and Transport Staff, and the Army Service Corps the Commissariat and Transport Corps. Only in 1888 would there be a full integration of the two branches into the Army Service Corps. Medical care on campaign suffered from organisational bottlenecks similar to those faced by transport and supply. In 1857 the Army Hospital Corps was created to provide orderlies and bearers, but it was only given officers in 1873 when doctors, who had previously been on the regimental strength, were transferred to the Army Medical Department. These two branches were only finally combined in 1898 into the Royal Army Medical Corps.

Communication between headquarters and military units and posts was by field telegraph line, brought into use in the 1870s, by heliograph, which had been developed in India at much the same time, by the traditional mounted orderly or by flag signal. The telegraph line was always vulnerable to being cut by the enemy, and in 1880–1881 the Boers kept on severing the telegraph wires between British garrisons, forces in the field and their headquarters in Pietermaritzburg. Cloudy weather halted the heliograph, rendering it useless for days at a stretch during Natal's rainy summer season. Nevertheless, if working, telegraph and heliograph were both superior to the dispatch rider or signaller. While it took a rider three to four days to make the journey from Colley's camp at Mount Prospect to Pietermaritzburg 250 miles away, it took the chain of heliograph stations only about three hours.

Colley was less free to exercise his own political and military judgement than previous wartime commanders in South Africa because since December 1879 submarine cable had linked Durban to the government in London via Aden; but no direct Cape Town–London link would exist until 1887. Yet the underwater cable could always break down, as Wolseley discovered to his annoyance when negotiating in the Transvaal in 1879–1880.[42]

British infantry in South Africa were armed with the Martini-Henry Mark II rifle, introduced in 1874. It was a single-shot, centre fire weapon with a falling block mechanism operated by a lever. The British Army did not adopt a magazine rifle until 1888, when the Martini-Henry was replaced by the bolt-action Lee-Metford Mark I. The Martini-Henry weighed 9 lbs, and fired a .450 calibre hardened lead bullet of 1.1 ounces with a muzzle velocity of 375 yards per second. It was sighted up to 1,450 yards, but was most effective at less than 400 yards. The Boxer pattern cartridge with its thin rolled brass case had a tendency to jam when the chamber was fouled and heated by the black gunpowder, and was often torn by the ejector. However, an improved cartridge was not introduced until 1885. Fouling also lodged easily in the rifled barrel with its seven deep, square-cut grooves. This increased the already severe recoil, made the barrel too hot to touch after excessive firing, and affected accuracy since the bullet would no longer spin properly. The Martini-Henry bullet flattened on impact, causing massive tissue damage and splintering bones lengthways, stopping its victim in his tracks. However, Martini-Henry fire did not cause the number of casualties that might have been anticipated, even against densely packed formations of Zulu. This was because the rifle depended for its effect on both range and volume. Even at point-blank range (below 100 yards) a skirmishing line, with regulation intervals of at least four paces and as many as ten, could not develop the necessary volume of fire at six shots a minute to stop a determined charge.

The concept of a new and flexible discipline in the battlefield slowly filtered through to training. Marksmanship was taught and encouraged, though not practised regularly enough, and sufficient emphasis was not given to individual fire. Firing from medium to long range (300 to 1,400 yards) continued to be delivered in volleys, generally by section, because officers found it easier to control the rate of fire and prevent wastage of ammunition. Independent fire was usually only ordered from close range (100 to 300 yards) when attackers began to emerge as individual targets. Volley firing might have been suitable in the open field, but in broken terrain it was more effective for men to fire independently, selecting their own target. Whatever the situation, it was important always to avoid premature firing until the enemy was within sufficient range, and to maintain fire discipline, as slower, deliberate, better-aimed fire was more effective. An accurate estimation of range was vital for full effectiveness of fire. Although rifle sights were calibrated, men relied upon correct orders to enable them to be set correctly. It was difficult to make a correct assessment of distance, and the system of 'combined sights' was often employed in which groups fired at the same target with rifles variously sighted to ascertain the correct range.

The Martini-Henry was fitted with a triangular socket bayonet, 22 inches long, which had been universal issue since 1876 and was known as the 'lunger'. When combined with the four-foot-long rifle it gave a formidable reach of over six feet in hand-to-hand combat, but was of poor quality and too often bent or broke. Officers still put considerable faith in the demoralising effect on the enemy (who were assumed to have no stomach for cold steel) of a well-timed bayonet charge. Of course, a charge was not attempted until the enemy had been heavily mauled by artillery and musketry fire and were on the verge of breaking. Even so, to expose oneself against a well-positioned enemy laying down a heavy fire meant taking considerable casualties, even if the position was carried. In defence, a rapid bayonet charge was still regarded as the best method of repelling an enemy break-through; and it played an important role in combat in confined spaces and in storming fortifications.

Officers carried privately-owned swords and double-action .45 revolvers (usually the Mark II Adams or the Webley Royal Irish Constabulary model of 1867) which were not accurate at more than 25 yards at best. It was not until 1900 that the Army insisted that officers carry the .455 Webley revolver.

Although the British cavalry remained wedded to the concept of close-quarter shock action with the sword or lance, the carbine had long been accepted as a secondary weapon. In 1877 the cavalry adopted the Martini-Henry carbine, which was sighted up to 1,000 yards. Mounted infantry also carried the carbine. The limited numbers of cavalry engaged in 1880–1881 operated mostly like mounted infantry, dismounting in action to make more effective use of their firearms. However, dismounted service was never popular, and cavalry continued to hanker after the traditional shock action. Otherwise, all varieties of mounted troops were required for the normal long-range reconnaissance and vedette duties, skirmishing, and for patrolling the lines of communication.

The artillery deployed in the Transvaal war were 9-pounder Rifled Muzzle Loaders sighted between 1,690 and 2,780 yards, and the light 7-pounder RML Mark IV steel mountain guns, mounted on light carriages. With a maximum range of 3,100 yards for explosive shells, their low muzzle-velocity rendered shrapnel-shot ineffective. In most small wars artillery was limited in quantity, so that it had to be used to provide immediate fire support for the infantry, rather than as a decisive force in its own right. In 1880–1881 targeting was made difficult by the dispersed deployment adopted by the Boers; while the absence of protective shields on gun-carriages left crews and teams vulnerable to Boer musketry, particularly at the Ingogo fight.

The Naval Brigade was equipped with 24-pounder Hale's rockets with explosive heads, approved in 1867. A rocket had three flanges at the exhaust vent for the propellant gases which caused it to spin in flight to help keep it on course, and was fired by a hand-lit fuse from a V-shaped trough on a stand. Effective range was no more than 1,300 yards and accuracy was very poor (the average deviation was 40 yards), though their hideous shrieking sound in flight and tail of smoke and sparks was supposed to have a demor-alising effect on the foe. The Gatling gun, which had come into service in 1871, was mounted on a carriage similar to a field gun. It could fire 200 Boxer .450 rounds a minute from ten rifled barrels rotated by a manually operated crank and was fed by gravity from a revolving upright case holding 40 cartridges, which was changed every four revolutions. With an effective range of up to 1,000 yards it could cause terrible casualties to an exposed enemy, but was unreliable on account of its tendency to jam. As a con-sequence it was under-utilised as an offensive weapon and confined to defensive positions.

It long remained one of the truisms of military history that the British army in the late-Victorian era was still caught in a Peninsular mind-set of shoulder-to-shoulder parade ground formations, of volleys in rigid lines and of wall-like bayonet assaults.[43] In reality, during this period tactical ideas were being transformed. As early as the North American campaigns of the eighteenth century, the British had learned that in fighting a highly mobile enemy over broken ground they could no longer rely on their well-tried dense column and line formations. Rather, individual soldiers had to be self-reliant and well-motivated, and be prepared to be deployed in open rather than mass formations in order to make better use of the terrain. These North American lessons tended to be forgotten in the early nineteenth century for lack of practical reminders, and skirmishing in extended order was relegated to supplementing the real attack, for which linear tactics continued to be prescribed. 'Bush-fighting' conducted by light infantry at the battalion level, with its emphasis on marksmanship, had to be relearned through culminating experience in the small wars of the Victorian age, and was pushed along by the advent of breech-loading rifles. These had a revolutionary effect on the battlefield since they not only made it possible to load and fire more rapidly, but to do so while kneeling or lying down.

The 1877 edition of *Field Exercise and Evolution of Infantry* incorporated all the new tactical ideas accepted by the War Office, and this was the manual with which the officers serving in the Transvaal War ought to have been familiar. A section on 'Extended Order' replaced the regulations on skirmishing, and allowed at least an interval of three paces between each file, and increased extension depending on circumstances.[44] When a company was extended as a fighting line, another was supposed to act in support about 150 yards to the rear with the company commander in front. Any part of the extended line could be reinforced by throwing forward supports, with the senior officer taking command of both companies. If men became separated from their own company they were to consider themselves under the command of the nearest officer who, in turn, could always take stray men under his command. If forced to retire, the extended firing line would fall back through the supporting line, and the two would continue falling back by alternate portions, each company covering the retreat of the other.[45]

In extended order at battalion level, when making an attack, the object was to bring up the battalion, with as little loss as possible, close enough to the enemy in order to pour in 'the hottest fire' and make the final assault as a 'compact body'. Emphasis was on attacking in depth, with a battalion deploying two companies as skirmishers, two further companies in line some distance behind in support, and the remaining four companies in line behind them. Supports would supply losses and reinforce the fighting line, which was attempting to dominate the enemy with its firepower, and protect its flanks. They and the main body would be brought up into the line as it closed to within 200 yards of the enemy for the final assault, taking advantage of all existing cover. The captain of each company and the section commanders were to remain six paces to the rear of their men to keep tight control over the commencement of firing, the choice of targets and adjustment of sights. In extended order the line was permitted to lie down, or single soldiers could use their individual judgement in choosing

cover. At all times they could assume the positions that were most convenient to make their fire most effective. When firing lying down both elbows
were supposed to rest on the ground to support the body and rifle. On
reaching charging distance in one general line, the drums and bugles would
sound the charge and the men would quicken their pace and cheer. Officers
had to be alert and quickly assume the defensive if the charge stalled, when
the best possible use had to be made of the ground gained, and the supports
would have to hurry up to assist them in laying down a heavy fire on the
attackers while the third line covered their retreat if it became necessary.
It was recognised that in extended order the commander would lose direct
control over portions of the battalion, so command had to be delegated to
company leaders who, thoroughly briefed concerning the objectives, would
be expected to exercise considerable freedom of action.[46]

The British army in southern Africa had essentially adopted these
methods, and learned while confronting more mobile adversaries to fight
in exactly this loose skirmishing order, making the most of the terrain and
natural cover. In the Ninth Frontier War of 1877–1879 the British had used
the extended firing-line with great success, and during the Anglo-Zulu War
of 1879 identical tactics proved equally effective in the running fire-fight
over broken terrain at the battle of Nyezane. However, at Isandlwana the
extended skirmishing line had not put up enough firepower to stop the Zulu
mass assault over open ground, and thereafter in the Anglo-Zulu War the
British adopted close-order, all-round defensive formations in order to concentrate their firepower and avoid being outflanked. Because the Zulu made
little effective use of their firearms, dense formations – such as the outmoded infantry square adopted at the battle of Ulundi – were not vulnerable
to enemy fire.[47]

Anachronistic, densely packed formations such as a square obviously
would not do against the Boers' sophisticated coordinated fire and movement tactics, superior marksmanship and mobility. Colley, who was, after
all, one of the best militarily educated commanders in the British army (he
had passed Staff College with the highest marks, been the Professor of
Military Law and Administration at Sandhurst and written the article on
'Army' for the *Encyclopaedia Britannica* of 1875)[48] entirely understood that
flexible attack formations were required, and that an assault against a Boer
position should be in depth and in open order. Furthermore, since the
terrain of the mountain pass into the Transvaal favoured the Boers, he followed the approved approach when he sought to fight and not manoeuvre,

thereby maximising his putative advantages of firepower, tactical flexibility, disciplined manpower and a readiness to engage in hand-to-hand fighting. Indeed, any possibility of successfully outflanking the Boers and causing them to fall back depended on a large force of well-trained horses, an arm in which Colley was sadly deficient. General Alison, the DQG, Intelligence, was fully aware of this, and eventually saw that Colley was sent a considerable force of cavalry.[49] It only arrived after the armistice, so whether or not its deployment in the difficult Natal terrain would have made an appreciable differences remains untested.

Ultimately, a military system is only as good as those who interpret and implement it, whether they be regimental officers or commanders. Failure is as much the consequence of not adhering to appropriate military doctrine at the tactical level as it is to making miscalculations in strategic planning or being unimaginative when confronted with novel or unexpected challenges. In any campaign the key is to adapt proactively both to the terrain and the enemy. Herein was to lie the chief British weakness in the Transvaal War.

Notes and references

1 This section draws heavily on a fine work of synthesis on the Boer military system by I. van der Waag, 'South Africa and the Boer Military System' in P. Dennis and J. Grey, eds, *The Boer War: Army, Nation and Empire* (Canberra, 2000), pp. 49–51, 53–62, 64, 67 and on the classic analysis by G. Tylden, 'The Development of the Commando System in South Africa, 1715 to 1922', *Africana Notes and News*, 13 (March 1958–December 1959), pp. 303–13. See also S. Trapido, 'Reflections on Land, Office and Wealth in the South African Republic, 1850–1900' in S. Marks and A. Atmore, eds, *Economy and Society in Pre-Industrial South Africa* (London, 1980), particularly pp. 352, 356, 361, and Duxbury, *David and Goliath*, pp. 2–3, 24–6.

2 J. Laband, *The Rise and Fall of the Zulu Nation* (London, 1997), p. 125.

3 E.A. Walker, *The Great Trek* (London, 3rd edn, 1948), pp. 350, 373–4.

4 J. Laband, 'War and Peace in South Africa' in P.B. Boyden, A.J. Guy and M. Harding, eds, *'Ashes and Blood': The British Army in South Africa 1795–1914* (London, 1999), pp. 14–15.

5 For a thorough account of Boer operations against Sekhukhune, see War Office, *Transvaal*, pp. 67–74.

6 WO 32/7806: memorandum by Maj-Gen Sir A. Alison, 14 February 1881.

7 WO 32 /7806: F. Schermbrucker to Lt-Gen Lord Chelmsford, 3 January 1881.

8 Colonel C.E. Callwell, *Small Wars. Their Principles and Practice* (London, 3rd edn, 1906), p. 31.

9 War Office, *Transvaal*, p. 51.

10 F. Machanik, 'Firearms and Firepower, First War of Independence, 1880–1881', *Military History Journal*, 5, 2 (December 1980), pp. 63–4; Kaptein R. von Moltke, 'Wapentuig van die Eesrste Vryheidsoorlog', *Militaria*, 1, 11 (1981), pp. 9–15.

11 P. Labuschange, *Ghostriders of the Anglo-Boer War (1899–1902): The Role and Contribution of Agterryers* (Pretoria, 1999), pp. ix, 4–5, 7–9, 14, 25–6; Warwick, *Black People and the South African War*, pp. 11, 25–6.

12 *Blue Book 1879*, pp. 116–17.

13 Haggard, *Last Boer War*, pp. 19–20.

14 By the time war broke out again in 1899, the increasing number of burghers who had grown up in towns were no better at musketry and field craft than their British counterparts, and were not nearly as hardened as the commandos who had come out in 1880.

15 This could be a vulnerable manoeuvre, disrupted in an ambush or running fight, as the Boers found to their cost at the battles of eThaleni and the White Mfolozi in 1838. See Laband, *Zulu Nation*, pp. 92–3, 103–5.

16 Barrett, 'Dutch Boers of South Africa', p. 179. See Laband, *Zulu Nation*, chapter 8, for a detailed description of the battle of Blood River (Ncome) where these classic tactics were used to great effect.

17 D. Friend, 'Training Doctrines of the Staatsartillerie of the Zuid-Afrikaansche Republiek', *Military History Journal*, 11, 5 (June 2000), p. 200.

18 Major D.D. Hall, 'The Artillery of the First Anglo-Boer War 1880–1881, *Military History Journal*, 5, 2 (December 1980), pp. 52, 56–7; von Moltke, 'Wapentuig', pp. 17–19, 25.

19 The Hon. E. Stanhope was Secretary of State for War in Lord Salisbury's second cabinet. His Memorandum is reproduced in E. Spiers, *The Late Victorian Army, 1868–1902* (Manchester and New York, 1992), p. 337. See also I. Beckett, *The Victorians at War* (Hambledon, London and New York, 2003), pp. 151–2.

20 The discussion below on army reform, organisation, recruitment, dress, weaponry, tactics, communications and logistics in 1880 is based – unless otherwise specified – on the following sources: E. Spiers, 'The Late Victorian Army 1868–1914' in D.G. Chandler and I. Beckett, eds, *The Oxford History of the British Army* (Oxford, 2003), pp. 187–200; H. Strachan, *European Armies and the Conduct of War* (London, 1983), pp. 76–89; Haythornthwaite, *Colonial Wars*, pp. 17–45, 48–60; I. Knight, *Go to Your God Like a Soldier: The British Soldier Fighting for Empire, 1837–1902* (London, 1996), pp. 12–32, 132, 138–52, 155–72, 182–202, 204–6, 247–9; H. Bailes, 'Technology and Tactics in the British Army,

1866–1900' in R. Haycock and K. Neilson, eds, *Men, Machines, and War* (Waterloo, 1988), pp. 35–47; Laband and Thompson, *Anglo-Zulu War*, pp. 21–30 and J. Laband, *The Atlas of the Later Zulu Wars 1883–1888* (Pietermaritzburg, 2001), pp. 9–19.

21 E.M. Spiers, *The Army and Society 1815–1914* (London, 1980), chap. 1. See W. Richards, *Her Majesty's Army: A Descriptive Account of the Various Regiments Now Comprising the Queen's Forces, from their First Establishment to the Present* (London, n.d., c. 1888), vols 1–3, *passim*.

22 See Spiers, *Army and Society*, chap. 5.

23 F. Emery, *Marching over Africa: Letters from Victorian Soldiers* (London, 1986), pp. 14, 18.

24 See Spiers, *Army and Society*, chap. 4.

25 The military academies at Woolwich and Sandhurst were amalgamated in 1947 as the Royal Military Academy Sandhurst. See R. Holmes, ed., *The Oxford Companion to Military History* (Oxford, 2001), p. 4

26 J. Laband, ed., *Lord Chelmsford's Zululand Campaign 1878–1879* (Stroud, 1994), pp. xxiii–xxiv.

27 Beckett, *Victorians at War*, pp. 179–90.

28 For his definition, see Callwell, *Small Wars*, pp. 21–2.

29 Preston, ed., *Wolseley's Journal*, p. 301, Appendix C: Wolseley, Memoir: the Boer command, 3 March 1881.

30 Laband, ed., *Chelmsford*, pp. xxvii–xxviii.

31 WC III/3/3: Wood to Cambridge, 21 November 1881.

32 Preston, ed., *Wolseley's Journal*, p. 304, Appendix C: Wolseley, Memoir: the Boer command, 27 May 1881.

33 Beckett, *Victorians at War*, pp. 7–10.

34 I.F.W. Beckett, 'Military High Command in South Africa, 1854–1914' in Boyden, Guy and Harding, eds, *'Ashes and Blood'*, pp. 60–3; Beckett, *Victorians at War*, pp. 6–7.

35 *Natal Advertiser*, 29 March 1881: extracts form the British parliament, 18 February 1881.

36 See WO 33/27: Report.

37 P.H. Butterfield, ed., *War and Peace in South Africa 1879–1881: The Writings of Philip Anstruther and Edward Essex* (Melville, 1987), p. 134: Anstruther to his wife, Zaida, 14 November 1880.

38 H.P. Holt, *The Mounted Police of Natal* (London, 1913), pp. 109–10.

39 See Jean Bou, 'Modern Cavalry: Mounted Rifles, the Boer War, and the Doctrinal Debates' in Dennis and Grey, eds, *Boer War*, pp. 99–105.

40 B. Martin, 'The Coming of the Railway to Pietermaritzburg' in J. Laband and R. Haswell, eds, *Pietermaritzburg 1838–1988: A New Portrait of an African City* (Pietermaritzburg, 1988), pp. 136–7.

41 For the geography, communications network and climate of the Transvaal, see War Office, *Transvaal*, sections A, C and G. The Appendix provides detailed reports on all the roads.

42 Beckett, *Victorians at War*, p. 98.

43 See J.F.C. Fuller, *The Last of the Gentlemen's Wars* (London, 1937), pp. 19–20.

44 Great Britain, War Office, *Field Exercise and Evolution of Infantry* (London, pocket edition, 1877), pp. 53–4.

45 War Office, *Field Exercise*, pp. 97–9.

46 War Office, *Field Exercise*, pp. 93–4, 96, 210–41.

47 For concise descriptions of the battles of Isandlwana, Nyezane and Ulundi, see Laband and Thompson, *Anglo-Zulu War*, pp. 82–5, 98–108, 165–9.

48 'George Pomeroy Colley' in de Kock, ed., *Dictionary of South African Biography*, vol. II, pp. 137–8.

49 WO 32/7806: Memorandum by Maj-Gen Sir Archibald Alison, 14 February 1881.

chapter 4

In open rebellion: the Boers seize the military initiative

The Transvaal Rebellion broke out while the Sotho 'Gun War', which was monopolising the attention of the British military in southern Africa, was still unresolved. The deployment of Imperial as well as Cape troops was required in Basutoland, and Lanyon (curiously oblivious of the simmering revolt about to explode on his own doorstep) reassured Colley in late September 1880 that it would cause no difficulties to withdraw troops from the Transvaal. He undertook to raise, equip and despatch two guns and 300 Transvaal volunteers (many of them veterans of the campaign against the Pedi) known as Ferreira's Horse.[1] Lanyon would later regret the crucial lack of mounted troops at his disposal, but in late 1880 his mind was still focused on the old bugbear of a widespread African uprising against white rule. Consequently, his overriding concern was not an apparently unlikely Boer revolt, but the possibility that disaffection in Basutoland might spread to other branches of the Sotho people living in Griqualand West and the Transvaal, and that any serious reversal in Basutoland might bring them all into the field against the British.[2]

Colonel Bellairs, Commanding the Transvaal District, took a very different view of the Transvaal situation from the Administrator. For him, the disgruntled Boers were becoming the most dangerous threat to British power in southern Africa, and the British troops in the Transvaal should be concentrating to face down any challenge. So, when the affair of Bezuidenhout's wagon blew up, he believed Lanyon's decision to detach a considerable portion of the Pretoria garrison and send it to Potchefstroom in the western Transvaal flew in the face of military common sense.[3] This field force, which arrived in Potchefstroom on 18 November where it hastily constructed a small, square earthwork fort outside the town, consisted of the Right Division of N/5 Brigade RA and two 9-pounder guns, 25 Mounted Infantry from the 2/21st Fusiliers, the 75 men of C Company of the same regiment, as well as medical and commissariat support personnel, all under the command of Major C. Thornhill, RA, the senior artillery officer in the Transvaal. Another company of the 2/21st Fusiliers, ordered up from Rustenburg, joined these troops on 20 November, making up a force of about 180 men.[4] Bellairs forcefully advised Lanyon on 16 November that instead of dissipating his inadequate forces as detached garrisons at scattered and distant outposts (of which only Standerton on the road to Natal was of any strategic importance), he should instead be concentrating them in Pretoria where there would be enough troops to mount an effective field force of about 700 men against any Boer concentrations.[5] Lanyon remained unconvinced. It was not until 23 November that he partially took Bellairs's counsel, and the orders finally went out for elements of certain garrisons to concentrate on Pretoria.[6] Yet Lanyon could not bring himself to abandon altogether any post held by British troops. So he simply compounded his strategic weakness by leaving such posts to be held by garrisons that were reduced and therefore more vulnerable, while condemning bodies of troops to make the hazardous march to Pretoria through an increasingly hostile countryside. To make matters worse, his unrealistic appreciation of the volatile Transvaal situation – or his pride – prevented him from telegraphing Colley in Pietermaritzburg for essential reinforcements until 25 November. And even then he failed to communicate any sense of real urgency.[7]

Unapprised of the true seriousness of the Transvaal situation, Colley was currently more concerned with the possible threat posed to Natal's western borders by the Gun War and by continuing unrest in Pondoland to the south.[8] It so happened that by the end of December the military situation in both these regions would have turned conclusively in the British favour, but Colley could not bank on that and allow Natal to be left ungarrisoned.[9]

Fort Napier, established on 31 August 1843 on the hill overlooking Pietermaritzburg from the west, remained the headquarters and supply and remount centre of the British garrison in Natal until the troops were finally withdrawn on 12 August 1914 for service on the Western Front.[10] The imperial garrison was stationed at Fort Napier not simply to provide physical security for white settlers apprehensive of the surrounding Africans, but because its presence was necessary in terms of global imperial strategy. In an era of increasing competition from rival colonial powers such as Germany, it remained necessary for Britain to protect the port at Durban from naval attack. The harbour still retained its importance as an alternative naval base on the Cape route to India if the Mediterranean and Suez Canal should be closed to naval shipping. Moreover, the Natal garrison served as a strategic reserve from which troops could be drawn to protect more important posts, such as the Cape, or be despatched on forward expeditions, such as to the Transvaal, to secure imperial interests.[11] Nevertheless, the garrison was always maintained at the lowest possible strength commensurate with the dangers of the military situation, not only in the interests of imperial economising and the limited budget of the War Department, but also (as we have seen) to promote colonial self-reliance and self-defence. Thus reinforcement during crises like the Anglo-Zulu War of 1879 was only a temporary expedient, and the garrison was always drastically reduced once peace returned. During the Transvaal Rebellion Fort Napier would serve as the base camp for the forces in the field and be temporarily occupied by a variety of units on their way to the front.[12] Since the British garrison in southern Africa was never strong enough to shoulder its full military burden unaided, it was always necessary to supplement it with units raised locally from among the colonists and the African population. However, the only reliable force Natal had at its disposal was the Natal Mounted Police, a small standing body of quasi-military police created in 1874. With its severely restricted military budget Natal proved incapable of taking on the burden of its own defence and continued to depend upon the imperial garrison.[13]

It was this knowledge which troubled Colley, for his military fief encompassed all of south-eastern Africa, and he had few troops available. The most he could do for Lanyon was to order up four companies of the 58th Regiment to relieve the companies of the 94th Regiment currently stationed at Newcastle in northern Natal and at Wakkerstroom in the south-eastern Transvaal. This would allow the bulk of that regiment to concentrate at Pretoria to maintain the authority of Lanyon's government and overawe seditious gatherings.[14] But this redeployment came too late, and on 16 December there were only 1,759 British soldiers in the Transvaal, still parcelled out among seven garrisons.

Telegraphic information that the Boers had declared the restored South African Republic in Heidelberg on 16 December only reached Colley in Pietermaritzburg on 19 December because the Boers had cut the lines north of Standerton. This intelligence prompted Colley to push ahead with plans to form a column preliminary to an advance into the Transvaal,[15] and he optimistically informed Lanyon that his whole force (such as it was) should be concentrated in Standerton by 20 January. Meanwhile, he ordered Lanyon to permit no movement of troops which could 'possibly bring on a collision' before his arrival[16] – a completely unrealistic directive since (as he would have known) various units were even then on the march to Pretoria from their garrisons. Colley understood that his available forces were dishearteningly dispersed and meagre, though he tried to assure Kimberley that they would be 'sufficient' for the task. It nevertheless still worried him that he would be leaving Natal 'denuded' at a very critical time, and applied for another regiment to be sent to garrison the colony and act as a reserve in time of need.[17] Meanwhile, A and C Companies of the 58th Regiment, which had marched out of Newcastle on 14 December under Captain H.M. Saunders, were on the way to Wakkerstroom. On 17 December Saunders relieved Captain G. Froom of the 94th Regiment stationed there. Froom then led out C and D Companies of the 94th and a company of the newly arrived 58th Regiment, intending to make for Pretoria.[18] But the Boers were already seizing the military initiative.

On 12 December Lieutenant-Colonel R.W.C. Winsloe assumed command at Potchefstroom, the epicentre of Boer resistance. Besides their fort to the west of the town, the British also occupied the gaol, a general dealer's shop, the landdrost's office and the courthouse in the town itself. Cronjé divided his forces to keep watch on these posts. Following the clashes of 16 December, the Boers took the offensive on 18 December and set fire to the thatched roof of the landdrost's office held by Major M.J. Clarke and 47 men, prompting their capitulation. Winsloe rejected Cronjé's ultimatum demanding the surrender of the rest of the garrison. He set about strengthening the fort with bags of mealies and corn, and during the night brought the men holding the gaol into the fort. The fort, only 25 yards square, was now packed to its limit because, besides the troops, there were also some 48 civilian men, women and children, and 60 African servants, wagon drivers and *voorloopers* [men who led the teams of wagon-oxen] taking refuge from the Boers. The inmates were in constant danger from concealed

Boer snipers well posted in vantage points on housetops or in trees who were regularly relieved by other burghers billeted around the town.[19]

To the north of Potchefstroom, Rustenburg was garrisoned prior to the outbreak of hostilities by two companies of the 2/21st Fusiliers and several commissariat and hospital personnel under the command of Captain Daniel Auchinleck. On 16 November one company was ordered to Potchefstroom leaving E Company of about 62 men without any artillery support to defend the small, 25 yards square earthwork fort (similar to the one in Potchefstroom) which was sited some 600 yards south of the town. Anticipating trouble after 16 December, the little garrison, reinforced by six men of the Rustenburg Rifle Volunteers, raised the fort's walls with sandbags.[20]

In Pretoria, as a result of the concern caused by the delivery of the Boer ultimatum on 17 December, and the reported presence of armed Boers in the vicinity, volunteers were called for to augment the garrison.[21] Meanwhile, Major LeMesurier, RE, set about organising Pretoria according to the principles of the defence of open towns. Royal Engineers knew that when time pressed it was necessary to barricade roads, construct abattis and shelter trenches, convert substantial buildings flanking the obstacles into keeps through blocking up their entrances and loopholing walls and windows, and generally create a strong shooting line. It was also recognised that not enough troops might be available to hold the whole of Pretoria, and LeMesurier was faced with the problem of how much of the town to defend.[22] For comprehensive defensive measures it therefore became essential that the troops recalled from the garrisons at Wakkerstroom, Marabastad and Lydenburg arrive soon.

Until 30 November 1880 two companies of the 94th Regiment held Marabastad, a village of only five or six houses in the remote Zoutpansberg District in the north-eastern Transvaal. Then one company was ordered to Pretoria, leaving B Company of about 50 men under the command of Captain E.S. Brook. Work had begun as far back as February 1880 on the typical earthwork fort, 25 yards square, but now the fort was hastily strengthened and a good supply of wood and provisions brought in. Apart from some minor civil disturbances, there was as yet no real outbreak of violence in the district.[23]

Lydenburg in the eastern Transvaal was garrisoned by the Headquarters and A and F Companies, 94th Regiment under Lieutenant-Colonel Philip R. Anstruther. On 27 November Anstruther received his orders to retire on Pretoria 188 miles away. Yet it was some time before he was ready to set out, because sufficient transport for removing an established garrison had to be hired from local civilians who haggled determinedly to make a handsome profit.[24] Anstruther delayed his march even longer than necessary because he insisted on assembling many more than the twelve wagons which the regulations allowed a column of his size, but they were necessary to evacuate all the quartermaster's stores as well as rations and personal baggage including mess kit and plate.[25] He finally moved out on 5 December with a train of 30 transport wagons, two mule carts, an ox-drawn ambulance, the ox-drawn regimental canteen and a water cart. Anstruther reported that the column consisted of Regimental Headquarters and A and F companies of the 94th Regiment, numbering 6 officers and 246 men, 2 officers and 4 or 5 men of the Army Service Corps and the surgeon of the Army Medical Department and 3 men of the Army Hospital Corps. With the wagons were the wives of Sergeant-Major Fox and Sergeant Maistré, and the widow of Bandmaster Smith, as well as 2 children. There were also about 60 black wagon drivers and *voorlopers*.[26]

In order to protect the large stocks of government stores and 200,000 rounds of ammunition being left behind in Lydenburg, Anstruther detailed a small force of 50 other ranks of the 94th Regiment (mostly the sick), 8 Royal Engineers, and a few men of the Army Service Corps and the Army Hospital Corps to guard them. Their food stores were sufficient for several months. On earlier orders from Pretoria, Second Lieutenant Walter H.C. Long, the young 22-year-old officer in command, had already set about removing the government stores from hired premises in the town to the camp, about 1,000 yards distant. The camp consisted of eight recently constructed stone-walled buildings, each 16 by 5 yards, set in two rows. After 5 December the garrison, with some hired help from the town, proceeded to join up these quarters with stone walls forming a strong defensive perimeter some 80 by 20 yards, and surrounded it with a ditch 2 yards wide and 1 yard deep. An old stone-walled laager, which had a commanding view of the camp, and a few nearby walls and old buildings, which might have provided cover for attackers, were demolished despite protests from the landdrost and his repeated assurances that there was not the slightest possibility of an insurrection.

Long offered the inhabitants of Lydenburg protection within the new fort, but even loyalists preferred to stay neutral. Seeing that no help could be expected from the townsfolk, Long set about strengthening the fort still further. He built an underground magazine for the ammunition, and began to add another wall about 3 yards outside the enclosure, although lack of labour and the march of events did not allow him to complete the fourth side facing the town. To provide safe movement within the enclosure, the garrison dug a trench network connecting the buildings. To complete the defensive works, the Engineers laid mines along the possible lines of approach which would be detonated by wires from the fort, and spread obstacles over the glacis. An old building, some 175 yards distant, which there had not been time to raze with the others, was also mined. After all these preparations, the garrison was ready to face even a determined assault. Only one woman remained in the fortified camp. This was Mary Long, the commander's young wife, and he named the fortified post Fort Mary after her.[27]

The Boers were naturally well-informed of these dispositions, and anticipated that Colley must march from Natal to secure Pretoria, the seat of the administration. The Triumvirate's strategy was not to storm the posts held by the British since (as we have seen) they possessed little artillery and were short of rifle ammunition besides, but to blockade them, repel any sorties and starve the garrisons into submission. In this way the British forces would be contained and prevented from concentrating and making a thrust towards either Heidelberg or Potchefstroom, and the main Boer forces disputing Colley's advance would not have to fear an attack from the rear.[28] As Acting Commandant-General H.P. Malan would write to Cronjé, who was prosecuting the siege of Potchefstroom more aggressively than most, the mountain pass to Natal was where the real danger existed, and that was where the war would be decided – and not around the town he was beleaguering.[29]

With these strategic objectives in mind, it was essential that the Boers intercept those British forces ordered to concentrate on Pretoria. They had already missed their chance with the company of the 94th Regiment stationed at Marabastad, for it had promptly begun its march on 30 November and had safely reached its destination on 10 December, six days before the opening of hostilities. That left Froom's force making its way to Pretoria from Wakkerstroom, and Anstruther's from Lydenburg.

Anstruther could have reached Pretoria before the Boers were ready to attack him, but his late start and slow progress dictated otherwise. The company from Marabastad had made good time on the road because it had marched with minimum transport, but with Anstruther it was exactly the reverse. Fully laden wagons, drawn by sixteen oxen or eight mules (which had to be rested every three to four hours and given five or six hours to graze), and struggling along rudimentary tracks turned into quagmires by rains, and over drifts [fords] across the swollen rivers, could hardly ever travel more than twelve miles a day, and sometimes as few as three. Such convoys were sitting ducks for mobile mounted Boer commandos and required all-round protection on the march, particularly on the flanks. Ideally, patrols ought to have moved parallel or in advance of the column to give early warning of enemy movements. However, since a single wagon in full span took up to 60 yards in column, this strung out a column on the march interminably and made it very difficult to guard.[30]

The progress of Anstruther's column was made even more labourious than customary by the incessant rain and thick mist (typical of summers in the eastern Transvaal) which set in only a day after it finally straggled out of Lydenburg. Along the way Anstruther found the Boers he encountered 'very friendly and civil' and in his good-humoured fashion did not suppose their apparent chaff about fighting to take back the Transvaal was in the least seriously meant.[31] The column averaged only 9 miles a day, and it was not until 15 December that it finally reached Middelburg, 93 miles from Lydenburg and still 97 miles from Pretoria. Throughout 16 December the column halted to rest the oxen, and resumed the march the next day, when it reached the banks of the Olifants River, which was in spate. While halted there Anstruther received at 06h00 on the morning of 17 December a letter of urgent warning from Bellairs, sent by mounted messenger on the evening of 15 December. Bellairs informed the dilatory Anstruther that 500 Boers were reported to have left their camp on the road to Potchefstroom, and that although no hostilities had yet taken place, he should take every precaution against being ambushed on the road to Pretoria, and that scouts should be sent forward to reconnoitre the hilly terrain before advancing. Very specifically, Bellairs singled out the Botha Hill range between Pretoria and Honey's farm as a likely place for a surprise attack. Since 'friendly' Boers had also warned Anstruther the day after he set out from Middelburg that Boer emissaries from Heidelberg were trying to stir up the people to oppose his march, he was doubly warned and ought to have been put thoroughly on his guard.[32] Yet even then Anstruther seemed unwilling to take the danger too seriously. He comes across in his letters to his wife as bluff, good natured and unfussed, with an amiable contempt for the Boers whose ability to take strong, concerted action he discounted. This culpable insouciance was fed by his superficial observation that the Boers he encountered en route (with the occasional exception) were disposed to be friendly and were willing to sell the British all the provisions they required.

On 19 December the Olifants River was at last low enough to cross, and that night the column reached Honey's farm, six miles east of a little stream called the Bronkhorstspruit. Here Anstruther did indeed take the proper precautions and formed a wagon laager and posted strong guards. There were no night alarms, and the column resumed its march on the fatal Monday, 20 December, passing Watkins' farm at about midday. Anstruther, Captain and Paymaster J.M. Elliott, Lieutenant and Adjutant H.A.C. Harrison and Conductor R. Egerton of the Army Service Corps, who was the senior warrant officer, rode at the head of the column. About 20 yards behind them came the band, including drummer boys, some 40 strong. Next followed F Company with 40 men. Behind them was the Colour Party of 5 sergeants carrying the Queen's Colour and the Regimental Colour, each on its 8 ft 7 in pike furled in its brass-capped black leather case.[33] Then marched A Company, with 38 men. Between them and the wagon train came the 21 men of the Quarter Guard and a Provost escort of 5 men with 18 prisoners. A rearguard of 20 men followed some 80 yards behind the last of the wagons which were thinly escorted by a baggage guard of mess and officers' servants, cooks and other regimental employees.[34] Curiously at odds with the precautions of the previous night the column continued to march very much at ease despite the clear warnings of Boer intentions. The men carried only 30 rounds of ammunition instead of the regulation 70 laid down for a combat situation. Many had their scarlet tunics unbuttoned. The band continued playing a medley of popular tunes with its arms (and those of some of the soldiers as well) stowed on the wagons. Despite his orders to ensure careful reconnaissance, Anstruther had sent forward only two mounted infantrymen as scouts and two more with the rearguard. At 300 yards both groups were too close to the column to be at all effective in the treeless, but hilly terrain. There were no outlying flank guards.[35] Such laxity was all the more extraordinary since every commander would have known how vulnerable a convoy was on the march, that protection on the flanks was essential, and that it was necessary to have patrols moving parallel as well as in advance of the column to give early warning of enemy movements.[36]

The Boer commando lying in wait for the British was under the command of Commandant Frans Joubert, uncle of Commandant-General Piet Joubert. His orders were to prevent Anstruther's column from reinforcing

Pretoria.[37] He had set out to Pretoria from Heidelberg on 18 December with a number of men and rendezvoused nearby with a force under S.P.E. Trichardt. On the way to Middelburg they were joined by more men under Nicolaas Smit and D.J.E. Erasmus. On the night of 19 December they bivouacked at Bothasnek, half way between Pretoria and Bronkhorstspruit. Early on the morning of 20 December the Boer commanders debated their next move. Some wanted to set a calculated ambush for the British column at Bothasnek or at the Honde River, but Smit, a veteran of the Pedi wars and a military commander of considerable dash and expertise, prevailed on them to be more flexible and to seize the best opportunity that presented itself. Accordingly, Joubert's force advanced east along the road to Middelburg. Meanwhile, the Middelburg commando, which Joubert had called up that morning, simultaneously moved westwards parallel to Anstruther without being detected by the British column. British officers noticed the unusual number of saddle horses at Honey's farm but made nothing of it at the time, not realising that the Boers shadowing them were using the place as a rendezvous.[38] In the course of the morning the two Boer commandos joined forces and off-saddled at Salmon Prinsloo's homestead near the Honde River where they remained until their scouts reported the British to be approaching. They then swiftly rode into a valley behind a low hill south of the Middelburg–Pretoria road where they halted and, still mounted, spread out into a long skirmishing line to await the British. The size of this commando has been a matter of considerable debate, with many contemporary British reports greatly exaggerating the numbers to explain away defeat. J.E.H. Grobler, who has carefully weighed the sources, has concluded that the number of about 300 is probably correct.[39]

When his scouts reported that the British convoy was directly north of him on the road, Joubert ordered his mounted men to move forward in line at intervals of ten paces through the sparsely scattered thorn trees and down the gentle forward slope of the low hill to the level ground about 200 yards south of the road. Contrary to most contemporary British accounts which give the impression that the Boers enjoyed the advantage of high ground, large numbers of boulders and thick bush, the open terrain (as is confirmed by contemporary photographs) offered little natural cover.[40]

At about midday, one of the two British scouts several hundred yards ahead of the column pointed out to Anstruther what he probably correctly took to be a mounted party of Boers ahead, moving off to a farmhouse on the flank. Anstruther, after a long survey through his glasses, declared that the scout must have seen nothing more sinister than some cattle. The column then pushed on for another 500 yards until it was about a mile from the Bronkhorstspruit, 38 miles from Pretoria, where Anstruther intended to make camp. Suddenly, at about 13h20, the band stopped playing, shocked by the menacing sight of the Boer horsemen lined up on their left flank.

The numerous accounts of the battle which followed are contradictory and confused, and not simply because such is ever the unreliable nature of the traumatised memory of combat. In the testimony carefully elicited after the battle witnesses were responding to loaded enquiries by military officers and officials who were anxious to discover why and in what ways the British military system had failed, and if it were possible to ameliorate the humiliation by pinning defeat on a specific failure in command, or on unanticipated treachery by the unscrupulous Boers.[41]

At first sight of the Boers Anstruther galloped back to the main body of the column and dismounted. He ordered it to halt, the wagons to close up, and the men to get into formation with their arms. The men responded with military precision and order, but no attempt was made to take cover behind the wagons. The band recommenced playing. While Anstruther was busy issuing his commands, Joubert's despatch-rider, Paul de Beer, approached within 100 yards of the head of the column under a flag of truce. After some parleying Anstruther, Captain Elliott and Lieutenant Harrison came forward on foot. Speaking in English, de Beer handed over the sealed despatch which Joubert had entrusted to him, and which Anstruther opened and read aloud. This terse communication, written in English from Heidelberg and dated 17 December, was signed by the Boer Triumvirate and informed the 'Commander-in-Chief of Her Majesty's Troops on the road between Lydenburg and Pretoria' that, until the Boers' 'diplomatic commissioner' had returned with a reply from Lanyon, they did not know whether or not they were 'in a state of war'. They consequently desired Anstruther 'to stop where you are'. The Boer leaders were at pains to state in their despatch that they were only 'recovering the independence' of their country, and had no wish to take up arms against the Queen or the 'people of England'. Nevertheless, they declared that any further 'movement of troops' would be taken by them as a 'declaration of war, the responsibility whereof we put on your shoulders, as we know what we will have to do in self defence.'[42]

De Beer informed Anstruther that five minutes were allowed for an answer. To which the Colonel replied with some heat that he had his orders to proceed to Pretoria and would do so, but that Joubert should be told that he had no wish for a hostile confrontation. De Beer seemed reluctant to leave without first receiving a more compliant response, and twice asked Anstruther whether he meant war or peace. Anstruther reiterated that he meant to go to Pretoria, and de Beer finally galloped off to find Joubert to make his report. The Boer sources make it clear that de Beer had trouble in locating Joubert, and that before he could do so Nicolaas Smit, evidently sensing that the advantage the Boers enjoyed was being frittered away as the startled British began to close up for combat, gave the signal for the attack. The Boers galloped forward, flung themselves off their horses about 140 yards from the road, and opened a devastating fire at close range standing, or kneeling or lying behind what cover they could find, and deliberately first picking off the British officers and NCOs.

When Anstruther and his companions had turned to walk back to the column after the fruitless parlay, they observed the Boers closing in and broke into a run. Anstruther shouted to F Company to spread out with an interval of five paces between each two men, for the regimental prisoners to be released and arms and extra ammunition to be doled out. Both companies of the 94th Regiment returned fire, but they had no time to complete their deployment and flung themselves down in the grass only partly extended, some apparently still bunched up in the scramble to take up firing positions. Most members of the band never managed to get back and retrieve their rifles from the wagons, while the Africans with the column ran off as fast as they could or hid under the wagons. While the main Boer force engaged the front and left flank of the British column, Commandant Erasmus led some horsemen in an outflanking movement and fell on the wagons to the rear, killing most of the rearguard and shooting or driving away the terrified African wagon drivers sheltering there, and executing those they found wounded with a shot to the head.[43]

It is evident that the British rifle sights were set to 400 yards, and that when the Boers moved forward they failed to resight their rifles correctly, most likely because all the officers fell dead or wounded in the first minutes of the battle and could not issue the requisite orders. Consequently, the British fire generally went high over the heads of the Boers.[44] In contrast, the Boers had set up stone range markers to assist their accuracy, and demonstrated just how deadly effective modern breech-loading rifles could be in the right circumstances in experienced hands. The Boers in any case made difficult targets, for not only were they wearing their usual drab clothes which blended in with their surroundings, but were heeding their emphatic orders to remain spread out and make use of what little cover there was as they worked forward towards the convoy. The British who, with few exceptions, were in exposed positions wearing scarlet or blue tunics made far easier targets and took heavy casualties. The effective Boer fire succeeded in pinning down the British and deterring anyone from trying to collect arms or reserve ammunition from the wagons. Anstruther, though repeatedly wounded, rode up and down the ranks to encourage his men, but saw within 15 minutes that the situation was hopeless and that he must surrender to save further life. He ordered his men to throw up their hats and wave handkerchiefs as a signal of surrender, and firing finally ceased when a man climbed onto a wagon and showed a white flag. The soldiers laid down their arms and the Boers formed a circle around the remnants of 94th Regiment to prevent any from escaping.

Joubert himself was appalled at the scale of the slaughter,[45] the precise extent of which is not quite clear. It would seem that during the battle one officer was killed and another eight wounded. Two of these died the same day and two more (of whom Anstruther was one) within the next three weeks. Fifty-six men were killed during the fight and ninety-two wounded, of whom at least another seven died within the month. Surgeon Ward, the senior medical officer, reported that the average number of wounds inflicted on the men was five each. Anstruther himself received five wounds in the legs and thigh and died on 26 December after one of his legs was amputated. Mrs Fox, Mrs Maistré and Mrs Smith were all subsequently awarded the Royal Red Cross Decoration for their courageous conduct and care of the wounded during the action. Mrs Fox was severely wounded, and died some years later of the effects. Only one Boer was killed in the attack and four others lightly wounded.[46]

The Boers were magnanimous in victory. De Beer brought Commandant Frans Joubert to Anstruther where he lay wounded on the ground. Joubert begged the Colonel not to be angry but, picking up the fatal letter still lying next to him, reminded him that the battle had been the result of his decision to press on to Pretoria. Anstruther, cleaving though in pain and humiliation to his code as an officer and a gentleman, was suitably gracious in response. The Boers were short of all war *matériel*, and everything they could loot from the stricken column – the arms, ammunition, boots, jackets, officers' swords, wagons and horses – was literally regarded as a godsend.[47] Anstruther wrote in pencil to Joubert the day after the battle invoking 'the custom of every civilized nation' to furnish the wounded with shelter, care, food and transport.[48] Joubert needed little prompting, and left 20 tents, blankets, the hospital wagon, water cart and rations to establish a camp for the British wounded in a pleasant spot near Bronkhorstspruit with its gum trees and springs. The Boers in the neighbourhood proved most kind and helped the wounded in many ways.[49] Joubert also allowed 20 unwounded men to remain to bury the dead and aid the wounded, but one unwounded officer and 62 men were taken prisoner to Heidelberg. Soon after Christmas the men were turned loose across the Vaal River and made their way to Natal through the neutral Orange Free State. Conductor Egerton and Sergeant Bradley were permitted to push on to Pretoria through the night for medical assistance, ambulances and supplies, which arrived in the wounded men's camp on 22 December. In early January some of the wounded were taken on to Pretoria for more intensive nursing. On 15 January the Boers took away about 30 of those who had recovered, subsequently releasing most of them over the border into the Orange Free State.

At the time of the British surrender some of the soldiers tore the silk 3 ft 9 ins by 3 ft Colours of the 94th Regiment off their pikes and hid them under the dangerously wounded Mrs Fox on her stretcher. They were then passed to Egerton who uncomfortably wound them around his waist under his coat and so got them safe to Pretoria. The British made much at the time of the saving of the Colours, the one spark of honour in a dismal day for British arms. Fortunately for the sake of the military system as a whole, the accumulated evidence permitted Bellairs in his official communiqué to lay the responsibility for the debacle squarely on Anstruther's shoulders. Of course, it helped that Anstruther died two days before his condemnation was published. Confident, therefore, that he would not be contradicted, Bellairs could draw attention to Anstruther's 'neglect' as a commander, blaming him for his 'absence of caution on the march', for issuing inadequate ammunition and not even having the ammunition boxes unscrewed in readiness of an emergency, and for not reconnoitring the ground adequately before advancing. Comfortingly, therefore, the defeat and surrender at Bronkhorstspruit were demonstrated to be a consequence of an individual commanding officer's failure to exercise leadership according to laid down military principles, which exonerated the other officers and soldiers who had 'all fought with gallantry and endurance'.[50]

From their perspective, their startling victory at Bronkhorstspruit gave enormous encouragement to the Boers of the Transvaal over whom God's hand was seen to be stretched in palpable protection. The news spread like an electric shock through the Afrikaner populations of the Orange Free State and the British colonies, stimulating their nationalist aspirations and winning support for their gallant blood-brothers in the Transvaal.[51] Commandant-General Joubert published a proclamation in which he 'bowed down in the dust before Almighty God' who had given the victory to the heroic burghers in their 'war of self-defence'; triumphant burghers, it needs be said, who were nevertheless Christian (if tartly political) in their compassion for 'the loss of the unfortunate victims of tyranny and deceit, who have not even the consolation of having lost their lives in a good cause.' Joubert ended his proclamation on an even more inflammatory note, accusing the British 'before the whole world' of having started the war 'without notice' and having conducted it 'contrary to all the rules of war accepted by civilized nations'.[52]

The tone of Bellairs's District Orders of 28 December 1880, in which he detailed the cautious procedures to be followed in future to guard against the Boers again carrying out their 'cunning, but savage designs' of advancing to battle stations under the cover of parlaying under a flag of truce,[53] must be understood as a direct and indignant response to Joubert's proclamation – as well as an effective means of attributing the British defeat to Boer perfidy. Certainly, this dubious action by the Boers introduced a very sour note into the war. Considerable and abiding damage was done to the popular perception of the Boers among the British public which persisted in regarding the Boer attack at Bronkhorstspruit as 'an act of black treachery' perpetrated by savage, hypocritical ruffians.[54] Nor was this hostile perception of the Boers effaced by their decent treatment of the wounded, which temporarily made a good impression on the British public,[55] because the subsequent 'infamy' of their treatment of two captured British officers compounded the furore over the fraudulent flag of truce.[56]

Two days after the outbreak of hostilities the Boers had captured Captain R.H. Lambart of the 2/21st Fusiliers who was bringing remounts into the Transvaal from the Orange Free State, and held him in Heidelberg where he was soon joined as a prisoner-of-war by Captain J.M. Elliott, the Paymaster of the 94th Regiment and the only officer not to have been wounded at Bronkhorstspruit. Both officers took up the Boer offer to be allowed to cross into the Orange Free State in return for giving their *parole d'honneur* that they would not bear arms again during the war. Despite having been assured of their safety by Commandant-General Joubert himself, their escort of four armed men forced them to cross the swollen Vaal River at Spencer's Drift on the evening of 29 December and, when their cart turned on to its side, opened fire on them. Lambart escaped to tell the tale in a detailed report, but Elliott died instantly, shot through four times.[57] His body was later recovered from the river. In Heidelberg State Secretary Bok swiftly tried to deflect the official and public indignation that flowed over the Transvaal – not only from the British, but from many Free Staters as well. While expressing the Triumvirate's regrets about 'a bad act' committed by a few people in 'an honest and noble war', like Joubert before him he went over to the attack against the 'evil deeds' being perpetrated by the British oppressor in South Africa.[58] The Elliott case would not go away, however, and after the armistice that ended hostilities and provisionally restored the British administration, his four killers were arraigned for murder to stand trial before the Chief Justice of the Transvaal.[59] However, despite the overwhelming evidence of their culpability, the Boer jury acquitted them.[60] This blatant miscarriage of justice only served to confirm the low British opinion of Boer treachery and hypocrisy, and during the South African War Elliott's murder would be revived to remind readers of the Boers' natural perfidy.[61]

Thus Bronkhorstspruit and its ancillary episodes tend to confirm John Lynn's reflections on what happens when sharply differing discourses on the conventional expectations of armed conflict and the soldierly values associated with it come into collision. The temptation is to become infuriated with the other side for its flouting of the perceived codes of honour and fair fight, and to justify in response an alternative and less restrained form of war.[62] The Transvaal Rebellion would not last long enough for these more extreme methods to take hold, but bitter memories of its lapses in soldierly ethics would prepare the ground for lowering the threshold of 'civilised' war in the greater war of 1899–1902.

Colley was still in Pietermaritzburg while these events unfolded in the Transvaal during December 1880, and he was growing ever more conscious that animosity between the Boers and British was waxing more bitter and unforgiving with every incident. He understood that it was becoming imperative to move as swiftly as he could with his relief force, not only to rescue the beleaguered garrisons in the Transvaal and restore British administration, but to bring the war to a rapid and successful termination before all of southern Africa was dragged into the maelstrom.

Notes and references

1 Theron-Bushell, 'Lanyon', p. 264.

2 GH 792, no. G464a/1880: Lanyon to Colley, 27 September 1880.

3 *BPP* (C. 2866), enc. in no. 77: Bellairs to Deputy Adjutant-General, 14 November 1880.

4 Bellairs, ed., *Transvaal War*, pp. 48–9; Bennett, *Rain of Lead*, pp. 45–6.

5 *BPP* (C. 2783), enc. in no. 49: Bellairs to Lanyon, 16 November 1880; Bellairs, ed., *Transvaal War*, p. 51.

6 *BPP* (C. 2838), enc. 2: Lanyon to Kimberley, 23 January 1881.

7 *BPP* (C. 2783), enc. 1 in no. 14: Lanyon to Colley, telegram, 25 November 1880.

8 *BPP* (C. 2783), enc. 3 in no. 14: Colley to Lanyon, 3 December 1880.

9 *BPP* (C. 2866), no. 3: Colley to Kimberley, 26 December 1880.

10 G. Dominy and H. Paterson, 'Fort Napier: The Imperial Base that Shaped the City' in Laband and Haswell, eds, *Pietermaritzburg*, pp. 102, 109.

11 G. Dominy, 'The Imperial Garrison in Natal with Special Reference to Fort Napier 1843–1914: Its Social, Cultural and Economic Impact' (unpublished PhD thesis, University of London, 1995), pp. 377–8; E.M. Spiers, 'The British Army in South Africa: Military Government and Occupation, 1877–1914' in Boyden, Guy and Harding, eds, *'Ashes and Blood'*, p. 76.

12 The vagaries of the transfer of troops on special duties from one area to another, the complex system of reliefs and the detachment of units on special expeditions into the interior makes it very difficult to be absolutely precise about Fort Napier's garrison strengths at any particular date. See H. Paterson, 'The Military Organisation of the Colony of Natal, 1881–1910' (unpublished MA thesis, University of Natal, 1985), pp. 47–51; P.B. Boyden and A.J. Guy, 'The British Army in Cape Colony and Natal, 1815–1877' in Boyden, Guy and Harding, eds, *'Ashes and Blood'*, pp. 44–7; I.F.W. Beckett, 'Military High Command in South Africa, 1854–1914' in *'Ashes and Blood'*, pp. 64–5; Dominy, 'Imperial Garrison in Natal', pp. 367–8.

13 Laband and Thompson, *Anglo-Zulu War*, pp. 22–3; Dominy, 'Imperial Garrison in Natal', pp. 320–2, 371–5; Paterson, 'Military Organisation of Natal', pp. 36–40, 52–4, 56–61. It was impossible for the Natal administration to contribute much more than 10 per cent of the total imperial expenditure required to maintain the garrison at Fort Napier, and during the crisis of 1880–1881 this dropped to a derisory 0.6 per cent.

14 *BPP* (C. 2783), enc. 3 in no. 14: Colley to Lanyon, 3 December 1880; no. 25: Colley to Kimberley, 13 December 1880; no. 37: Colley to Kimberley, 19 December 1880.

15 WO 32/7797, no. 079/3492: Colley to QMG, London, telegram,
9 December 1880.

16 *BPP* (C. 2783), enc. 1 in no. 49: Colley to Lanyon, 19 December 1880.

17 *BPP* (C. 2783), no. 37: Colley to Kimberley, 19 December 1880; enc. 1 in no. 41:
Colley to Childers, 19 December 1880.

18 Bellairs, ed., *Transvaal War*, pp. 350–3; J. Crouch, 'The Defence of
Wakkerstroom' in J. Crouch and I.J. Knight, eds, *Forged in Strong Fires:
The Transvaal War 1881. A V.M.S. Centenary Publication* (Chippenham, 1981),
p. 20.

19 For the early stages of the siege of Potchefstroom, see Bellairs, ed., *Transvaal War*,
pp. 242–53; Bennett, *Rain of Lead*, chaps 4–7; J. Orford, *95 Days: The Siege
of the Fort at Potchefstroom 16th December, 1880–21st March 1881* (Potchefstroom,
1973), pp. 15–41, 52–3. J. Orford, 'Five Flags at Potchefstroom' in Crouch
and Knight, eds, *Forged in Strong Fires*, pp. 12–14; BV 1, 3, 5, 7–9, p. 76: Report
by Cronjé, December 1880; BV 17, p. 10: Private memorandum by Major
Clarke.

20 See Bellairs, ed., *Transvaal War*, pp. 276–7; J. Crouch, 'The Siege of Rustenburg'
in Crouch and Knight, eds, *Forged in Strong Fires*, p. 23; L. Wulfsohn, *Rustenburg
at War: The Story of Rustenburg and its Citizens in the First and Second Anglo-Boer
Wars* (Rustenburg, 1987), pp. 8–9.

21 Bellairs, ed., *Transvaal War*, pp. 68–9.

22 War Office, *Text Book of Fortification and Military Engineering, For Use at the
Royal Military Academy, Woolwich, Part I* (London, 2nd edn, 1884), pp. 94–100.
A summary, using the same diagrams is in Maj-Gen J.E. Portlock, RE, and
Col Sir C. Nugent, KCB, RE, 'Fortification', *The Encyclopaedia Britannica*
(Edinburgh, 9th edn, 1879), pp. 435–6.

23 Bellairs, ed., *Transvaal War*, pp. 285–9.

24 *BPP* (C. 2866), enc. F in no. 76: Bellairs to Anstruther, 23 November 1880; enc. G
in 76: Anstruther to Bellairs, 30 November 1880.

25 Butterfield, ed., *War and Peace*, pp. 137–8: Lt-Col P. Anstruther to his wife, Zaida,
29 November 1880. Battalion transport was supposed to consist only of eight
company wagons to carry the officers' and men's personal baggage, as well as
additional wagons for reserve ammunition, rations and camping equipment. See
Laband and Thompson, *Anglo-Zulu War*, p. 29.

26 *BPP* (C. 2866), enc. H in no. 76: Anstruther to Bellairs, 5 December 1880: 94th
Regiment Marching-Out State; enc. T in no. 76: Surgeon Ward to the senior
Medical Officer, Transvaal, 22 December 1880; enc. S in no. 76: Anstruther to
DAAG, Transvaal, 26 December 1880: notes in margin. Note that there are slight
discrepancies between these tallies.

27 *BPP* (C. 2866), enc. H in no. 76: Anstruther to Bellairs, 5 December 1880; Long,
Fort Mary, chap. II; Bellairs, ed., *Transvaal War*, pp. 300–3.

28 See J.E.H, Grobler, 'Die Beleëring van die Britse Garnisoene' in Van Jaarsveld, Van Rensburg and Stals, eds, *Eerste Vryheidsoorlog*, p. 130; Davey, 'Siege of Pretoria', pp. 275–6.

29 BV 17, p. 48: H.P. Malan to P.A. Cronjé, 6 January 1881.

30 Laband and Thompson, *Anglo-Zulu War*, pp. 28–30.

31 Butterfield, ed., *War and Peace*, p. 139: Anstruther to his wife, 15 December 1880; *BPP* (C. 2866), enc. J in no. 76: Anstruther to Bellairs, 15 December 1880.

32 *BPP* (C. 2866), enc. L in no. 76: Bellairs to Anstruther, 15 December 1880; enc. K in no. 76: Anstruther to AAG, Pretoria, 16 December 1880; enc. M in no. 76: Anstruther to Bellairs, 17 December 1880; enc. in no. 76: Bellairs to DAG, Pietermaritzburg, 30 December 1880: Remarks on the defeat experienced by Lt-Col Anstruther on the 20th December 1880; Butterfield, ed., *War and Peace*, p. 140: Lt J.J. Hume's account.

33 For Regimental Colours, see Knight, *Go to Your God like a Soldier*, pp. 190–1.

34 Butterfield, ed., *War and Peace*, pp. 141–2: Lt Hume's account.

35 *BPP* (C. 2866), enc. Q in no. 76: Cpl Stewart's and Pvt Weston's statements; *Natal Witness*: 1 July 1881.

36 War Office, *Field Exercise*, pp. 305–10; Laband and Thompson, *Anglo-Zulu War*, p. 30.

37 J.C. 26, no. 2451: P.J. Joubert to J.H.G. van der Schyff, 22 December 1880.

38 Butterfield, ed., *War and Peace*, pp. 140–1: Lt J.J. Hume's account.

39 For a full discussion on all aspects of the Boer commando at Bronkhorstspruit, see J.E.H. Grobler, 'Die Sege by Bronkhorstspruit' in Van Jaarsveld, Van Rensburg and Stals, eds, *Eerste Vryheidsoorlog*, pp. 118–20.

40 The terrain today is considerably more wooded than it was in 1880.

41 The ensuing account of the battle and its immediate aftermath is based on the following sources: *BPP* (C. 2866), enc. in no. 27 (repeated in enc. O in no. 76): Conductor R. Egerton's and Sgt J.F. Bradley's statements; enc. 2 in no. 29: statements by Sgt R. Gordon (see also WO 32/7803, enc. 1 in no. 079/3768), Pvt D. Campbell (see also WO 32/7803, enc. 2 in no. 079/3768) and Pvt P. King (see also WO 32/7803, enc. 3 in no. 079/3768); enc. Q in no. 76: evidence of canteen-waiter Lance-Cpl Fisher, Cpl Stewart, Pvt Wood, Pvt Weston, Conductor McCanlis, Mule-Driver Frederick and Pvt Carroll; enc. R in no. 76: statement of Lance-Sgt F.G. Briggs; enc. S in no. 76: Anstruther to DAAG, Transvaal, 26 December 1880; enc. T in no. 76: Surgeon Ward to Senior Medical Officer, Transvaal, 22 December 1880; enc. V. in no. 76: Surgeon-Major Comerford to Senior Medical Officer, Transvaal, 6 January 1881. Note that these enclosures can also be found printed in WO 32/7807. See also WO 32/7825: Surgeon Ward to Lanyon, 29 April 1881; Lt J.J. Hume to Lanyon, 27 April 1881; translated statement by de Beer, 29 December 1880; translated statement

by J.M. Engelbrecht, 29 December 1880. Bellairs, ed., *Transvaal War*, pp. 73–91; Norris-Newman, *With the Boers*, pp. 117–24; Carter, *Boer War*, pp. 129–46; Lehmann, *First Boer War*, pp. 114–30. See WO 32/7801, enc. in no. 079/3752: Capt M. Churchill's sketch of Bronkhorstspruit, 21 December 1880.

42 *BPP* (C. 2838), annex. 3: S.J.P. Kruger, M.W. Pretorius, P.J. Joubert and W. Edward Bok to the Commander-in-Chief of Her Majesty's Troops on the Road between Lydenburg and Pretoria, 17 December 1880.

43 Haggard, *Last Boer War*, p. 132: testimony of a Zulu driver.

44 *BPP* (C. 2866), enc. in no. 79: Bellairs: District Orders, 28 December 1880.

45 BV 3, p. 90: P.J. Joubert to Kruger and M.W. Pretorius, 21 December 1880.

46 WO 32/7812, enc. 2 in no. 079/3974: Surgeon Ward, 22 December 1880: Nominal rolls of killed and wounded at Bronkhorstspruit; Surgeon-Maj H. Comerford, 8 January 1881: Died of wounds since return of 22 December; WO 32/7819, no. 079/4623: Report by Surgeon Ward, 27 March 1881; *BPP* (C. 2866), enc. S in no. 76: Anstruther to DAAG, Transvaal, 26 December: Killed and wounded; enc. S in no. 76: Surgeon Ward to Senior Medical Officer Transvaal, 22 December 1880; Grobler, 'Bronkhorstspruit', p. 123.

47 See J.C. 26, no. 2452: P.J. Joubert to J.H.G. van der Schyf, 22 December 1880.

48 J.C. 26, no. 2460: Anstruther to Joubert, 21 December 1880.

49 WO 32/7819, no. 079/4623: Report by Surgeon Ward, 27 March 1881; *Natal Advertiser*: 3 February 1881.

50 *BPP* (C. 2866), enc. U in no. 76: Capt M. Churchill, DAAG: District Orders, 28 December 1880. When Bellairs initially wrote to the War Office explaining the débâcle he referred to Anstruther's 'culpable negligence', a phrase the War Office thought prudent to omit from the published *British Parliamentary Papers*. See WO 32/7801, enc. in no. 079/3752: Bellair's report on Bronkhorstspruit, 21 December 1880.

51 Grobler, 'Bronkhorstspruit', p. 126.

52 *BPP* (C. 2866) enc. V in no. 76: Proclamation by Cmdt-Gen Joubert and the Triumvirate, 23 December 1880; brought to Lanyon on Christmas Day.

53 *BPP* (C. 2866), enc. U in no. 76: Capt M. Churchill, DAAG: District Orders, 28 December 1880.

54 Garrett Fisher, *Transvaal and the Boers*, p. 206. See Lehmann, *Boer War*, pp. 122–4 for the popular denigration of the Boers in the British press.

55 J. Nixon, *The Complete Story of the Transvaal* (London, 1885), p. 214.

56 Garrett Fisher, *Transvaal and the Boers*, p. 207.

57 See WO 32/7803, enc. in no. 079/3765: Capt R.H. Lambart to Colley, 5 January 1881.

58 Norris-Newman, *With the Boers*, pp. 136–40.

59 *BPP* (C. 3098) enc. 5 in no. 17: *In re* The Queen *versus* R.J.J. Van Nieuwenhuijs *et al.*

60 *BPP* (C. 3098), appendix: Criminal Sessions of the High Court, 20 to 22 July 1881: Alleged Murder of Captain Elliott.

61 Creswicke, *South Africa and the Transvaal War*, vol. I, pp. 73–6: 'The Fate of Captain Elliott'.

62 Lynn, *Combat and Culture*, pp. xxi, 249, 280.

chapter 5

'Cribbed, cabined, confined, bound-in'[1]: the blockaded garrisons

Wolseley's fears for the English community in the Transvaal were to prove all too well founded when the Boer rebellion finally broke out in December 1880. Lanyon published Boer warnings that there could now be only two sorts of men in the Transvaal, 'those who were for, and those who were against, the Boers, in their opposition to the Government', and that it clearly appeared that 'civil war was now being carried on'.[2] However, as Lanyon had already recognised, it would be difficult in many cases for 'people well-disposed towards the Government' to rally effectively to its support for they were so 'mixed up with and dependent on the Boers in trade and other pursuits'.[3] Yet, since Boer strategy (as Colley explained to Kimberley) was one of 'surprising and attacking in detail our troops while spread in peace garrisons',[4] the active role of loyal inhabitants could in any case only be a limited one. Colley did what he could, though. He ordered all landdrosts and field cornets to call public meetings, prepare lists of all persons in their districts whose loyalty could be relied upon, and enrol loyalists as volunteers to defend their homes and government laagers. Volunteers were to help the garrison troops with supplies and transport, and to act as scouts. While troop reinforcements were being concentrated at Newcastle in Northern Natal they were to hold out as best they could until relieved, but were not to resist if the odds against them seemed irresistible.[5]

In Pretoria, Potchefstroom, Standerton and Wakkerstroom many of the loyalist civilians took refuge from the besieging Boers with the British garrisons in their forts, or behind hastily erected defences, and the men duly helped the troops in their defence and organised themselves into volunteer units. Elsewhere, in Rustenburg, Lydenburg and Marabastad, where the forts were rudimentary and the garrisons small, the civilians prudently decided to remain neutral. In the towns under siege, the defenders saw incessant military action and suffered considerable privations. Siege conditions produced special hardships for women, not least on account of their concern for their children and men out fighting. As Jacklyn Cock has argued, war uses and maintains the ideological construction of gender, and besieged women in the Transvaal were no exception. For while they were excluded from direct combat, they performed their traditional nurturing roles as nurses, cooks and comforters.[6] In 1880–1881, and again in 1899–1902, some of these women recorded their experiences and dangers, an act which gave some order to their disrupted lives and placed them at the centre of events in which they played a more passive part than the men.[7] Two such were Mary Long in Lydenburg and Sarah Heckford in Pretoria.[8]

On 20 December, the same day their regimental comrades suffered disaster at Bronkorstspruit, C and D Companies of the 94th Regiment, and one company of the 58th Regiment, were making for Pretoria from Wakkerstroom.[9] Captain Froom, the commander of the column, was handed a letter, its wording identical to that delivered to the unfortunate Colonel Anstruther, warning him to advance no further. Unlike Anstruther, Froom had taken earlier warnings seriously. Like Anstruther, he was not prepared to heed rebel threats, but his column was not similarly laden down with goods and civilians. So Froom resolved to run the gauntlet and make for Standerton, a small town of some 50 houses on the north bank of the Vaal which he knew to have the nearest garrison. The Boers were indeed planning to attack the column while it was strung out crossing the Vaal (a repetition of Bronkhorstspruit), but Froom pressed on with such haste that he made the crossing before Commandant van der Schyff could muster all the outlying Boer forces and position them for the assault. So although Froom saw Boers flanking his column the rest of the way to Standerton, they kept their distance and he made it safely into town.[10]

The Boers had already cut the telegraph line between Standerton and Pretoria, where he had been marching, and Froom decided that, without further orders, it would be best to halt and assist in building Standerton's defences. One company of the 94th Regiment was already in camp, together with some Royal Engineers and Hospital and Commissariat personnel. The three companies of the 94th Regiment mustered 257 men and the company of the 58th Regiment, 76. Mounted Infantry and locally raised volunteers added another 40 mounted rifles, which a trickle of additional volunteers eventually increased to 75. Major W.E. Montague of the 94th Regiment joined the garrison and assumed command of the defence. The military camp and hastily constructed earthwork fort (late called Fort Alice) were sited over a mile south-west of the town, unavoidably commanded from the north by the looming bulk of the flat-topped Standerskop Mountain.

On Christmas Day Commandant-General Joubert learned that the British were fortifying Standerton.[11] He decided to make a show of force in that direction and set off from Heidelberg on 27 December with a commando of 800 men. The first shots with the Standerton garrison were exchanged on 29 December when the Boer commando surprised a reconnaissance party, killing one and wounding four others. Joubert then pressed on to hold the Transvaal–Natal border against Colley, detaching 100 men under Commandant Lombard to blockade the garrison. This force swelled periodically whenever more Boer forces were passing through on their way to the laagers on the Natal border, and in late February Commandant-General Joubert estimated their number to be about 300.[12]

Lombard's men took up positions on a flat-topped hill south of the Vaal River, to the north-west behind Standerskop and also to the east of the town. By 29 December the garrison and civilian population of about 150 were completely invested and constantly sniped at by Boer marksmen. British soldiers, when taking up their positions, were permitted by Montague to do so at the run, but no ignominious bobbing and ducking was tolerated. Supplies were plentiful, and as Colley (according to his last message before the line was cut) was expected to reach the town on 20 January, there was no alarm in that respect. The garrison was made a trifle apprehensive, however, when it was learned that the Boers for months past had been stockpiling ammunition and gunpowder in preparation for a long siege.

Although the besiegers seemed content to remain at a safe distance and snipe, fire from Standerskop in particular made movement in the camp difficult, and on 4 January Montague decided on a sortie to be rid of this nuisance. Thirty of the mounted troops were to swing to the north of the mountain while he, with about thirty of the 94th Regiment, would proceed to Stander's farmhouse at its foot, which the Boers were reported to be using as their headquarters. Montague's men soon ran into a large body of Boers sent to oppose them, and a heavy fire-fight ensued. The company of the

58th Regiment sallied out in support and the Boers broke off the engagement, allowing the British to withdraw to their camp.

Soon after successfully repelling this sortie, the Boers established themselves in a well-constructed earthwork they threw up on high ground south
of the Vaal, and which they continued to improve and extend. This second
commanding position not only threatened the camp, but all movement
between the camp and the town. The British were forced to dig a system of
trenches as protection from the sniping. Standerskop remained the greatest
thorn in the British side, and to bolster their defences the British built
several outworks to the north and east of the town in support of the fort
guarding the camp.

News of the declaration of the Boer republic reached Wakkerstroom
on 18 December,[13] followed on 24 December by word of Bronkhorstspruit.
The garrison and loyal townspeople prepared to defend themselves against
attack. Wakkerstroom consisted of a well-built church, a courthouse, a store
or two and a few dozen houses. Captain Saunders's command comprised
approximately 120 men of the two companies of the 58th Regiment and
about 40 volunteers from among the townspeople. Saunders stationed about
100 of these men in an earthwork enclosure surrounded by a ditch which
passed for a fort, but which was unfortunately commanded by the hills.
Somewhat in accordance with the principles of defending an open town,
Saunders divided up the rest of his forces between the well-built church,
which was sandbagged and made ready for defence, and the courthouse,
also placed in a state of defence, but subsequently abandoned and dismantled. The town's two stores were also prepared for defence and occupied by
the volunteers.[14] One old ship's cannon, mounted on the chassis of a water-
cart, was placed in front of the church more as a symbol of resistance than
anything more effective. The garrison had adequate stocks of food, but only
limited supplies of ammunition.

News of an impending attack by the Boers under Commandant van
Staden reached the town on 28 December. Van Staden's forces threw a
loose cordon around Wakkerstroom and were fairly comfortably housed and
provisioned at the surrounding farms. The Boers made no serious attempt to
capture the town, even though reinforcements could have been brought
over from the Boer laagers nearby on the Natal border. Joubert himself rode
across in early January to inspect the British defences, and decided they
were too strong to attempt without artillery.[15] Thereafter, the Boers remained
content to keep the British bottled up. Sniping was frequent, though, and

the Boers occasionally raided for cattle and horses that strayed too far from the vicinity of the defended posts, and the British retaliated in kind.

Kruger arrived in Potchefstroom from Heidelberg on 23 December to discuss with Cronjé his plans for the reduction of the British garrison. It is true that the town was the original capital of the Transvaal, and that its capture would be a moral coup, and that it was also the main commercial link with the Free State, the only outside source for ammunition and supplies. Yet there was a more significant reason for committing 450 men – or close to a quarter of the total of 2,000 or so Boers blockading the British garrisons[16] – to this particular siege. As Bennett argues, the British garrison's two 9-pounder guns were the prize, for they were essential to neutralise the British artillery in Pretoria if the town were to be quickly taken. For if both Potchefstroom and Pretoria fell, then it would be possible to reinforce Joubert with both men and artillery for his decisive encounter on the border. The ultimate success of the Boer campaign thus depended in large measure on getting hold of these guns, undamaged, and the Boers prosecuted their siege of Potchefstroom with that object in mind.[17]

Nor did Boer hopes of taking Potchefstroom seem, at first, too far-fetched. Finding adequate water in the British fort for some 200 soldiers and 50 civilians, plus their horses, mules and cattle, presented an immediate problem.[18] The defenders sank a well, but by 21 December no water had been found. A few days later a second well struck a plentiful supply of water. That problem solved, concern began to grow that supplies of food would not last a protracted siege. With no relief in sight, the garrison released all the horses and mules, and the Boers shot any cattle which strayed from the fort. Over the succeeding weeks most of the black drivers and *voorloopers* absconded, running the grave risk of being shot by the Boers for disloyalty. On Christmas Eve a number of women and children tried surreptitiously to leave the fort, but the Boers opened fire, killing a boy and wounding a girl. Following this tragedy all but 13 of the civilian men, women and children gained Cronjé's permission to leave the fort. Cronjé denied the same privilege to those who later wished to leave. Constant, well-directed Boer sniping forced the defenders to strengthen their earthworks and to raise the parapet to an ultimate height of about three yards. This backbreaking work never ended, for although sandbags were added every night, bullets and the summer rains caused them to deteriorate so quickly that they had to be replaced daily. When stocks of bags ran out they were made from tents. The tents, when not cannibalised for sandbags, provided ever less shelter from the elements since they were shot full of holes. Fuel ran out and most of the wagons and carts had to be broken up and used for firewood. There were no luxuries such as sugar, tea, coffee or tobacco. Even the supplies of army biscuits were finished and were replaced with a ration of mealies and, on every third day, tinned bully beef.

During the early hours of New Year's Day the Boers opened up a heavy fire for three hours preparatory, the British believed, to storming the fort. 'Ou Griet', the famous carronade said to have been used at Blood River in 1838 and buried at Potchefstroom at the time of the British annexation, was exhumed and mounted on wagon wheels to join in with its 5 lb shot until silenced by return fire from the two 9-pounders. To the garrison's relief, the anticipated assault did not materialise. On 3 January the Boers opened fire on the town magazine which was a small solidly built building about 200 yards from the fort and began energetically digging a trench straight towards it. The garrison considered it prudent to remove its contents and kept 10,000 rounds of Martini-Henry ammunition for their own use, but destroyed a ton of gunpowder and 21,500 rounds of Westley Richards which the Boers could have used for their weapons. They then threw out a sap to the magazine, removed its roof and occupied it to prevent the Boers using it as an uncomfortably close strong point.[19] From 3 January Ou Griet fired almost daily on the fort and the Boers busily sapped towards both sides of it. Despite considerable return fire from the fort by both rifles and 9-pounders, the Boers also made dangerous progress towards the rear of the fort with a third sap. On 22 January the British launched a determined counter-attack and after some fierce fighting took the trench. Four Boers were captured and a couple wounded, while three of the British were wounded, one dying the following day. The Boer prisoners were exchanged for four members of the 2/21st Fusiliers. On this occasion Cronjé was unexpectedly chivalrous, returning the stretchers used for conveying the Boer wounded back to their lines loaded with fruit for the British wounded and some carbolic acid which the two British medical officers had requested to treat their wounded.[20]

Certain decencies were in fact maintained throughout the siege. Early on both sides ceased firing on the Sabbath. When one of the civilians, Mrs Sketchley, died of enteric fever on 28 February, Cronjé allowed a coffin to be sent from the town, and granted a brief truce to enable the burial to take place. The Boers were reasonably well-disposed to the British soldiers they captured, eventually allowing two lance-corporals and fourteen men of the

Fusiliers to cross into the Orange Free state, and so back to the British lines. But they were determined to punish any captured civilians who had taken service with the British whether as officials, military volunteers or intelligence agents (this last being deemed the most reprehensible). Under Cronjé they commenced a series of courts martial which handed down severe sentences ranging from death to forced hard labour digging trenches which brought prisoners under British fire from their fort. Loyalists in the town who did not defer satisfactorily to the new regime were also punished; while storekeepers were compelled by Cronjé's war council to supply goods on the punitive terms required.[21] There is no doubt that in Potchefstroom Boer animosity and resentment towards the loyalist commercial and administrative communities was allowed to play out under Cronjé's command with little disguise or hindrance, much as it was in several other towns taken by the Boers.

Anstruther's column had marched from the little village of Middelburg on 16 December. The landdrost, C. von Brandis, began to make preparations on 20 December to defend it with walls and barricades, and the following day signed up potential defenders. But there were only 25 loyalists in the town willing to come forward, and most of these promptly backed out that same day when news came in of the Bronkhorstspruit encounter and the presence of Boer forces in the vicinity. Von Brandis consequently gave up all hope of holding the town and dismantled what defences had been erected. On 23 December 120 Boers under Commandant Grové entered the town and took formal possession of it without a shot being fired. The Boers seized the government weapons and ammunition, imposed a curfew on the inhabitants, arrested the leading loyalists, levied a war contribution in cash and livestock on those who had intended to resist, and commandeered goods from all the stores. They then mounted guards on the town and effectively cut it off from the rest of the world for the duration.

The fates of Zeerust and Utrecht were very similar to that of Middelburg. On Christmas morning 150 mounted Boers arrived in Zeerust in the far western Marico District and ordered the English to assemble on the stoep of the courthouse to be informed of the change of governments. Some of the loyalists tried to raise the Union Jack before being overpowered, and Moffatt, the Native Commissioner, was beaten with rifle butts for refusing to tell the Africans that they were now under the Republic's law. The Boers then looted the town of powder and stores.[22] No troops were available to garrison Utrecht, close to the Natal border north-east of Newcastle, and

Colley instructed the landdrost, G.M. Rudolph, not to attempt a defence if outnumbered. Although Rudolph believed many of the townspeople to be loyal, only nine volunteered to stand by him. Consequently, when on 28 December 1881 a force of Boers under Field Cornet Ignatius Ferreira rode into Utrecht and raised the Vierkleur, Rudolph had no choice but to surrender. He was considered a determined loyalist and traitor to his people, and on 3 January was taken a prisoner to Heidelberg. As in Middelburg, the loyalist suffered exactions from the Boers, and the Africans in the neighbourhood had many cattle seized from them to feed the Boer commando who also commandeered their horses and labour.[23] The Boer force did not hold Utrecht, however, and withdrew by the end of December, having first destroyed the town's stonework settlers' laager and the military earthwork built adjacent to it in 1877. In Luneburg on the Zululand border to the north-east of Utrecht, where German settlers of the Hermannsburg Mission Society had established themselves in 1869 and were holding themselves strictly neutral in the conflict, the Boers nevertheless took the precaution of likewise demolishing their stone-built civil laager and Fort Clery (the military earthwork thrown up in 1878).[24]

On 27 December Joubert's representative, Diederik Muller, demanded the surrender of the Lydenburg garrison.[25] Lieutenant Long refused, but played for time by successfully requesting to refer the matter to Pretoria and used the respite to improve Fort Mary's walls, ditches and obstacles. Assistant Commandant-General J.P.Steyn's commando of about 200 men entered Lydenburg on 6 January and formally proclaimed the Republic at a flag-raising ceremony. Steyn then once more demanded that Long surrender the fort and offered him the honours of war if he marched out. Long stoutly refused. The Boers then launched the first of their many attacks on the fort, taking up position in the demolished laager, only 100 yards away, and brought a heavy fire to bear. The garrison, who had no artillery of their own, were consternated on 8 January when the Boers fired on Fort Mary with an old ship's cannon. Another cannon joined it on 12 January, and during six hours of bombardment many round-shots began to penetrate the walls and roofs of the buildings. Exchanges of small arms fire were remarkably heavy, and Steyn reckoned that on a single day 6,000 shots came from the fort,[26] which eventually subdued the cannon fire. As a result, the Boers moved one of the cannons back on 13 January to a properly prepared earthwork redoubt. An attempt by the defenders to open a sap in its direction was abandoned under heavy harassing fire. The Boer bombardment resumed and reached the same intensity on 18 January as it had on 12 January. The Boers mounted their most determined attack on 23 and 24 January with heavy rifle fire on the fort from all directions supported by about a hundred rounds from the cannons. However, no actual assault followed, and although the cannons kept up the bombardment for another two days, rifle fire died away.

On 27 December the 200 or so Boer forces under Commandant M.A. van der Walt,[27] which had been hovering within several miles of Rustenburg, occupied the town and disarmed the townspeople.[28] The investment of the fort began the same day when the garrison refused the Boer demand to surrender and were fired upon. The following days the defenders noticed that the Boers were pushing forward a sap from a point close to the town and about 500 yards from the fort. The Boers made good progress under constant covering fire, especially from a small hill some 1,000 yards away. Captain Auchinleck was wounded in the face on 29 December by this long-range fire, and temporarily relinquished command to Lieutenant H.T. Despard. On 1 January the Boers sent in a flag of truce demanding surrender, but were again stoutly refused. The Boers next brought up one of their home-made Ras guns on 8 January 1881 and fired at the fort from a range of 2,000 yards. Ineffective at that range, it was moved forward to within 1,200 yards. After firing 45 rounds it approached still closer and fired another 14 rounds at 600 yards. Then it suddenly ceased fire. The British believed they had silenced it with rifle fire, but in fact its breech had blown. Van der Walt was replaced as commander on 11 January by Kruger's son-in-law, Sarel Eloff. His attitude to the British was altogether more antagonistic than his predecessor's, and he squeezed the loyalists in town for money. Eloff forcibly sent three of those who would not pay up to the '*gat*' [hole], as he called the fort, to 'starve'.[29]

Word of Bronkhorstspruit reached Marabastad on 29 December and the garrison prepared for an attack. Captain Brook declared martial law and called upon loyal civilians to come into the fort.[30] The garrison of regulars was augmented by about 30 volunteers and a detachment of 43 black Transvaal Mounted Police under Captain Thompson. So far the Boers had shown no hostility towards the garrison, but were known to be in several laagers in the vicinity. On 11 January Commandant Barend J. (Swart Barend) Vorster advised Brook that unless he desisted from further seizures of corn and other farm produce to victual the fort, he would take active steps. Vorster followed this message the next day with a demand that the landdrost surrender his keys as a symbol of the transfer of civil authority, and then attacked his office when he would not. The 100 or so Boers invest-ing Marabastad were quartered in four laagers 7 or 8 miles distant from the fort.[31] Each day Vorster detailed some Boers to keep watch on the garrison from behind the earthworks they threw up all around their position. On 19 January Captain Thompson, 15 Mounted Police and 10 volunteers under Conductor Stott of the Commissariat set out to reconnoitre a Boer laager at Sandspruit, 8 miles from the fort. Before they reached their objective they were ambushed by a numerically superior force of mounted burghers. Forced to retire, they suffered one man killed and four wounded, two of whom the Boers captured.[32] The Boers, who had previously kept their distance, were buoyed up by their success, and now became more active in sending out patrols to capture the garrison's horses and cattle grazing near the fort.

Pretoria was naturally the great prize, the military and administrative capital of the British occupation. In the early hours of the morning of 21 December word of the ambush of the 94th Regiment at Bronkhorstspruit reached Pretoria. Deeply shocked, Bellairs abandoned not only his previous plans to send out flying columns to break up the large parties of Boers gath-ering to attack Pretoria, but gave up his intention to defend the town itself.[33]

Reports differ as to the strength of the Pretoria garrison. There were the Headquarters of the 2/21st Fusiliers, with four companies, the company of the 94th Regiment which had safely marched in from Marabastad on 10 December, and a troop of Mounted Infantry raised from the same regiment. For artillery there were two 9-pounder guns of the N/5 Brigade, RA, and further guns dug out of ordnance stores and pressed into service. These consisted of two 7-pounders and a rocket-launcher manned by the bandsmen of the 2/21st Fusiliers, four Krupp 4-pounders and a 3-pounder Whitworth which were worked by the volunteer Transvaal Artillery, and an old Mitrailleuse. Bellairs reckoned he had 590 regulars excluding artillery-men, but with them and some Royal Engineers, as well as Army Service and Army Hospital Corps personnel, the figure was probably closer to 650.

Loyal civilians were also available for defence. On 19 December Colley had proposed that Lanyon employ any volunteer forces raised as far as pos-sible in defence of the towns and that he avoid bringing them directly into contact with the Boers because '[t]he feeling that would be aroused by such civil war would be more bitter and enduring than any resulting from a direct conflict with the government.'[34] This made sense, but could hardly be com-plied with if volunteers were to play any active role, especially on essential patrol duties, and Colley's advice was ignored. Although only a third of the civilian men in Pretoria capable of bearing arms initially volunteered for service, the number of volunteers grew as the siege progressed. Thus the 120 men of D'Arcy's Horse (or Pretoria Carbineers) grew to about 150, the 68 men of Nourse's Horse to some 100 (including Melvill's Scouts who were Africans attached to Nourse's Horse), and the six companies (or 400 men) of the Pretoria Rifles to 500. There was also an indeterminate Civic Guard intended as a purely defensive body. The lack of regular cavalry made the role of the volunteer irregular horse very important in patrolling outside the town (patrols averaged an arduous 60 miles a day). They also played a prominent part in all sorties. Even so, Bellairs and his senior officers could not rid themselves of the usual prejudices of hidebound regulars towards colonial units, and tended to ascribe all military failures to their unprofessional door. In addition to the volunteers already enumerated, there were those posted to the artillery, engineers and other services, making a total of some 600 volunteers initially, rising to about 750. Thus a total of between 1,250 and 1,500 men were available to hold Pretoria; double the number of Boers investing them. The thousand or so Africans in Pretoria formed a useful labour pool and also acted as scouts, messengers and scavengers. However, the usual ambivalence among the settlers towards Africans manifested itself, and wavered between dependence, uncertainty and hostility. The pass system was consequently still rigorously applied during the siege, but Bellairs also issued a notice warning civilians and the military against ill-treating Africans.

Bellairs initially believed as many as 6,000 Boers (a gross over-estimation) were preparing to attack Pretoria, so that Pretoria was far too open and sprawling a town to be held against them. It made far better sense to concentrate his regular and volunteer forces, together with the white civilian population (975 men, 676 women and 718 children) and their 1,331 African servants, in a defensible perimeter. There was another advantage to organising a confined defensive area: it would be far easier to supervise and neutralise potential supporters of the Boer cause among the townsfolk. Lanyon concurred, and to enforce Bellairs's plan proclaimed martial law on 21 December now that 'certain of the inhabitants' of the Transvaal were self-evidently 'in open rebellion'.[35] All civilians in Pretoria, including the hastily recruited volunteers, were ordered to move into the established military camp about half a mile to the south-west of Pretoria, and also into what became known as the Convent Redoubt about 600 yards north-east of the camp. This was an enclosure which incorporated the Loreto Convent and the gaol. Under martial law, Bellairs, as military commander of the Transvaal, took precedence over Lanyon in the defence of Pretoria. As a result, there was the inevitable friction associated with having a prominent official (who was also a professional soldier) at headquarters, though the frustrated Administrator did accept that Bellairs's military arrangements were effective.[36] Lanyon was in any case neutralised since he was cut off from Colley and his directives as High Commissioner for most of the siege, though blockade runners did sometimes manage to get messages through.[37]

Not unexpectedly, many townsfolk vocally protested against being herded into military enclosures, for they still believed that the Boers would quickly be defeated, and that their property should not be so cavalierly abandoned to pillage. They were only somewhat mollified by assurances that they would be compensated for any losses by later mulcting the defeated rebels. So it was with considerable reluctance that the civilians submitted over several chaotic and ill-tempered days to the commandeering of arms, ammunition, dynamite, horses, forage and any other useful military equipment, as well as provisions of every kind deemed essential to maintaining the besieged camp and redoubt until Colley was able to march to their relief. Over the succeeding weeks prices of goods inevitably rose, and shortages occurred. It was fortunate that it remained possible to graze cattle and horses under the shelter of the garrison's guns. But with no relief in sight disaffection grew, and not just among open Boer partisans who were treated as virtual prisoners. Supposed loyalists grew ever more grudging in their support, and the numbers of unenthused trimmers grew.

With the reluctant civilians under their control, the military immediately set about pushing out and strengthening their defences. In order to cover the main routes to Pretoria, which was encircled by hills, a number of fortified posts were built. To secure the southern approach, Fort Tullichewan was erected on the heights to the east of the South Poort [a 'poort' is a narrow pass] and Fort Commeline to the west. Both were covered forts each holding 25 men and a 4-pounder Krupp gun.[38] A block-house for 12 men was built to guard the entrance to the Poort. Fort Royal, about 600 yards east of the camp, commanding the entrance on that side between Fort Tullichewan and the town, was designed to hold a company and a 4-pounder Krupp gun. At the Convent Redoubt the gaol was strengthened and a bastion added in the south-east corner for the fourth 4-pounder Krupp gun. At the military camp, which was to the north of Fort Commeline overlooking Daspoort, the west of the town and the road to Rustenburg, the few buildings enabled the defenders to form a series of posts or defensive squares styled on Fort Victoria. Improvements were still being made to these defences when the first encounter with the Boers took place on 28 December.

The garrison habitually over-estimated the Boer forces blockading Pretoria, and had some difficulty in collecting intelligence concerning their positions and numbers. However, by 6 February 1881 Bellairs was able to report reasonably accurately that two Boer wagon laagers were established to the west and south-west of Pretoria, three more to the south or south-east, two to the east, and a final three to the north-east or north. All were within an average radius of 10 miles of Pretoria across the main approaches to the town. (Bellairs did not know to include in his count the even smaller wagon laagers of very compact groups of Boers who were constantly on the move around Pretoria.) The numbers manning the laagers ranged, Bellairs calculated, between up to 200 men at Wonderboom Poort and down to a few dozen at Derde Poort nearby, with a total of about a thousand all told.[39] Yet Bellairs was probably still over-estimating the investing forces which, though the single largest Boer contingent committed to a siege, likely numbered no more than 800.[40] Commandant D.J.E. Erasmus directed operations from the Doornkloof laager. The skilfully placed Boer laagers made patrolling easier and movement against the flanks or rear of any British force sallying out possible. However, being summer, this was the season for horse-sickness, which hampered extensive operations by mounted men.[41] With some consideration the Boers evacuated civilians on farms too close to the theatre of operations, though they usually confiscated the possessions of obvious loyalists. Unhappily, abandoned farms were inevitably ransacked by patrols from both sides.

Open hostilities began on 28 December when a mounted British patrol reconnoitring the Boer positions south of Pretoria encountered a party of burghers from Red House Laager 10 miles south-west of Pretoria and 3 miles west of the Heidelberg road. Two volunteers were wounded and one Boer killed.[42] Lieutenant-Colonel George Gildea, the spirited officer commanding the 2/21st Fusliers, decided on retaliatory action, the first British offensive of the war. On 29 December he marched on Red House Laager (which he believed to be held by 150 Boers) with a force of two 7-pounder guns, 158 mounted men (of whom 10 were the black Melvill's Scouts) and 198 infantry.[43] Gildea's advance can only be described as cautious to a fault. As the few Boers he encountered all fell back skirmishing in the direction of

Red House, he periodically detached troops to hold tactical points along his line of retreat. This so depleted his column that he soon decided he could go no further without endangering it. The disappointed mounted volunteers with his force were all burning to make a good showing, however, and when they saw an apparently abandoned kraal filled with cattle, they requested Gildea's permission to rustle them. Gildea was wary and unenthusiastic, and made it clear that if they ran into trouble they should not look to him for support. Undeterred, the volunteers galloped off straight into a cleverly laid ambush. A heavy Boer volley wounded four of them, and it was only with the greatest difficulty that the chastened volunteers were able to extricate themselves and make it back to camp.

For a few days after the Red House debacle the British attempted no more sallies, and life went on routinely in the camp with all its petty military duties, irksome tasks and relative hardships which the civilians bore with varying degrees of fortitude. Being the rainy summer months water was relatively plentiful, but in early January the garrison built dams and reservoirs against the dry season. Basic foodstuffs, including meat, were adequate, but luxuries like sugar were rationed, or simply unavailable. Life was generally monotonous, and since they were not being subjected to a close siege, many of the civilians could see little reason why they should not return to their homes.

Then on 5 January 1881 a foraging party ranging north-east of Pretoria brought back word of a Boer laager some 13 miles away at Zwartkoppies on Venter's (or Cockcroft's) Farm near Pienaar's River. To test the strength of the Boers' perimeter in the direction from which a relief force was expected, Gildea once more sallied forth on the morning of 6 January with one 9-pounder gun, 148 mounted troops and 190 infantry.[44] This time he also had a train of 15 wagons to transport the infantry during the advance and the forage they intended to collect on the way back. Forty Boers under Field Cornet Hans Botha held the Venter's Farm Laager. They were actually taken by surprise by the British who managed to swing around the laager undetected and attack it from the rear. The Boers made a determined defence, but this time the British overwhelmed them, taking 17 prisoners, several of whom were wounded with 2 subsequently dying. However, in storming the laager in a conventional frontal attack at bayonet point, the British had also suffered severely, losing 4 killed and 15 wounded. Nor could they hold the dearly won position. Since Boers from other laagers in the vicinity were seen to be approaching, they began hastily to retire on Pretoria. At one stage it seemed that a body of some 40 troops, left as a rearguard to hold some high ground along the line of withdrawal five miles from camp, might even be cut off. But the Boers evidently decided it was too risky to become fully engaged when British reinforcements were available from Pretoria close by, and broke off the encounter.

During this skirmish a young burgher, in a panic under British fire, raised a white flag. The British then ceased firing, but Field Cornet Botha, enraged at this unauthorised act of capitulation, tore down the token of surrender, and firing had resumed. Two British officers, who had gone forward in good faith to negotiate, and who were carrying white flags, were shot down. The British, already infuriated by the 'treachery' of the Bronkhorstspruit ambush, chose to regard 'such savage proceedings' as another incidence of Boer perfidy, and Bellairs indignantly warned his troops against similar Boer subterfuges in future.[45] Indeed, the Pretoria garrison was beginning to learn something about the Boer way of war. In his report on this affray, Gildea included a passage which was omitted in the published despatches, but which nevertheless accurately (too accurately?) summarised the nature of the war being fought, and pointed out tactical realities that Colley in turn was going to learn the hard way on the Natal front. Gildea wrote:

. . . the Boers will never attack in the open; they are most tenacious to stones and cover, and it is very hard to get them out. Their principal tactics are traps, and as they are all well mounted, and have a thorough knowledge of the country, they can travel fast, and take up positions wherever they like. Cavalry with light Artillery are the only troops that can be used with any effect against the Boers. Infantry are only useful for holding positions, as the Boers will never let them come near enough to them in the open.[46]

For their part, the Boer setback, relatively minor though it was, and some-what compensated for by the competent pursuit of the retiring British, was nevertheless enough to ruin Commandant Erasmus. He was replaced by the more dynamic Assistant Commandant-General Hendrik J. Schoeman who set up his headquarters at Wonderboom Poort. Schoeman increased the state of Boer alertness and set up a series of signal fires to allow rapid com-munication between laagers so that reinforcements could be rushed to any stronghold under attack and a repetition of the Venter's Farm affair be avoided.

Following this last relative success, Gildea decided to probe the Boer laager at Elandsfontein on the Daspoortrand about 10 miles west of Pretoria, held by no more than 100 men under Henning Pretorius. At daybreak on 16 January Gildea led out the largest column thus far, consisting of two 9-pounder guns, one 7-pounder gun, 181 mounted troops and 314 infantry.[47] Six Royal Engineers created a diversion in the opposite direction from the one Gildea was taking with a series of dynamite explosions. Much emphasis was placed on the artillery support Gildea considered so essential for flushing out the Boers, and in a spirited attack Gildea's forces slowly drove the outnumbered Boers back. For their part, the Boers put up a lively and tenacious defence, and Schoeman's new signal system saved the day for them. Duly alerted, Schoeman rapidly brought up between 100 and 150 men to the scene of action. Facing ever stiffer opposition as these reinforcements were fed into the Boer positions, Gildea broke off the engagement. In a repetition of the sortie of 6 January, he fell back on his camp hotly pursued all the way by the Boers. The British lost two men killed and eight wounded in the skirmish, while six Boers were wounded. Gildea was particularly disappointed that his artillery (on which he had pinned high hopes) had not performed as effectively as anticipated, despite firing about 70 rounds.[48]

For both sides in the Transvaal it seemed apparent by the end of January that a stalemate had been reached. The Boers had failed to reduce any of the British posts, and seemed to have little prospect of doing so. Kruger, in apparent acceptance of this fact, ordered the Boers' forces on 31 January to use ammunition sparingly, and to take no offensive action against the forts unless first attacked.[49] If the Boers had initially viewed overrunning the British garrisons as ancillary to their main effort in the field on the Transvaal–Natal border, that prospect had now been firmly relegated to a strategic side-show. For their part the British garrisons, whether less or more closely and uncomfortably invested, had succeeded in their passive objective of standing fast and tying down Boer forces (which might have been deployed more effectively on the Natal front) while waiting to be relieved.

Only the Pretoria garrison was large enough to mount a field force capable of significant offensive action, and the intention of relieving the garrison at Potchefstroom – the Transvaal's second town after Pretoria – took a while to fade. Gildea's repulse on 16 January finally made up Bellairs's mind. He had now seen enough of Gildea's sorties to realise that any relieving column would have to maintain a running fight for over 100 miles with the Boers hanging tenaciously on its flanks and rear, and that if it succeeded in reaching its objective (which was by no means certain) it would be too much weakened either to be of much assistance to the beleaguered garrison or to be strong enough to make it back to Pretoria. Since it was also clear that a relief column would require all the regular troops stationed in Pretoria, this would leave the town to be defended by the relatively untrained and not necessarily loyal volunteers units: a sure recipe for disaster. Closer to home, Bellairs was fast losing faith even in Gildea's limited sorties which were using up precious 9-pounder ammunition and costing casualties and the loss of horses to no appreciable effect. The wisdom of adopting a more passive defence in future was brought home to him when, on 7 February, he learned that Colley's force had been repulsed at Laing's Nek on the Transvaal border. With relief no closer, Bellairs considered it his primary duty to keep the Pretoria garrison sufficiently up to strength to offer material aid to Colley's advancing column[50] – should it ever succeed in breaking into the Transvaal.

Notes and references

1 The motto of *The News of the Camp. A Journal of Fancies, Notifications, Gossip, and General Chit Chat*, the news letter published in Pretoria during the siege. The editors were Charles Du-Val, an Irish itinerant entertainer, and Charles Deecker, the former editor of the *Transvaal Argus* on whose presses the paper was printed.

2 *BPP* (C. 2866), enc. in no. 75: Memorandum by His Excellency the Administrator in Council, 1 January 1881.

3 *BPP* (C. 2740), enc. in no. 73: Lanyon to Colley, 26 November 1880.

4 *BPP* (C. 2866), no. 74: Colley to Kimberley, 10 February 1881.

5 *BPP* (C. 2866), enc. 5 in no. 3: Colley to Landdrosts, Field Cornets, &c., of the Transvaal, n.d. [December 1880].

6 J. Cock, *Colonels and Cadres: War and Gender in South Africa* (Cape Town, 1991), p. x.

7 See E. van Heyningen, 'The Voices of Women in the South African War', *South African Historical Journal*, 41 (November 1999), pp. 25, 31, 32–3.

8 See Mrs Long, *Fort Mary, passim* and Mrs S. Heckford, *A Lady Trader in the Transvaal* (London, 1882), pp. 348–412.

9 For the defence of Standerton until the end of January, see WC III/2/13: Maj W.E. Montague to Wood, 27 March 1881: Report on the siege of Standerton; WO 32/7833, no. 079/4715: Maj W.E. Montague to Wood, 29 March 1881: Report and enclosures of the siege of Standerton; Bellairs, ed., *Transvaal War*, pp. 327–44; Carter, *Boer War*, pp. 341–52; Norris-Newman, *With the Boers*, pp. 244–7.

10 For Froom's dash to Standerton, see Bellairs, ed., *Transvaal War*, pp. 91–6.

11 BV 16, p. 11: Joubert to Kruger, 25 December 1880.

12 BV 13, p. 423: Joubert to Kruger, 21 February 1881.

13 For the defence of Wakkerstroom until the end of January, see WO 32/7833, no. 079/4814: Capt J.M. Saunders to Wood, [?] April 1881: Report of Officer Commanding Troops at Wakkerstroom from 14 December 1880 to 24 March 1881; Bellairs, ed., *Transvaal War*, pp. 352–63; Carter, *Boer War*, pp. 445–8; Crouch, 'Defence of Wakkerstroom', in Crouch and Knight, eds, *Forged in Strong Fires*, pp. 20–1.

14 See WO 32/7829 [1], Map MFQ 297: Sketch of Wakkerstroom.

15 BV 11, p. 55: Joubert to Kruger, 10 January 1881.

16 BV 13, p. 423: Joubert to Kruger, 21 February 1881.

17 Bennett, *Rain of Lead*, pp. 119–20.

18 For the siege of Potchefstroom from late December 1880 until mid-January 1881, see WO 32/7831, no. 079/4720: Lt-Col W.R.C. Winsloe's report to the AAG, Pretoria, on the defence of Potchefstroom, 23 March 1881; WC III/3/8: copy of same to Wood; WC III/3/8: Maj C. Thornhill, RA to DAAG, Pretoria, [?] April 1881; Bellairs, ed., *Transvaal War*, pp. 253–8; Carter, *Boer War*, pp. 392–414; Norris-Newman, *With the Boers*, pp. 238–43; Orford, 'Five Flags at Potchefstroom', in Crouch and Knight, eds, *Forged in Strong Fires*, pp. 13–15. For the most recent and most comprehensive description, see Bennett, *Rain of Lead*, chaps 7–12.

19 J. Orford, 'The Siege of Potchefstroom, 16 December 1880–21 March 1881', *Military History Journal*, 5, 2 (December 1980), p. 92.

20 Bellairs, ed., *Transvaal War*, p. 260.

21 Bennett, *Rain of Lead*, pp. 122–3, 157–8, 164–6. Hans van der Linden and Dr Christian Woite were vindictively executed for earlier 'spying' for the British at Paardekraal.

22 *Natal Advertiser*, 12 February 1881: letter from 'Englishman of Zeerust'.

23 Landdrost Rudolph's report, 8 April 1881, quoted in Carter, *Boer War*, pp. 448–50; Norris-Newman, *With the Boers*, p. 252; J. Crouch, 'Middelburg' in Crouch and Knight, eds, *Forged in Strong Fires*, pp. 24–5.

24 *BPP* (C. 2740), enc. in no. 75: Colley to Childers, telegram, 31 December 1880; *BPP* (C. 2950), enc. 2 in no. 64: G.M. Rudolph to Chief of Staff, Newcastle, 26 April 1881; Laband and Thompson, *Anglo-Zulu War*, pp. 134–5, 137.

25 See WO 32/7820, no. 079/4665: 2/Lt W. Long's report on the defence of Fort Mary, Lydenburg, n.d. [recd 10 April 1881]; Mrs Long, *Fort Mary*, chaps III–VIII; Bellairs, ed., *Transvaal War*, pp. 303–16; Carter, *Boer War*, pp. 433–4; Norris-Newman, *With the Boers*, pp. 248–9.

26 BV 17, p. 21: J.P. Steyn to J.G. Marais, 15 January 1881.

27 BV 13, p. 423: Joubert to Kruger, 21 February 1881.

28 For the siege of Rustenburg up to the end of January, see WO 32/7833, no. 079/4722: Capt D. Auchinleck to DAAG, Pretoria, 7 April 1881: Defence of Rustenburg and enclosures; Bellairs, ed., *Transvaal War*, pp. 277–80; Wulfsohn, *Rustenburg at War*, pp. 9–10. For map of Rustenburg under siege, see WO 32/7816, enc. in 079/4457: Rustenburg.

29 Maj C.G. Dennison, *A Fight to the Finish* (London, 1904), pp. 9–10.

30 See WO 32/7833, no. 079/4724: Capt E.S. Brook to DAAG, Pretoria, 7 April 1881: Diary of siege of Marabastad; Bellairs, ed., *Transvaal War*, pp. 289–3; Carter, *Boer War*, pp. 438–9; Norris-Newman, *With the Boers*, p. 251.

31 BV 13, p. 423: Joubert to Kruger, 21 February 1881.

32 BV 11, p. 151: B.J. Vorster to Kruger, 22 January 1881.

33 For accounts of the siege of Pretoria, see the detailed and copious reports in WO 32/7831, no. 079/4569 and WO 32/7832, no. 079/5220 upon which Bellair's book is based; Bellairs, ed., *Transvaal War*, pp. 97–171; Carter, *Boer War*, pp. 365–78; Norris-Newman, *With the Boers*, pp. 231–5; Capt A.E. van Jaarsveldt, 'Pretoria Gedurende die Eerste Vryheidsoorlog', *Militaria*, 1, 11 (1981), pp. 48–56; Davey, 'Siege of Pretoria', pp. 277–300, 305–7.

34 *BPP* (C. 2783), no. 37: Colley to Kimberley, 19 December 1880.

35 WO 32/7812, enc. 2 in no. 079/3974: Proclamation by Lanyon, 21 December 1880.

36 Davey, 'Siege of Pretoria', pp. 277–8.

37 For a tiny message in minute handwriting smuggled out of Pretoria in March 1881, see WC III/2/12.

38 See R. Tomlinson, 'Fort Tullichewan, Pretoria: An Exercise in Site Excavation and Historical Research', *Military History Journal*, 6, 5 (June 1985), pp. 156–63.

39 See WO 32/7831 [1], Map MFQ 311: Rough plan of Pretoria and the Boer camps. Also see WO 32/7814, enc. 1 in no. 079/4352: Bellairs to DAG, Pietermaritzburg, 6 February 1881.

40 BV 13, p. 423: Joubert to Kruger, 21 February 1881.

41 Grobler, 'Beleëring van die Britse Garnisoene', in Van Jaarsveld, Van Rensburg and Stals, eds, *Eerste Vryheidsoorlog*, p. 134; Davey, 'Siege of Pretoria', pp. 305–6.

42 WO 32/7812, enc. 3 in no. 079/3974: Lt J. de C. O'Grady to the Garrison Adjutant, Pretoria, 28 December 1880.

43 WO 32/7812, enc. 3 in no. 079/3974: Lt-Col F. Gildea to DAAG, Pretoria, 29 December 1880.

44 WO 32/7812, enc. 3 in no. 079/3974: Gildea to DAAG, Pretoria, 7 January 1881.

45 WO 32/7812, enc. 2 in no. 079/3974: District Orders by Colonel Bellairs, 9 January 1881. Davey, 'Siege of Pretoria', p. 289.

46 WO 32/7812, enc. 3 in no. 079/3974: Gildea to DAAG, Pretoria, 7 January 1881.

47 WO 32/7812, enc. 3 in no. 079/3974: Gildea to DAAG, Pretoria, 17 January 1881.

48 BV 17, pp. 27–9: Pretorius to Malan, 20 January 1881.

49 BV 19, pp. 273–4: Kruger to Cronjé, 31 January 1881.

50 WO 32/7812, enc. 3 in no. 079/3974: Bellairs to Lanyon, 17 January 1881; WO 32/7816, enc. in no. 079/4391: Bellairs to DAG, Pietermaritzburg, 4 March 1881.

chapter 6

The Natal Field Force

Sir Garnet Wolseley's political machinations had ensured that Major-General Sir George Pomeroy-Colley succeed him in July 1880 in the dual offices of Governor of Natal and High Commissioner for South-East Africa.[1] Military and civil powers were thus effectively combined in his person,[2] which meant that the disputes between competing civil and military authorities which had marred the conduct of operations in Zululand in 1879 were avoided in 1880–1881.[3] As High Commissioner, Colley was the imperial agent in southern Africa outside of Cape Colony, which had its own Governor and High Commissioner. Colley was directly responsible to the Secretaries of State both for the Colonies and for War, and superior to Sir Owen Lanyon, the Administrator of the Transvaal (who nevertheless also reported to the Colonial Secretary). As High Commissioner, Colley was also designated Commander-in-Chief, which meant that the framing and implementation of defence policy in South-East Africa were his preserves alone, and overrode the inferior authority of other administrators. However, whether these powers meant that in practice he exercised actual control over all military planning and operations, or whether these fell within the sphere of the General Officer Commanding Her Majesty's Forces in South Africa, with his Headquarters in Cape Town, was something of a problem. The GOC was himself responsible to the Secretary of State for War, who framed imperial military policy and had supreme control of the army. To complicate matters further, the GOC was also responsible to the Field

Marshal Commanding-in-Chief at the Horse Guards, the Duke of Cambridge.[4]

This complex tangle around the demarcation of military authority had been decided earlier in the nineteenth century (though only after considerable indecision by the imperial government) in favour of the High Commissioner, in whom supreme military control was thereafter vested.[5] Thus the will of High Commissioners prevailed over that of GOCs who, in the nineteenth-century South African context, were seldom officers of high calibre or ambition. The relative smallness of the imperial garrison, and the subordination of military to civil authority, meant that South Africa was not a significant or highly prized military command. Not surprisingly, second-rate GOCs often proved relatively supine and unequal to conducting operations during a real crisis. When Lieutenant-General the Hon. Leicester Smyth (whom General Buller described as 'a feeble creature' who did not know 'his own mind for five minutes together'[6]) was appointed to the Cape in 1880, it was made clear that Colley would act independently of him.

Colley first learned on 19 December 1880 by telegraph from Standerton of the Boer uprising, and immediately began to make urgent preparations to despatch all available troops to the Transvaal.[7] Although he had distinguished himself as an able administrator and possessed a considerable theoretical grasp of military strategy, his ability to exercise an independent command over troops in the field had yet to be put to the test. Yet such was his reputation that none doubted his success.[8] His forward base was to be the village of Newcastle in the far northern apex of Natal, sited on the main road north to the Transvaal where it functioned as an entrepot and forwarding agency for the Overberg trade. Like so many up-country towns it was not attractive, its main feature being a gridiron pattern of wide open streets with scattered houses and stores built of corrugated iron with a few better-built public buildings. Newcastle was the magisterial seat of the remote Newcastle Division whose small settler population of about 1,500 mirrored similar communities in the Transvaal. The majority were Afrikaans farmers, while the English colonists (who numbered less than 300) were concentrated mainly in Newcastle or at stores and accommodation houses along the rudimentary roads.[9]

At the outbreak of hostilities there was only one company of the 58th (Rutlandshire) Regiment stationed at Newcastle, though two more companies and the HQ were at the village of Estcourt, halfway on the road back to Pietermaritzburg. At Fort Napier in the Natal colonial capital were a division of N/5 Brigade, RA with two 9-pounder guns, another two companies of the 58th Regiment and the HQ and two-and-a-half companies of the 3/60th Regiment (King's Royal Rifle Corps). The depot of the 1st (King's) Dragoon Guards, consisting of some 35 unmounted men, and No. 7 Company of the Army Service Corps (without transport), both with details of invalids and time-expired men, were waiting at Fort Napier for the arrival of HMS *Humber* so they could proceed home to England. A further half company of the 3/60th Rifles was stationed in Durban, and two more companies of the same battalion were on the road to Pietermaritzburg from Harding in far southern Natal where they had been watching the unsettled Pondoland frontier. Yet two more companies were stationed even further away in Fort Harrison (now Port St John's) at the mouth of the Mzimvubu River where they were intended to overawe the Pondo. Fort Harrison fell under the Cape command, and despite requests to the Governor of the Cape, Colley never succeeded in getting his hands on that last detachment of the 3/60th Rifles. The Cape government had insisted as early as late November 1880 that it had no available force to send to relieve them should they be withdrawn.[10] The Governor (the newly arrived Sir Hercules Robinson) finally confirmed in mid-February 1881 that the withdrawal of the Fort Harrison garrison would be 'highly inexpedient', and that the suggested alternative of stationing a gunboat as a guard ship at the mouth of the river would not answer.[11]

Denied these two companies, Colley did what he could with inadequate materials. The mounted portion of his relief column was cobbled together from 25 men drawn from the 1st Dragoon Guards and Army Service Corps, with another 60 men from the 58th Regiment and 3/60th Rifles. This nascent mounted infantry still had to be mounted (there was difficulty in procuring horses because of the drain of the Gun War and additional horses had to be purchased from the Cape) and properly equipped. Colley was understandably concerned that his force would be much too weak in mounted men. This deficiency was only somewhat made up for with 140 men of the Natal Mounted Police (NMP) under their commandant, Major J.G. Dartnell.[12] Yet Colley firmly turned down all offers to raise mounted volunteer forces in the Cape and Natal because he believed that political expediency should take precedence over military need. As he explained to Kimberley on 26 December:

My greatest anxiety at present is lest this rising should turn into a war between the two white races in South Africa, an internecine war the results of which I hardly dare to contemplate. There is undoubtedly strong sympathy with the Boers throughout the Dutch population of Natal and the Cape Colony; and in the Free State it is rumoured that it has taken the form of active assistance.

Colley hoped that the 'upright, able and experienced' President Brand of the neutral Orange Free State would exert all his influence to prevent such intervention, but could not be sure he would succeed. It was for these reasons that he was 'anxious to restrict the contest within the very narrowest possible limits'.[13] Consequently, as he informed Childers, he had no alternative but to restore order with available forces aided by reinforcements when they arrived.[14]

Colley had therefore to nurse his precious mounted men carefully until British cavalry regiments could be sent out. So he issued them special instructions, reminding them that their principal functions were scouting and guarding the column against surprise when it advanced, and that in action they were to act as cavalry, supporting and covering the flank of an infantry attack, and charging and pursuing only when the opportunity arose. Revealing that he had indeed studied Boer military practices, he advised his mounted troops to avoid becoming involved in a prolonged skirmish with the Boers (whom he acknowledged were more accurate shots and better trained at mounting and dismounting quickly), and proposed that they should rather charge at the Boer horses which were left in the rear when the Boers dismounted to take up position. Boers, Colley reasoned, were not used to hand-to-hand fighting and feared being left dismounted, so such a demonstration would force them to abandon their position. Accordingly, he armed his mounted men with swords, as well as carbines.[15] Even so, it was never supposed that engagements with the Boers would be anything but rare. In practice, the main function of Colley's mounted men became that of patrolling along the borders of Natal, which meant watching the drifts over the Buffalo River to the east, the passes over the Drakensberg to the west, and the main road from the Transvaal over Laing's Nek to the north, as well as acting as mounted escort to important officers. This left few mounted men to guard the lines of communication, and supplies usually had to be brought up from Pietermaritzburg without a mounted escort.[16]

Nor could Colley be confident that the artillery component of the column was sufficiently strong. All he could do for the moment to remedy this was to attach two 7-pounder mountain guns from the garrison at Fort

Napier, manned by men of the 3/60th Rifles under an NCO of the N/5 Brigade RA, to the division of two 9-pounders already at his disposal. Meanwhile, he also requested any artillery that could be spared from the Cape Command. Commodore F.W. Richards, commanding HM's Vessels, Cape of Good Hope and West Coast of Africa, understood Colley's need and took it on himself to convince the cautious and hidebound General Smyth to release a Naval detachment from the garrison battery in Cape Town. On 30 December Richards was able to offer Colley a Naval Brigade from HMS *Boadicea* of 120 men with two Gatlings, three rocket-tubes and two 9-pounder guns. Royal Navy crews were routinely trained in the use of small arms and light artillery to serve as landing parties in coastal areas when regular troops were not available. The Naval Brigade arrived in Durban on 5 January 1881 to Colley's real gratification, and marched the following day for Pietermaritzburg under Commander Francis Romilly.[17]

Meanwhile, Colley ordered the companies of the 58th Regiment at Estcourt forward to Newcastle on 19 December. Two days later the guns from Fort Napier and two companies each from the 58th Regiment and 3/60th Rifles set off in the same direction, as did the NMP. Colley's headquarters remained for the time being in Pietermaritzburg, but on 26 December Colonel Bonar Deane, the Deputy Adjutant-General, who had seen considerable service in India, but who had never exercised a field command, went forward to Newcastle on 30 December to take command of what Colley designated the Natal Field Force (NFF).[18] In Durban some much-needed drafts for the under-strength companies in Natal arrived on 26 December.[19]

Colley established his general depot at Fort Napier with remount depots there and at Newcastle. Bringing up supplies was no easy matter, however. Colley tried to avoid the great expenses and all 'the heavy losses, the numerous claims, and the constant labour and friction which a heavy transport train gives rise to' by contracting with private individuals for the carriage of all stores as far as Newcastle. Much would depend, though, on the efficiency and honesty of the contractors. Colley also had to arrange with Commodore Richards the tricky business of landing troops and supplies at Durban, for the sandbar across the harbour in the bay meant all had to be brought ashore in lighters. Medical preparations also had to be made, and Colley established a base hospital of 100 beds in huts at Newcastle, three field hospitals of 25 beds each to accompany the troops as they advanced, with more beds and medical equipment to follow later.[20]

Despite all his energetic efforts, the forces at Colley's disposal (as he confided to his sister on New Year's Day, 1881) were still hardly 'sufficient' for a major offensive, and he and his staff were 'sad and anxious'.[21] Indeed, as soon as he had learned of the Bronkhorstspruit disaster he started pestering the War Office for the quick despatch of a cavalry regiment.[22] The Duke of Cambridge and Childers urgently held a conference at the War Office with Kimberley on 25 December, and their military advisers convinced the Colonial Secretary of the necessity of sending Colley reinforcements immediately. On 28 December the War Office advised Colley that it was despatching a regiment of cavalry and a complete, mounted field battery from England, and that it was prepared to send an additional cavalry regiment, infantry regiment and field battery, all of which were about to embark from Bombay for England on the expiry of their Indian service.[23] The difficulty was that these cavalry and artillery units would be unmounted, and Colley feared that the already considerable drain on horses in Natal would make it impossible to mount them unless the Cape was of some assistance in supplying horses.[24]

Even if all the reinforcements came and were mounted when appropriate, the question then arose how best to deploy them. Colley suggested that the troops sailing from India should reinforce him in Natal, and that the troops coming from England should land in Cape Town and form part of a column to be sent up to the Transvaal by way of Beaufort West and Kimberley.[25] This westerly column would take the Boers in the rear around Potchefstroom and distract them from their operations in Natal. The advantages from a military point of view, as Colley enumerated to General Smyth in the Cape, were an easy road without any mountain passes, a reduction of the pressure on transport and supplies in Natal, the effect this would have on suppressing pro-Boer agitation in the Orange Free State which was unsteadily maintaining its neutrality in the war, and the likelihood of distracting Transvaal strategy.[26] The political wisdom of such a movement was another matter. The Administrator of the Cape, Sir G.C. Strahan (who was holding the fort until Sir Hercules Robinson arrived in January 1881 to take up his posts as High Commissioner and Governor) consulted the Cape premier, John Sprigg, and came to the conclusion that such a manoeuvre would greatly add to the pro-Boer agitation already evident in the Cape. So while the Cape administration continued to profess itself eager to help its sister colony of Natal, it saw only too clearly the adverse consequences of direct military involvement on its own internal stability.[27] Cape military

THE SCHOOL OF MUSKETRY.

Plate 1: Boer (to F.-M. H.R.H. the Commander-in-Chief). 'I say Dook! You don't happen to want a practical "Musketry Instructor", do you?'. *Punch*, 7 May 1881. © Punch, Ltd.

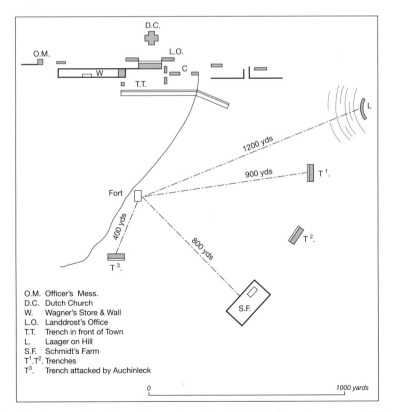

Plate 2: Diagram of the Siege of Rustenburg. From British Parliamentary papers, 1881, *LXVII* (C. 295.), South Africa, Correspondence, 1880–1881. The text of this Bill and the typographical arrangement of the text are Parliamentary Copyright.

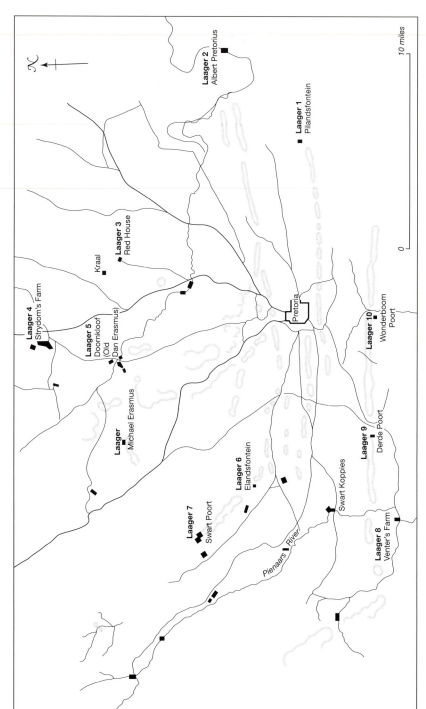

Plate 3: Plan of Pretoria and the Boer Camps. Courtesy of the National Archives Image Library.

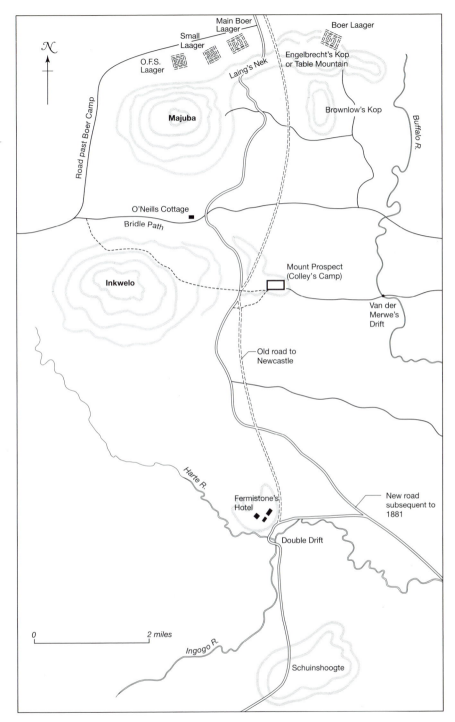

Plate 4: The theatre of operations in Northern Natal, 1880–1881. Courtesy of South African National Museum of Military History, after Geo. R. Duxbury, *David and Goliath: the First War of Independence, 1880–1881* (1981).

Plate 5: A panoramic view of the theatre of operations from the heliograph station on the hill above Fort Amiel, Newcastle. Note Majuba with the nearer bulk of Inkwelo Mountain to its left. To its right the road to the Transvaal can be seen passing over Laing's Nek. *The Illustrated London News*, 9 April 1881.

Plate 6: The British assault on Laing's Nek, 28 January 1881. The 58th Regiment on the right is storming the heights with the 3/60th Rifles drawn up below in support. The Naval Brigade, stationed on the left near Laing's farmhouse in advance of the Royal Artillery batteries in the foreground, is firing a rocket. Note the ambulance wagons in the left-hand corner. *The Graphic*, 19 March 1881.

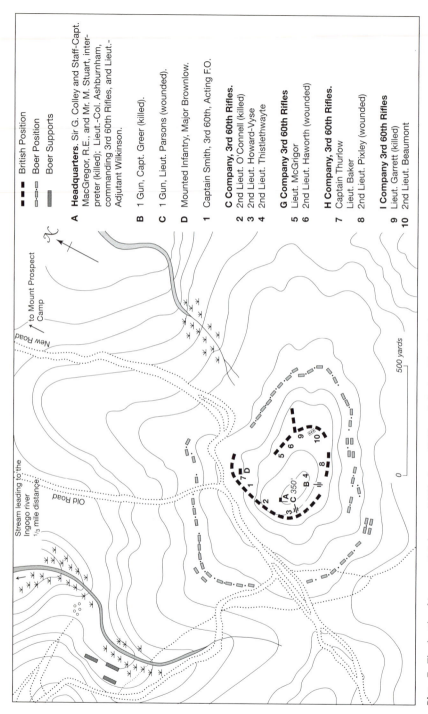

Legend:
- ▬▬▬ British Position
- ▭▭▭ Boer Position
- ▬▬▬ Boer Supports

A Headquarters. Sir G. Colley and Staff-Capt. MacGregor, R.E. and Mr. M. Stuart, interpreter (killed); Lieut.-Col. Ashburnham, commanding 3rd 60th Rifles, and Lieut.-Adjutant Wilkinson.

B 1 Gun, Capt. Greer (killed).

C 1 Gun, Lieut. Parsons (wounded).

D Mounted Infantry, Major Brownlow.

1 Captain Smith, 3rd 60th, Acting F.O.

C Company, 3rd 60th Rifles.
2 2nd Lieut. O'Connell (killed)
3 2nd Lieut. Howard-Vyse
4 2nd Lieut. Thistlethwayte

G Company 3rd 60th Rifles
5 Lieut. McGrigor
6 2nd Lieut. Haworth (wounded)

H Company, 3rd 60th Rifles.
7 Captain Thurlow
8 Lieut. Baker
8 2nd Lieut. Pixley (wounded)

I Company 3rd 60th Rifles
9 Lieut. Garrett (killed)
10 2nd Lieut. Beaumont

Plate 7: The battle of Ingogo, 8 February 1881. From William F. Butler, *The Life of Sir George Pomeroy Colley*, John Murray, Ltd. 1899.

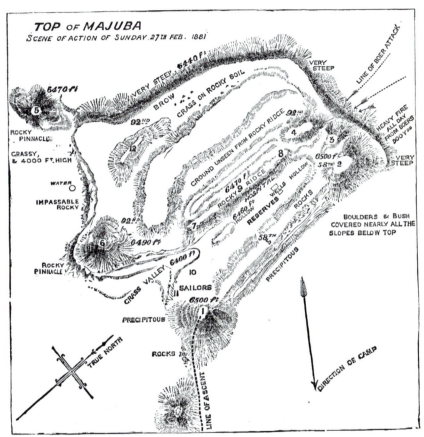

Plate 8: The British positions on the summit of Majuba, 27 February 1881. *The Illustrated London News*, 14 May 1881.

Plate 9: The British in flight from Majuba, sketched from the hill above Mount Prospect Camp. *The Illustrated London News*, 23 April 1881.

cooperation was not immediately put to the test, however. When Colley realised that the reinforcements from England, who were fully equipped and ready to take the field immediately, would arrive in Natal almost as soon as the less prepared troops from India, he changed his tune and informed Kimberley that he believed the reason for the second column had disappeared.[28] Yet it was doubtless just as well that Colley was not compelled to pin his hopes on Cape military cooperation. Even when it came to the uncomplicated matter of despatching military stores from Cape Town to Natal to assist Colley, selfishness and caution overcame altruism. Smyth insisted it could not be done without creating 'dangerous deficiencies' for the Cape garrison should it ever have to take the field.[29]

It was Colley's plan that the NFF concentrating at Newcastle would move up to the Transvaal early in the new year and reach Standerton by 20 January. Meanwhile, he firmly ordered Lanyon on 19 December not to risk any collisions with Boer forces before his arrival with the NFF.[30] The shocking news of the disaster at Bronkhorstspruit which was received on Christmas Day, and word of the disturbing state of the beleaguered garrisons which was also filtering in, upset these intentions and timetables. Colley became alarmed at the effect the Boer success would have on waverers, and realised that any chances for a peaceful settlement had evaporated. He was particularly concerned that a protracted guerrilla war might ensue, and requested a cavalry regiment against the contingency.[31] On 28 December he issued a general order to the troops from Pietermaritzburg informing them of the disaster and expressing his faith in their 'courage, spirit and discipline' to vindicate British honour. Worried that anger at Boer 'treachery' might tempt them to abandon normal military constraints, he exhorted them not to allow anger with the 'misled and deluded Boers' to 'degenerate into a feeling of revenge'. And with a complacency that was to prove fatal, he declared: 'It is scarcely necessary to remind soldiers of the incalculable advantages which discipline, organization, and trained skill give them over more numerous but undisciplined forces.'[32]

Because Colley was unavoidably taking considerable time in building the NFF up sufficiently to risk marching on the Transvaal, Commandant-General Joubert was being given welcome breathing-space to mobilise a commando to block his path. He had earlier anticipated a British thrust from Natal, and had arranged to monitor the border until his commando was ready to advance.[33] Consequently, by the last week of December mounted Boers began patrolling their border with Natal.[34] On 27 December Joubert led his commando of 800 riders out of Heidelberg, the provisional Boer capital, and advanced without undue haste towards the vicinity of the strategic pass at Laing's Nek from where he intended to direct operations. Operations against the British garrisons within the Transvaal were left to acting Commandant-General H.P. Malan to direct from Heidelberg. It was Joubert's belief that since the shortest wagon road from Natal into the Transvaal passed over Laing's Nek that Colley must take that route. On 29 December the commando was at Standerton, where it was involved in an indecisive skirmish with the British garrison, and by 2 January it off-saddled at the farm of two traders, the Meek brothers, above Laing's Nek, just within the Transvaal border. Joubert did not anticipate that Colley would advance until his concentration at Newcastle was complete. Nevertheless, as a precaution against surprise, every night he posted a mounted guard of 25 men at Laing's Nek, just inside Natal territory, to keep an eye on British movements.[35] During the next few weeks Joubert's commando was reinforced by a trickle of men from various parts of the Transvaal, but in repeated letters to Kruger, Joubert complained that his force was too small for the task assigned it. Indeed, far from all eligible burghers had responded to his call to mobilise, and there were many cases of desertion too. By the end of January there were probably no more than 1,000 burghers in the field in the Standerton–Wakkerstroom–Laing's Nek area of operations, and numbers of the reinforcements intended for Laing's Nek had stopped off to assist burghers in their investment of the British posts at these two villages.[36] Besides inadequate forces, Joubert's commando was further weakened by insufficient ammunition for any prolonged engagement. Each man carried about 75 rounds of his own, but there was no reserve ammunition. The men did not have bullet-moulds to manufacture their own, the heavy rains after 24 January damaged much of what they had, Kruger was slow in sending more ammunition down from Heidelberg, and none was supplied from the neutral Orange Free State.[37]

Intelligence reached the British camp in Newcastle on 31 December that the Boers were patrolling their border, so the next day Colley sanctioned the raising of scouts among the settlers and Africans of the Newcastle Division and put them under the command of K.C. Birkett who had been an officer in the 2/1st Natal Native Contingent during the Anglo-Zulu War.[38] Birkett rode north to Coldstream, just within the Natal border, recruiting eight white and seven black scouts as he went who were designated the 'patrol section of the Transport Department'. Over the next few days he ascertained that the Boers had established a laager at the Meeks' white-washed store three miles beyond Coldstream where the road levels out beyond the steep climb to Laing's Nek,[39] and reported increasing activity from Boer patrols. On 4 January the British scouts saw that 150 Boers had taken up position at Laing's Nek, and were sending out scouts south along the road, over the heights to its west and down the valley of the Buffalo River as far as the Ingogo River, only 16 miles north of Newcastle. In response, an officer and 12 men of the NMP who, as colonial forces, technically fell under the command of the civilian Resident Magistrate of Newcastle, were requested by Deane to patrol in the direction of the Ingogo, but to avoid engaging the Boers if possible.

Meanwhile, the troops which had set off from Pietermaritzburg on 21 December reached Newcastle on 2 January, so that 622 officers and men were now assembled there. British intelligence led them (with the grossest exaggeration) to believe that the Boers had between 4,000 to 5,000 men in the field between the Meeks' store and Laing's Nek, when in fact the numbers of the two adversaries were fairly even. The assembled NFF thus believed itself outnumbered, but its officers had enough confidence in its professionalism to consider it not dangerously so, and plans were put in train to advance on 10 January. The column's forward base where its supplies would be assembled was to be Fort Amiel at Newcastle, which a detachment of the 80th Regiment (Staffordshire Volunteers) had constructed in 1878 on the high ground north of the Ncandu River overlooking the town. Its stone wall and ditch already enclosed officers' quarters, barracks, a hospital and stores,[40] but on 4 January it began to be enlarged and strengthened. A month's supply of provisions was loaded on wagons which formed parts of the sides of the fort, and batteries were constructed for the guns. A laager of wagons was formed in the hollow below the fort for the oxen, mules and horses. Major William Ogilvy of the 3/60th Rifles was put in command of the garrison. A telegraph line was laid from the fort to the main Pietermaritzburg line, and on 6 January the tented military camp next to the river was drawn in towards the protection of the fort.

The atmosphere in the British camp was nevertheless unsettled, for the full, gory details of the Bronkhorstspruit disaster came in from Pietermaritzburg on 6 January; while the NMP reported they believed that the Boers concentrating on Laing's Nek were intending to descend on Newcastle.[41] Vedettes were consequently pushed out, the line of piquets strengthened at night and the men in camp cautioned to turn out at any time fully equipped. Two further companies of the 3/60th Rifles on the road to Newcastle (a total of 126 all ranks), who had merrily been singing 'My Grandfather's Clock' to the accompaniment of two whistles and a drum played on a canteen with two sticks,[42] were ordered to push on over the last 20 miles without halting for the night. Scouts and patrols continued to encounter small Boer patrols within only a few miles of Newcastle. During the evening of 8 January Colonel Deane and his staff attended a meeting of the townsfolk and informed them, on Colley's instructions, that, unless they were prepared immediately to undertake the defence of the town with the assistance of the garrison, their arms and ammunition would be removed from the Court House to Fort Amiel to prevent their falling into Boer hands. The meeting selected a committee and dithered about taking immediate defensive measures, so Deane acted on his instructions and removed their weapons.

The Resident Magistrate of Newcastle, under Colley's instructions, had written to Joubert on 6 January noting the presence of armed Boers on Natal territory, and informing him that Natal wished to hold a neutral position, but that future Boer actions would determine this. Joubert replied on 8 January that it was not his intention to do anything inimical to Natal, and that his patrols were being sent out to prevent the passage of hostile troops. However, that same morning the Resident Magistrate received a disapproving telegram from Lord Kimberley instructing him to inform Joubert to withdraw his patrols from neutral Natal at once. Meanwhile, the British continued to send out patrols of their own along the Buffalo River valley (which bordered the Utrecht District in the Transvaal) as far north as the Ingogo River close to Laing's Nek. They reported that while Boer vedettes and scouts were holding or watching the drifts over the Buffalo and the passes over the Drakensberg,[43] the country on the Natal side of the border seemed relatively free of them. As the Boer threat to Newcastle appeared to have diminished for the time being, and as the weather continued very hot, bathing parades were ordered for the troops. This could not have given them much pleasure for, as a Newcastle storekeeper saw with regret, the soldiers in camp had no better place to wash themselves and their clothes than in filthy pools of water on the flats, and afterwards to lay out their washing on the wet grass to dry.[44]

On 11 January Colley and his personal staff, escorted by Commandant Mansel and the NMP, rode into Fort Amiel, where he established his new headquarters. Finding the inhabitants of Newcastle now willing to defend their town, he had their arms and ammunition returned to them. On 14 January a detachment of 58 mounted troops under Major William Brownlow marched into camp.[45] The Remount Committee and the Transport Department were kept busy finding the horses, mules, oxen and wagons required for the impending advance, and in coralling and parking them. Heavy rain on 16 and 17 January caused the rivers to rise several feet and delayed the arrival of the latest detachment from Pietermaritzburg until 18 January. On that day Lieutenant-Colonel Cromer Ashburnham of the 3/60th Rifles marched in with another 364 officers and men, including 50 very necessary mounted infantry. The NFF had now come close to doubling its strength since 21 December, and was altogether a more reputable force than it had been. But the Boers also seemed to be consolidating, and conflicting reports continued to come in of their movements and concentrations. What did seem certain is that by 18 January the Boers had again occupied Laing's Nek in some strength, thus barring the road to the Transvaal.

Colley still believed his augmented force to be outnumbered by the Boers on Laing's Nek, and it must be queried why he did not therefore wait for the large reinforcements promised from overseas to come up before he attempted to force the Boer position. Colley was certainly prey to uncertainties which he argued out and resolved to his own satisfaction in his letter of 17 January to Wolseley, his mentor and patron. Colley's first concern was to wonder if public opinion in Britain – so vital for military reputations and promotions – thought him too slow in moving forward, and his second was to question Wolseley whether he considered his decision to advance without major reinforcements too rash. Colley answered the second question himself, and in justifying his announced determination to march at once even though he anticipated a 'stiff fight' at Laing's Nek if he did, he explained that his mind was made up after Bronkhorstspruit. It was not simply a matter of vindicating British honour, but a question of relieving the invested garrisons. He believed most posts could hold out for several months, but saw Potchefstroom with its inadequate supplies as 'our weak point', making it the determining factor in his planning. Colley explained that he was persuaded that, unless it was relieved before the middle of February, Potchefstroom would fall to the Boers. He calculated that if he were repulsed in trying to break through he could always hold on at Mount Prospect – a wide ridge south of Laing's Nek which the Boers called Kokshoogte – until reinforced. However, if he penetrated the Boers' lines he could push on to Standerton and hold on there until reinforced or, strengthened by the Standerton garrison, advance towards Heidelberg and try to bring the Boers to a decisive battle. Not that any of these alternatives came without real risks, especially without sufficient mounted support, and Colley admitted to Wolseley the general anxiety of his force under a veneer of cheery confidence, and reported that his devoted staff 'shake their heads gloomily at my venturing on without any regular cavalry'.[46]

With a general advance increasingly imminent, on the moonlit night of 18 January Major J. Ruscombe Poole, RA,[47] Colley's DAAG, left camp with an escort of 50 NMP and reconnoitred some distance up Laing's Nek. He reported the road clear. More welcome reinforcements were coming up, and the Naval Brigade of 128 officers and men, which had landed in Durban on 5 January, marched into camp on the evening of 19 January with 21 more Mounted Infantry and other details, making a total of 329 all ranks. Heavy rain fell over the next few days during which period the men drew reserve rations and ammunition, and final arrangements for the line of march were worked out. On the hot, dry Sunday afternoon of 23 January Colley reviewed the NFF, which marched past him and then formed a square for him to address them in encouraging terms.

Colley had already written to Kimberley and Childers a few days before carefully justifying his intentions. He told them that as far as he could make out (though his information concerning Boer numbers was exaggerated), the Boer forces were considerably dispersed with some 2,000 facing him and twice that number blockading the British garrisons. He believed the Boers to be ill-supplied and tired of being in the field, with their commanders finding it difficult to keep them together, though he admitted that they were nevertheless reported to be fully confident that they could repel any British troops sent against them. He conceded, as he had to Wolseley, that in the circumstances it might have seemed sensible to await the promised reinforcements from England and India in order to take the offensive with an overwhelming force. But, he explained, these reinforcements were still weeks away and he feared the political consequences in South Africa of continued inaction. He also invoked the danger of the early capitulation of the Potchefstroom garrison if not speedily relieved. It was his decision, therefore, to move forward with the force he had and bring the Boer force holding the Transvaal passes to battle. But, he assured the two Secretaries of State, so as not to leave Natal entirely denuded of troops, he was delaying the advance until he heard confirmation of the imminent arrival of the 97th (Earl of Ulster's) Regiment at the Cape from Nova Scotia via Gibralter.[48]

On the same day he addressed the NFF in Newcastle, Colley wrote Commandant-General Joubert a letter quite stunning in its arrogance and condescension, and unintentionally provocative in its tone. Nothing could better express the gulf of incomprehension that divided the two sides, nor more effectively expose the ingrained arrogance of the imperial stance. Colley began by assuring Joubert that he was still 'anxious to avoid un-necessary bloodshed' (which was true enough) and called on him to dismiss his followers, following which Colley undertook to consider their grievances (a promise repeated by various British officials, administrators and officers since 1877, and destined to be scorned by any right-thinking Boer). Having offered these inadequate blandishments, Colley proceeded with threats. Extraordinarily, in describing Britain's unlimited imperial might – of which the NFF was but the vanguard – he coolly made the assumption that the Boers in general were as ignorant as untutored savages about the great world outside their borders, and compounded the insult by assuring Joubert that the Commandant-General was himself a rare exception. Colley wrote:

The men who follow you are, many of them, ignorant, and know and understand little of anything outside their own country. But you, who are well educated and have travelled, cannot but be aware how hopeless is the struggle you have embarked upon, and how little any accidental success gained can affect the ultimate result.[49]

In confirmation of how blind Colley was to the Boer outrage his letter must surely elicit, he went on to assure Kimberley on 10 February that he had always maintained 'relations of official courtesy' with the Boer leaders, and had avoided 'all language or acts which would tend to embitter the relations' between them and the British government![50] Joubert's response, which (on account of delays in the post over terrible roads) he was only able to pen after the battle of Laing's Nek, was predictably indignant. Joubert declared himself shocked that Colley had begun military operations before he had had a reasonable chance to discuss his letter and terms with his gov-ernment in Heidelberg, and bitterly declared: 'I am at a loss to understand the justice of this attack unless it might be called a principle of international or public law, that men in our position, are not entitled to even the slightest consideration.'[51]

Still secure in his imperial presumption, Colley led the NFF out of Newcastle at 05h00 on 24 January. After its steady trickle of reinforcements, the column (if only the British had realised it) was now more than a match numerically for the Boers holding Laing's Nek. It was made up of a total of 1,462 officers and men – of whom the Mounted Squadron and NMP constituted an inadequate 191 – 6 guns and 2 Gatlings. The infantry and Naval Brigade carried 70 rounds per man of Martini-Henry ammunition in their pouches, and the Mounted Squadron 60. The order of march had the transport in the centre with flanking infantry, and artillery and more infantry to front and rear. With Anstruther's fatal lapse regarding proper scouting doubtless in mind, the mounted men scouted in front and rear. The column did not get far that day, however. Many of the 23 wagon conductors and 161 drivers were new to their work and found it difficult to get their vehicles into the prescribed order of march; while the rain-sodden ground and steep hills out of Newcastle meant that the wagons had to be dragged one by one up the slope by double teams. (The road from Newcastle continued to present real difficulties, and in mid-March 200 infantry under the supervision of Royal Engineers were still repairing the road on Ingogo Hill where the mud was 'fully two feet deep'.[52]) It was 15h30 before the 82 ox-wagons, 23 mule wagons, 3 American wagons, 7 Scotch carts, 8 water carts, the field forge and 10 ambulances drawn by 1,338 oxen, 369 mules and 77 horses had made the ascent. Colley was left with no choice but to form laager for the night only five miles from Fort Amiel.[53]

The column faired better the next day, which was fine and hot, for the countryside was now flat and open, and the wagons could move four or five abreast, covering twice the distance of the previous day. However, on descending the slopes of Schuinshoogte towards the Ingogo River, the road narrowed so that the convoy had to proceed in single file and be pulled up the other side by double spans and drag ropes while troops and guns occupied the heights to cover the operation. They were watched by distant Boer patrols operating from the base Joubert had set up that day on Laing's Nek to monitor their advance. The NFF laagered for the night on the right bank of the Ingogo River. On the morning of 26 January the column again moved very slowly, for it had to cross two drifts and pass through what was almost a defile, with a company of infantry posted at either side, before the heights were reached and the oxen could outspan to rest and graze. The Mounted Squadron scouting ahead of the column spotted large parties of Boer horsemen in the distance. The march resumed later that day until the column reached a spur below Mount Prospect about 5 miles from Laing's Nek. The British noticed many Boers on the Nek for Joubert and his commanders were following the laborious British progress through their telescopes, and all were of the opinion that Colley would attack the following day[54] – which is indeed what he intended.

Colley ordered the wagons to form a wagon laager and three entrenchments were prepared at almost opposite angles of the laager to be occupied as posts by the garrison left in charge of the wagons and animals when the bulk of the column attempted to force Laing's Nek the following day. Colley had conducted his march in exemplary fashion, and he was again following the textbook in his creation of a secure entrenched camp. This, as all officers were instructed, was necessary when the intention was to keep a large force at a particular point, usually on or near some 'important line of communication', ready 'to strike a blow in any direction, or to give shelter to an army that has been worsted in the field, and to enable it to reorganise'.[55] In the early afternoon, soon after the laager was formed, a violent thunderstorm broke over the camp and heavy rain fell throughout the night.

The Boers were ready early on the morning of Thursday, 27 January, to face the British attack, but the continuing rain and thick, heavy mist caused Colley to postpone his intended advance. He continued to gather what intelligence he could, and a reconnaissance party found the road to the Nek in such poor condition from the rain and neglect that it would be impassable for the NFF's wagons once the advance was resumed following the taking of Laing's Nek. Another road, apparently a Boer wagon track, appeared more practicable even though it crossed a bad drift, and a working party was immediately set to improving it. During the course of that wet day, whenever the mist lifted, the British caught sight of the Boers on the Nek and surrounding heights where the Boers' officers were holding their men in position then and throughout the coming night in case the British should make a sudden advance.

The Boer and British forces had not been manoeuvring in a void, however. As South Africa and Europe became increasingly informed of the escalating conflict, efforts were being made to contain it. Problematically for the British, much of the sentiment expressed favoured the Boer cause. Throughout the Cape Colony and Orange Free State meetings were held and resolutions passed calling on the British not to enforce their will at the point of the bayonet lest they fatally alienate Afrikaner opinion. In the Netherlands, which felt a strong cultural and ethnic affinity with the Boer republics, a mass appeal for a peaceful settlement was signed by 7,000 people and presented to the British parliament. In Natal, which had strong trade and business links with the Transvaal, there were vigorous calls for neutrality in both official and commercial circles despite the fact that most settlers were English-speaking. In what amounted to a repudiation of the war, the Natal Legislative Council passed a motion washing its hands of any responsibility for the costs that the colony might incur in its prosecution. Even more pointedly, subscriptions were got up in the Cape and Orange Free State to start a Red Cross Society for helping the Boer wounded, and large quantities of provisions, arms and ammunition were increasingly sent to the Transvaal through the Orange Free State, despite its official neutrality. In this increasingly polarised atmosphere the one voice of statesmanship was that of President Johannes H. Brand of the Orange Free State, who nurtured a political vision that encompassed the benefits for South Africa as a whole of Boer–British cooperation. On 25 January he telegraphed Lord Kimberley suggesting mediation, and at the Cape the recently arrived Sir Hercules Robinson caught gratefully at this initiative and lent his encouragement. This promising flow of telegrams, aimed at preventing further bloodshed, was interrupted on 28 January with news that the British and Boers had fought a battle at Laing's Nek.[56]

Notes and references

1 Beckett, *Victorians at War*, p. 97.

2 See Benyon, *Proconsul and Paramountcy*, pp. 7–11, 69–70, 212–13, 358–61.

3 See Laband, 'Divided Command', pp. 343–55.

4 Laband, ed., *Chelmsford's Zululand Campaign*, p. xxvii.

5 V.T. Harlow, 'Cape Colony, 1806–1822' in E.A. Walker, ed., *The Cambridge History of the British Empire, Volume VIII: South Africa, Rhodesia and the High Commission Territories* (Cambridge, 1963), pp. 206–8.

6 WC III/2/5: Buller to Wood, 15 December 1880.

7 Unless otherwise specified, details concerning the operations of the Natal Field Force are taken from the Journal of the Natal Field Force kept by an experienced staff officer and veteran of the Anglo-Zulu War, Brevet Major Edward Essex, 75th Regiment, whom Colley first appointed Deputy Assistant Adjutant and Quartermaster-General, South Africa, on 9 December 1880, and then on 2 January 1881 Staff Officer to the Natal Field Force. Essex kept his official diary of operations from 19 December 1880 until Major Hart relieved him on 12 March 1881. The Journal is printed in Butterfield, ed., *War and Peace*, and the entries from 19 December up to the eve of the battle of Laing's Nek on 28 January 1881 are to be found on pp. 170–92.

8 'Colley' in de Kock, ed., *South African Biography*, vol. II, p. 138.

9 J. Laband and P. Thompson with S. Henderson, *The Buffalo Border 1879: The Anglo-Zulu War in Northern Natal* (Durban, 1983), pp. 4–5, 8–10.

10 *BPP* (C. 2783), enc. 3 in no. 14: Colley to Lanyon, 3 December 1880.

11 CTAR, GH 30/17: Sir Hercules Robinson to Lt-Gen the Hon Sir Leicester Smyth, 17 February 1881.

12 *BPP* (C. 2783), enc. 1 in no. 41: Colley to Childers, 19 December 1880; enc. 2 in no. 49: Colley to Childers, 26 December 1880; (C. 2866), enc. 1 in no. 20: Colley to Childers, 10 January 1881.

13 *BPP* (C. 2866), no. 3: Colley to Kimberley, 26 December 1880.

14 *BPP* (C. 2783), enc. 2 in no. 49: Colley to Childers, 26 December 1880. See also Butler, *Pomeroy-Colley*, pp. 277–8: Colley to his sister, 1 January 1881 in which he explains how anxious he was to suppress all suggestions of race or civil war in South Africa.

15 Holt, *Mounted Police*, pp. 97–8.

16 Holt, *Mounted Police*, pp. 96–8.

17 *BPP* (C. 2866), enc. 1 in no. 20: Colley to Childers, 10 January 1881, no. 37 and encs: Commodore F.W. Richards to the Secretary of the Admiralty, 10 January 1881.

18 WO 32/7803, enc. 3 in no. 079/3765: Col B.M. Deane to AAG, Pietermaritzburg, 3 January 1881.

19 *BPP* (C. 2740), enc. in no. 75: Colley to Childers, telegram, 31 December 1880.

20 *BPP* (C. 2866), enc. 3 in no. 29: Colley to Childers, 10 January 1881.

21 Colley to his sister, 1 January 1881, quoted in Butler, *Life of Pomeroy-Colley*, pp. 276–7.

22 WO 32/7798, no. 079/3516, Colley to Childers, telegram, 24 December 1880.

23 Passage for troops ships from India to Durban took about five weeks, and between three and four weeks from England to Cape Town, when further time was required to sail the 730 miles to Durban. Mobilisation for embarkation could add months to this timetable. See Beckett, *Victorians at War*, pp. 98–9.

24 WO 32/7798, no. 079/3516: Kimberley to Childers, telegram, 25 December 1880; Childers to Colley, telegram, 26 December; no. 079/3522: Childers to Colley, telegram, 28 December 1880; Colley to Childers, telegram, 28 December 1880; no. 079/3531: R.G.W. Herbert (Under-Secretary of Colonies) to R. Thompson (Under-Secretary of War), 28 December 1880.

25 WO 32/7811, no. 079/3821: Colley to Sir G. Strahan, telegram, 30 December 1880.

26 WO 32/7806, no. 079/3930, Appendix A: Colley to Smyth, 31 December 1880.

27 WO 32/7811, no. 079/3720: Strahan to Kimberley, 4 January 1881; *BPP* (C. 2754), enc. 2 in no. 45: Strahan to Kimberley, telegram, 3 January 1881. See also CTAR, GH 30/17: Robinson to Smyth, 14 February 1881.

28 WO 32/7811, no. 079/3821: Colley to Kimberley, 6 January 1881.

29 CTAR, GH 36/19, Military 8/81: Strahan to Smyth, 9 January 1881; Smyth to Robinson, 12 January 1881.

30 *BPP* (C. 2783), enc. 2 in no. 37: Colley to Lanyon, 19 December 1880.

31 *BPP* (C. 2866), no. 3: Colley to Knutsford, 26 December 1880.

32 Lt-Col A.H. Wavell, AAG, to the troops, 28 December 1880, quoted in Norris-Newman, *With the Boers*, pp. 129–30.

33 JC 25, no. 2389: P.J. Joubert to J.J.G. van der Schyff, 13 December 1880.

34 BV 16, pp. 26–7: Van der Schyff to Joubert, 31 December 1880.

35 BV 16, p. 30: Joubert to Kruger and M.W. Pretorius, 7 January 1881; JC 26, no. 2452: Jooernaal Geschreven door de Heer A. Faure vanaf de Zesde January 1881 oor die Oorlog tusschen de Boeren en Ingelsche.

36 BV 11, pp. 106–7: Joubert to Kruger, 17 January 1881; p. 157: Joubert to Kruger, 24 January 1881; pp. 177–8: Joubert to Kruger, 26 January 1881; JC 26, no. 2424: Kruger to Joubert, 4 February 1881.

37 BV 11, pp. 177–81: Joubert to Kruger, 26 January 1881; pp. 182–3: Joubert to Kruger, 26 January 1881.

38 Laband and Thompson, *Buffalo Border*, Appendix VII: Natal Native Contingent.

39 Norris-Newman, *With the Boers*, p. 187. The Boers later used the store as a hospital.

40 The fort, which had functioned as a rear depot and hospital during the Anglo-Zulu War, continued in use by the British during the South African War of 1899–1902. Since restored to the way it looked in *circa* 1902, it now houses a museum. See Laband and Thompson, *Buffalo Border*, pp. 88–9, and Laband and Thompson, *Anglo-Zulu War*, pp. 144–5.

41 *BPP* (C. 2740), no. 77: Colley to Childers, 5 January 1880.

42 Reminiscences of Lt Percival Marling, quoted in Emery, *Marching over Africa*, pp. 102–3.

43 WO 32/7806, no. 079/3903: Colley to Childers, 19 January 1880.

44 *Natal Advertiser*, 24 February 1881.

45 Major Brownlow had not embarked in November 1880 with the King's Dragoon Guards on HMS *Orontes* for India because he was in command of the regimental depot in Pietermaritzburg, and was still awaiting transport when the war broke out. See E. Cox, 'The First King's Dragoon Guards in South Africa, 1879–1881', *Military History Journal*, 6, 5 (June 1985), p. 165.

46 Colley to Wolseley, 17 January 1881, quoted in Butler, *Pomeroy-Colley*, pp. 282–4.

47 Ruscombe Poole had been the exiled Zulu King Cetshwayo's custodian in Cape Town during the earlier stages of his captivity.

48 *BPP* (C. 2866), no. 49: Colley to Kimberley, 19 January 1881; no. 58: Colley to Childers, 19 January 1881.

49 JC 26, no. 2462: Colley to Joubert, 23 January 1881.

50 *BPP* (C. 2866), no. 74: Colley to Kimberley, 10 February 1881.

51 JC 26, no. 2463: Joubert to Colley, February 1881.

52 WO 32/7833, no. 079/4743: Report by Lt T. Brotherton, RE, 19 April 1881.

53 For an extremely detailed report, intended for the eyes of the Duke of Cambridge and Childers, on the deplorable state of communications in the Natal theatre, see WO 32/7830, no. 079/4999: Brig-Gen J.W. Baker, Inspector General of the Lines of Communication and Base to the QMG, Horse Guards, 31 May 1881.

54 BV 11, pp. 182–3: Joubert to Kruger, 26 January 1881; JC 26, no. 2452: Jooernaal Geschreven door de Heer A. Faure.

55 Great Britain, War Office, *Text Book of Fortification and Military Engineering, For Use at The Royal Military Academy, Woolwich, Part I* (London, 2nd edn, 1884), p. 122. This 1884 edition is essentially the same as that of the first in 1878 which would have guided officers in 1880–1881.

56 Norris-Newman, *With the Boers*, pp. 131–3, 142–5. Brand's and Robinson's telegrams are quoted on pp. 144–5.

chapter 7

Laing's Nek

The pass over Laing's Nek (named after Henry Laing whose farm lay below by the side of the wagon road) pushed through the centre of a rough semi-circle of hills, six miles in length. These hills culminate in the west with Majuba Mountain (*amajuba* means 'doves' in Zulu), flat-topped with steep sides and deep wooded ravines, and in the east with the Buffalo River swirling through a deep and rugged gorge. The road skirted the lower spurs of Majuba, from which it was commanded, before rising up from the undulating grassy plain below the hills to the nek, or pass. Between the nek and Majuba is a series of ridges and shoulders and deeply furrowed kloofs, or ravines. A low, rocky hill (later known as Brownlow's Kop), about one-and-a-half miles east of Laing's Nek, formed the extreme left of the Boer position, after which the ground fell away to the deep valley of the Buffalo. Two further hills rose between Brownlow's Kop and the nek. The hill nearer to Laing's Nek was a flat-topped feature about 1,000 yards in length and 600 feet above the plain which the British called Table Mountain, and the Boers Engelbrecht Kop.[1] It commanded both the road over the nek and the most easterly of the three Boer laagers established on the reverse slopes to its north. The further hill was a round, rocky feature of the same height as Table Mountain. From the eastern end of Table Mountain a broad spur about 200 yards wide falls away very steeply for 100 yards in a south-easterly direction, and then descends more gradually for another 300 yards when it is cut by a donga, or gulley, leading sharply down to a stream. Sir Evelyn Wood later conceded that this was a position of great natural strength for defence, lending itself to effective flanking fire across bare, steep slopes.[2]

Because of the nature of the terrain, Joubert and his officers did not suppose that Colley could advance except by way of the wagon road, and made their dispositions accordingly. They placed their two strongest contingents under Joubert's own eye across the nek itself and to the west of the road. A smaller detachment under Commandant Greyling was positioned on Table Mountain, another under Commandant Engelbrecht on Brownlow's Kop, and a third under Commandant Basson held the ground between them.[3] There is uncertainty over the number of Boers holding these positions, though Joubert himself put the number at 600.[4]

On the evening of 27 January Colley called his senior officers together and informed them of his plan.[5] His intention was first to distract the Boers by opening fire on their positions across the nek with his artillery from a broad, low spur from Majuba about 2,300 yards away and 300 feet below. For this barrage he had at his disposal four 9-pounders of the respective divisions of the N/5 Brigade, RA and 10/7 Brigade, RA, the two 7-pounders taken from Fort Napier and the Naval Brigade's three 24-pounder rockets. The artillery would be supported in threatening the nek by the 66 Natal Mounted Police, the 88 men of the Naval Brigade and the 334 men of the 3/60th Rifles. Meanwhile, the 494 men of 58th Regiment (the largest body of regulars Colley had available) would advance up the spur at the eastern end of Table Mountain, rest and reform near the top, and then rapidly move forward to gain possession of Table Mountain which Colley considered the key to the whole Boer position. One company would then be detached to cover any enemy movement against the rear, and the remaining companies would swing to their left along Table Mountain to command the nek, thus rolling up the Boer defences. If their advance up the spur were threatened on their right flank, a company would be detached to join the Mounted Squadron of 119 men advancing up the hills further to the right to turn the Boers' left flank. Once the Boers fell back from the nek, the artillery would be able to move up and support the Mounted Squadron as it harassed the retreating Boers. Colley afterwards admitted that if he had had enough infantry available he would have commenced by storming Brownlow's Kop on the Boers' left which would have allowed him to take their whole position in flank, but he believed that to have done so would have extended his force too much and have exposed it to a counter-thrust through its attenuated centre.

It must be questioned why Colley did not plan to make active use of the Natal Mounted Police who had the distinct edge over the Mounted Squadron both in terms of training and practical knowledge of operating in the kind of terrain that confronted them. It is probable that Colley kept them in reserve, not only on account of the professional British officer's notorious distrust of the discipline and effectiveness of white colonial troops – a prejudice that remained firmly in place during the South African War of 1899–1902[6] – but because Colley remained anxious to suppress any suggestions of race or civil war between the white populations of southern Africa. To have given a prominent role in the assault to the NMP (the closest thing Natal had to a standing army) might well have inflamed Boer opinion.

The Movable Column (as it was officially named), numbering 1,211 officers and men, marched out of camp at about 06h15 with the NMP as an advance-guard. The infantry carried 70 rounds a man and a reserve of 7,200 rounds in a Scotch cart. Each man also carried two pounds of biscuit and bully beef. Ambulances and water carts were also taken. The entrenched camp was left under the guard of 248 officers and men – which was just as well, for during the course of the day a large party of mounted Boers reconnoitred the laager and moved off when they saw it was securely held.

At 07h45 the leading units halted on an undulating ridge about 2,000 yards from the hill on the left of the Boer position. The rest of the Column came up steadily, and by 09h20 had completed its approach. It was deployed with a company of the 3/60th Rifles on the left in extended order below the spur from Majuba about 1,500 yards from the nek. The Naval Brigade was also in extended order on its left, its rocket tubes on its left flank sheltered by a stone kraal wall near Henry Laing's small farmhouse. About 200 yards in the rear were five companies of the 3/60th Rifles just below the crest of the spur. Behind these, on the summit of the spur, were the guns, the 7-pounders on the right, Division 10/7 Brigade, RA in the centre and N/5 Brigade, RA on the left. The 58th Regiment was a little in the rear, ready to advance with the Mounted Squadron to their rear on the right, and the NMP to their rear on the left. The ambulances and water carts were kept about 200 yards in rear of the centre.

At 09h25 the artillery and rockets opened fire as planned at the rate of one round a minute on the Boer positions across the nek and on the reverse slopes where many men and their horses were collected. The Boers duly took cover from the shrapnel and common shells behind rocks and natural folds in the ground.[7] The British confidently anticipated that the Boers would not be able to face an artillery barrage, and the artillery officers were betting that they would clear the nek in a quarter of an hour. When a few panicky Boer horsemen were seen galloping over the skyline in the initial shock of the bombardment, the British broke into cheers thinking that the enemy were on the run.[8] But even though the Boers, as Joubert later admitted, had 'at first a dread of artillery fire' (and were especially taken aback by the erratic rockets), they quickly realised it was relatively ineffective, so they kept their heads down and held their fire.[9]

After 15 minutes of what was in fact a rather ineffectual artillery barrage of the nek, Colley launched the second phase of his plan at 09h40 when he commanded Major William Hingeston to lead the 58th Regiment forward and ordered five of his staff, including Colonel Deane, who nominally commanded the NFF, to accompany the attack. Deane immediately took personal command, relegating the regimental officers, whom the men would have seen as their natural leaders, to a subordinate role. Covered by rapid artillery fire directed at Table Mountain, and supported far away on its right flank by the Mounted Squadron under Major Brownlow, the 58th Regiment started its difficult advance. Deane and the other staff officers remained mounted, which compelled Hingeston and his adjutant, Lieutenant Monck, to follow suit, making them obvious targets for the Boer marksmen. The men had to cross two spurs and two streams before they even reached the beginning of the spur 1,000 yards away leading up to Table Mountain, and were already becoming exhausted by the hot summer weather. At 10h10, as the five companies of the 58th Regiment began to move up the steep spur in a tightly packed column four abreast, they came under some fire to their right from 50 Boer skirmishers under Gert Engelbrecht well concealed behind big rocks, occasional trees and other natural features some 900 yards away on the western slopes of Brownlow's Kop. The open, grassy slopes of the spur (which nowadays are covered in commercial timber plantations) offered the British little natural cover. Nevertheless, the distant Boer fire was largely ineffective. Yet Brownlow, at the head of Mounted Squadron, acted in the impetuous style of the cavalry officer which he was, rather than as a commander of mounted infantry. His orders were to protect the flank of the 58th Regiment if they came under attack. Without coordinating his attack with a company of the 58th Regiment as Colley had intended, and without first scouting the ground ahead and ascertaining the best way to reach the Boers on Brownlow's Kop (he would have found a much gentler ascent only a little further on which would have allowed him to take the Boers in the flank), he immediately wheeled his men sharply to the right. With one troop extended and the other in support, he led them in a charge straight up the steepest part of the hill. The consequence was that most of the horses were 'completely blown'[10] before they were even half way to the top.

Brownlow, with Troop Sergeant-Major Lunnie, KDG at his side, were the first to reach the crest held by the Boers, followed closely by the first troop. The second troop was still huffing up behind. The Boers rapidly fell back down the reverse slope before the British were in striking distance, keeping to the natural cover. They were hurriedly reinforced by the 33 Boer horsemen under Commandant Basson stationed to their right who dismounted and opened fire at close range. Brownlow's horse fell and he was thrown. Lunnie flung himself at some Boers still on the crest, killing a Boer and wounding another with his revolver before being shot dead. Behind them, wounded and exhausted horses wheeled and reared in panic, while their unseated riders scurried about attempting to find cover or flee. Brownlow's servant, Private John Doogan, KDG, despite being wounded in the charge, scrambled off his own horse and insisted that Brownlow take it. While under galling Boer fire Doogan was again wounded, but both men managed to make their escape. Doogan won the Victoria Cross for his selfless valour.[11]

With half their horses dead or wounded, attempts to rally the first troop failed, and the Boers quickly moved back to the crest to fire on the second troop coming up in support. The men of this troop had all recently been mustered as mounted infantry. Their riding skills were inadequate and they were mounted on mostly ill-trained horses that could not be brought to face fire. Not unnaturally these men became thoroughly demoralised by the heavy firing and careering riderless horses ahead of them, and turned tail before they reached the crest and blundered their way down the hill again as fast as they could go, leaving the survivors of the Mounted Squadron to make their way back as best they could under fire.[12] Brownlow was so thoroughly disgusted with the craven performance of his men, and felt himself so 'broken-hearted' by their flight before the eyes of the whole army, that he refused to speak to them once he returned to camp.[13] What they thought of his irresponsible, derring-do leadership is another matter. As Norris-Newman commented, it would have been more to the point if Brownlow had handled his men like proper mounted infantry instead of cavalry, and had led them unmounted up the slope in skirmishing order.[14] It must be supposed that the NMP, if only Colley had employed them, would have done just that.

Joubert fully appreciated the advantage Brownlow's inept failure gave the Boers.[15] The British mounted troops were now out of the picture, and the right flank of the 58th Regiment exposed. Colley also understood the danger they were now in, but since they were becoming engaged he feared the dire effects if he ordered them to withdraw. All he could do was concentrate as much artillery fire as he could to cover them, though once again it seemed to have no effect on the Boers even though most were no longer under cover. As for the 58th Regiment, its only option was to move forward as fast as it could go to minimise casualties. So after a short breather in a ravine which had offered good cover it was 'hustled up at a tremendous pace' over the rough ground which, being a 1 in 15 gradient, was far steeper than had appeared through the officers' field glasses the previous day.[16] To make matters worse, the hillside was covered in the long thick grass of early summer, made slick by the rain. It slipped though the hands of the men using it as handholds as they pulled themselves up on hands and knees, boots could find no purchase and it clung around ankles bringing the troops down. Officers had the greatest difficulty in urging their horses forward. The Boers on Brownlow's Kop, some mounted and some unmounted, and now numbering perhaps 100, moved forward without fear of interference towards the top of the spur almost parallel to the 58th Regiment and opened a heavy and effective fire on its right flank and rear. To counter this new threat on their flank, a company of the 58th Regiment wheeled to the right and, now bereft of the planned support of the routed Mounted Squadron, engaged the Boer riflemen as best they could. Stung by the Boer flanking fire, the rest of the 58th Regiment broke into an exhausting, stumbling, crouching half-run to make the summit where the Boers were being steadily reinforced, though they still probably did not number much more than between 70 and 80 in number. The British clearly saw several armed *agterryers* among them and were shocked that Africans were fighting in the Boer lines against white men.[17]

At about 10h40 Colonel Deane, who was leading his men still mounted, reached the ridge where the spur finally joined Table Mountain. He found himself facing a further hillside as smooth and devoid of cover as the glacis before a fort, with the Boers snugly ensconced 160 yards away behind rocks and roughly erected stone breastworks. The British thought the Boers were in trenches, but Boer sources are insistent that no trenches were built until after the battle.[18] Even so, this was a classic killing ground. Deane had not yet extended his men who arrived panting and unprepared in a confused mass at the foot of the lethal slope still in the close formation of column of companies (though now strung out over 120 yards) with their left flank completely exposed to the Boer marksmen on Table Mountain. Deane urgently attempted to extend his men out of column into line, but they were too exhausted by the climb and beset by heavy Boer fire to deploy effectively. Still far too closely bunched and at a considerable disadvantage in the fire-fight, the British were in an untenable position. In such circumstances to fix bayonets and charge was the only remaining option. So Deane, who was tasting action for the first time in his career,[19] gave the order though many of his men were so fatigued that they could barely stand, let alone lift their rifles. Nevertheless, the 58th gallantly responded and advanced cheering with both Colours flying, the last time (as it turned out) that a British regiment would carry them into battle.

Deane, who was still mounted, presented an obvious target. He was shot in the arm and got off his horse which he could no longer control and, revolver in hand, gallantly went forward well ahead of the rest of his troops. He was shot dead through the head.[20] As at Bronkhorstspruit, the Boers were clearly picking off the officers, and Lieutenant Inman of the 3/60th Rifles, Deane's orderly officer and a member of Colley's staff, fell just behind him. Major Hingeston, once more in active command of his regiment, urged his men forward, only to fall mortally wounded. At much the same time, two more members of Colley's staff, Major Ruscombe Poole and Lieutenant Elwes, were also shot dead. Of the five men on Colley's staff who had joined the attack, only Major Edward 'Lucky' Essex survived, as he had also lived to tell the tale of the route at Isandlwana in January 1879. Captain Lovegrove succeeded Hingeston in command of the 58th Regiment, and when he too fell wounded the command temporarily devolved on Lieutenant Jopp before Major Essex took control.

The 58th Regiment's bayonet charge came as close in places as 30 to 40 yards of the Boers' positions, but the men could maintain their momentum no further under the heavy fire and took heavy casualties. Keeping as low as they could to the ground, for there was little if any cover, they managed at least to return fire. Boer reinforcements were being fed into the front line all through the action, and soon after 11h00 Major Essex accepted that the Boer position was too strong to be carried by a frontal attack, and that the spent and demoralised men could not be called on to attempt another charge. He therefore began a withdrawal from the right of the line where the three companies were least heavily engaged, and they slowly fell back down the open slope to the ridge above the spur, covered by the two left-hand companies who had borne the brunt of the fighting. The artillery and rockets opened up an accurate fire to cover the retirement, which, although it kept the Boers in check, unfortunately also killed some of the British wounded lying on the hillside. Finding that the 58th Regiment halted and resting on the ridge were still enfiladed by Boer fire from Table Mountain and Brownlow's Kop, Essex retired them in good order further down the spur. Though under the cover of the artillery barrage, they remained under fire from all sides and from those Boers who broke cover to pursue them.

The 58th Regiment's disciplined retirement was partly covered by two companies of the 3/60th Rifles which Colley had moved to their right at 11h10 in order to pin down the Boer pursuers. One of the companies of the 58th Regiment was still holding together sufficiently well to form line and put up a very effective rearguard action against the Boers. Lieutenant Baily, who was carrying the Regimental Colour, now fell mortally wounded. The Colours were carried by the two junior officers of a battalion, escorted by a Colour party, to encourage the line forward in an attack, or to serve as a rallying point in defence. To lose a Colour to the enemy was the ultimate disgrace, and Lieutenant Peel, who carried the Queen's Colour, offered his assistance, but Baily refused, saying 'Never mind me, save the Colours'.[21] So Peel took up both Colours, but shortly thereafter stumbled in an antbear hole and fell. Sergeant Bridgstock, presuming he was wounded, took both Colours and scrambled them away, first on horseback and then on foot, until he reached the bottom of the spur where he handed them over to the quartermaster, who took them safely out of action. Meanwhile, Lieutenant Hill attempted to rescue the wounded Baily. Unable to hoist him into the saddle of his restive horse, Hill carried him in his arms down the spur, but Baily was fatally shot on the way. Undeterred, Hill went twice more up the spur to rescue wounded men, and was later awarded the Victoria Cross for his gallant conduct. This incident, which had inflicted so many unnecessary casualties on the officers and sergeants of the Colour party, compounded the temporary loss of the Queen's Colour at Isandlwana in January 1879 during the Anglo-Zulu War and the loss of both the 66th Regiment's Colours in July 1880 during the Second Afghan War. Colours were clearly at risk in the scrambling fighting typical of Victorian small wars, and certainly no longer had any place on a battlefield dominated by accurate long-range rifle fire. Wolseley believed that to order young officers to carry the Colours into battle was nothing short of murder, and in 1882 it was ordered that they were no longer to do so.[22]

The 58th Regiment, once it regained the foot of the spur and was almost out of the reach of enemy fire, reformed and marched back to its original position, taking proud care to maintain its order and soldierly bearing as best it could. The two companies of the 3/60th Rifles then advanced and opened fire on the Boers who soon withdrew beyond range.

Earlier, when the 58th Regiment had begun to retire down the spur, the Boers attempted a complementary attack on the British left flank. During the previous night Joubert had sent a detachment to the deep kloof west of the road above Laing's farm,[23] and at 11h00 these mounted Boers issued from their position above and beyond the left of the company of the 3/60th Rifles and the sailors of the Naval Brigade who were stationed in advance of the guns on the spur from Majuba. Despite being surprised, the British suffered few casualties on account of the protection of the stone kraal wall, and their effective return fire drove off the Boers.

With the 58th Regiment back at its starting line on the ridge facing the Boers, the NMP, who had gone forward as vedettes on the British left were also withdrawn. Clearly, the British were in no condition to renew the attack, but Colley entertained the hope that the Boers might be foolhardy enough to follow up their success with an advance, and maintained his position. The Boers made no move however. Many of his men believed that Joubert was indecisive and too prudent, and should have seized the opportunity to pursue and destroy the retreating British. But Joubert sensibly decided against abandoning his strong defensive position and risking his men against the British in the open.[24] He had a healthy respect for the British artillery and calculated that he would suffer too many casualties to make an attack worthwhile, though he was later to write that if he had had 200 men more he would have attempted it.[25]

Accepting at length that the Boers would not attack, at noon Colley ordered a staff officer escorted by two troopers of the NMP to carry forward a flag of truce to enable the wounded to be removed and the dead buried. Joubert insisted he would not allow it so long as Colley maintained his advanced position, and not before the Boers had removed the arms from the British wounded and dead littering the slopes.[26] Colley then agreed to pull back. He divided the column into two sections which withdrew alternately very slowly towards Mount Prospect camp, which was reached at about 16h00. It would still have saved his reputation if only the Boers had tried to storm his camp and been repulsed but, as he wryly confided to Wolseley, he did not 'expect such luck'.[27] More realistically, he expected to be 'gibbeted' by his critics and deeply regretted his casualties, especially the loss of so many of his loyal and closely-bonded staff.[28]

The good order maintained in falling back on the Mount Prospect camp could not disguise that the Movable Column had suffered a stinging and humiliating reverse. Colley had no feasible option left but to hold his camp until sufficiently reinforced to renew the attack when, as Lance-Sergeant Morris put it, 'we will pepper them for what they have done'.[29] Certainly, the British had done some 'peppering' that day, expending 8,635 rounds of rifle ammunition, 845 of carbine and 80 pistol rounds. That was an average of over 17 rounds per man, almost double the 10 Colonel Callwell reckoned normally shot away in a typical 'small war' battle, and nearly triple the 6.4 the infantry had fired at the battle of Ulundi on 4 July 1879 and which had proved sufficient to break the might of the Zulu army. Then the artillery had fired only 90 rounds compared to the 187 shrapnel and 13 common shells fruitlessly thrown at the Boers on Laing's Nek.[30] And in final proof, if any more were required, that this was warfare of a very different nature from the sort that had been so successful against mass assaults by poorly armed 'savages', all this great expenditure of ammunition had only resulted in Joubert's official tally (numbers do vary in various accounts) of 16 Boers killed or died of their wounds and another 27 wounded, mainly as a result of artillery fire.[31] In stark comparison, between 500 and 600 Zulu had been killed within close range of the British infantry square at Ulundi, and another 600 in the mounted pursuit.[32]

Something else struck Colley forcibly about his failure to force Laing's Nek. The Boers, he reported ruefully, had fought 'with great courage and determination', and during the close range fighting from 20 to 200 yards 'had shown no fear' of the British troops. Indeed, they had intrepidly advanced to meet them. Not only were the Boers tougher and braver soldiers than the British had believed, but they were more courteous than cultural stereotyping had anticipated in permitting the care and removal of the British wounded.[33]

Forty men of the 58th Regiment and 20 of the Naval Brigade were detailed to bury the dead, and the medical personnel went forward to tend the wounded. They found the Boers busy on the hillside rifling the dead and stripping them of their rifles, ammunition, boots, leggings and accoutrements, all of which Joubert considered both natural and necessary considering the

Boer shortages of these items.[34] At the same time, the Boers were generally considerate to the wounded, though the youngsters among them (still stirred up by the fighting) tended to be more full of 'bragging insolence' than their more regretful and shaken seniors.[35] Nothing in Boer behaviour that day warranted the shrill cries in certain sections of the British press concerning 'Boer atrocities', including the reported killing of British wounded.[36] It took until 20h00 to clear the field of the wounded, who were carried back to Mount Prospect by 40 Africans, where they lay groaning and crying out in the makeshift hospital.[37] Unlike the egalitarian Boers, who recognised no social distinctions in death, it was British practice to bury other ranks in mass graves on the battlefield, and remove officers for individual burial near the headquarters camp.[38] The British burial detail accordingly brought back the corpses of the slain officers, but had not had sufficient time to complete the task of burying the dead on the battlefield. A burying party of 60 men went the next day under a flag of truce with the Reverend George Ritchie, Chaplain to the Forces, to finish the business. In the afternoon the remains of the officers were buried about 200 yards west of the camp. Two German missionaries tended the wounded Boers who were brought back to the Meeks' house at Coldstream, but they were very short of medical supplies.

British losses were unacceptably heavy, particularly among the officers and NCOs, since, as Lance-Sergeant Morris put it, 'the Boers were dead nuts on them'.[39] Though there are the usual minor discrepancies in the various tallies, it was certainly the 58th Regiment which bore the brunt. According to the returns kept by Major Essex, the regiment lost 3 officers and 71 other ranks killed and 2 officers and 99 men wounded, or a shattering 35 per cent of its total strength.[40] The Mounted Squadron lost 4 killed and 13 wounded, and the Naval Brigade 2 killed and 1 wounded.[41] Throughout the force 7 officers were killed and 3 wounded and Colley's staff virtually wiped out. In all, this was 16 per cent of Colley's effective force, a casualty rate indicative of a thorough-going defeat. Edouard Bok, the Secretary of the South African Republic, forwarded a letter found on the body of Trooper Joseph Venables of the KDG to his relatives, commenting in his covering note that '[w]e feel very sorry indeed, the more so because he and so many with him fell and shall fall victim to a mischievous policy of the English government – who send brave soldiers against men who only defend their liberty and the independence of the country'.[42]

The evening of the battle a badly rattled Colley, accepting as best he could 'the verdict of failure',[43] spoke to his demoralised officers and men and assured them that the entire blame for the day's repulse rested entirely upon him, not them, and that in their actions they had 'not lost one atom of the prestige of England'. Colley concluded lamely by assuring them that 'we certainly shall take possession of that hill eventually'.[44] Though his men appreciated his organisational ability and personal courage, this self-abnegation was hardly calculated to restore their confidence in his leadership in the field. As Lieutenant-Colonel Cromer Ashburnham, the Officer Commanding the 3/60th Rifles, was reported to have snorted contemptuously, 'You don't win a battle by making speeches or writing despatches'.[45] In Britain, Colley's repulse (the press could not bring itself to describe it as a 'defeat'), was not received any better, especially since it had been administered by contemptible 'undisciplined bands of yeomen'.[46] Colley's own ingrained confidence in his superior tactical skills, though shaken, took only a couple of days to reassert themselves. Exposing a surprisingly inflexible inability to learn from experience, he assured Wolseley with inappropriate cocksureness that if he were to attack Laing's Nek again with the same number of men he would do it again 'in exactly the same manner that I originally intended'.[47] In stark contrast, Joubert humbly wrote on the evening of the battle from the Meeks' farm in simple, devout relief to the Assistant Commandant-General, P.A. Cronjé, informing him that the British had attacked him that day, and that, '[w]ith the help of God, they have been repulsed with heavy losses . . . Looking up to God that he may further bless us'.[48]

Notes and references

1 After the battle the British called it Deane's Hill after Colonel Deane who died in the failed assault.

2 WO 32/7818: Wood to Childers, 30 March 1881.

3 Grobler, 'Die Britse Terugslag by Laingsnek' in Van Jaarsveld, Van Rensburg and Stals (eds), *Eerste Vryheidsoorlog*, p. 149.

4 BV 11, p. 205: Joubert to Kruger, 30 January 1881.

5 For the first-hand reports of the battle upon which the following account is primarily based, see WO 32/7810, no. 079/4016: Colley to Childers, 1 February 1881; Butterfield, *War and Peace*, pp. 192–8: Journal of the Natal Field Force, Friday, 28 January 1881, which was written by Major Essex; *BPP* (C. 2837), no. 2: Colley to Childers, telegram, 28 January 1881; Colley to Childers, telegram, 29 January 1881; *BPP* (C. 2866), no. 69: Colley to Kimberley, 1 February 1881;

enc. in no. 73: Commander F. Romilly to Commodore F.W. Richards, 29 January 1881; Colley to Wolseley, 30 January 1881, quoted in Butler, *Pomeroy-Colley*, pp. 285–9; Carter, *Boer War*, pp. 161–72. T.F. Carter, the correspondent for the *Times of Natal*, had been delayed by the appalling roads and had only reached Newcastle, 24 miles away, on the day of the battle (p. 159). But he was able to interview the British participants on the days immediately following. Also see Norris-Newman, *With the Boers*, pp. 146–53, 177–8; Lady Bellairs, ed., *Transvaal War*, pp. 373–6; Ransford, *Majuba Hill*, pp. 43–51; Lehmann, *Boer War*, pp. 132–59; Grobler, 'Laingsnek', pp. 149–56.

6 For British reluctance again in 1899–1902 to make effective use of the Natal Volunteers, see M. Coghlan, 'The Natal Volunteers in the Anglo-Boer War, September 1899 to July 1902: Reality and Perception' (unpublished PhD thesis, University of Natal, 2002), pp. 413–18.

7 On 24 March 1881 Wood inspected a trench about 150 feet long dug across the roadway with a bank of earth thrown up before it which he described as 'paltry and ill-traced'. However, it is clear that this was only dug *after* the battle. See WO 32/7818: Wood to Childers, 30 March 1881.

8 Holt, *Mounted Police*, p. 101.

9 WO 32/7818, no. 079/4532: Wood to Childers, 30 March 1881. However, several Boers later told Sir J.L. Vaughan, who had been sent out rather belatedly by *The Times* to cover the war, that their defences were so inadequate that if the British artillery had continued to fire only a little more they would have retreated. See Sir J.L. Vaughan, *My Service in the Indian Army – and After* (London, 1904), p. 248.

10 Carter, *Boer War*, p. 163.

11 Under the original warrant of 1856 the Victoria Cross was available only for 'some signal act of Valour or devotion' or to those whose personal bravery contributed to the success of an operation. Until May 1881 it was not to be awarded for an act of gallantry considered merely in the performance of duty, and was only awarded posthumously after January 1907. See Beckett, *Victorians at War*, pp. 38–41.

12 See the accounts of this attack given by Sergeant Madden and Private Venables, both British prisoners-of-war in the Boer camp, quoted in Norris-Newman, *With the Boers*, pp. 151–2.

13 Colley to Lady Colley, 30 January 1881, quoted in Butler, *Pomeroy-Colley*, pp. 291–2.

14 Norris-Newman, *With the Boers*, p. 147.

15 BV 11, p. 193: Joubert to Kruger, 28 January 1881.

16 Emery, *Marching over Africa*, p. 105: officer [possibly Lt P.S. Marling, 3/60th Rifles] in the *Citizen*, 19 March 1881.

17 Carter, *Boer War*, p. 165.

18 Grobler, 'Laingsnek', p. 152.

19 Deane's wife had tried to 'keep him in a glass case', but seeing him increasingly unhappy at his lack of active military service, had lobbied in support of his appointment to South Africa. After Laing's Nek she was treated with enormous respect because of his gallant death on the field of battle. See Beckett, *Victorians at War*, p. 26.

20 Emery, *Marching over Africa*, p. 104: Lance-Sergeant W.J. Morris to his mother, the *Northampton Mercury*, 19 March 1881.

21 Carter, *Boer War*, p. 165.

22 Knight, *Go to Your God Like a Soldier*, pp. 191–3.

23 Grobler, 'Laingsnek', p. 149.

24 Meintjes, *Commandant-General*, pp. 78–9.

25 BV 11, p. 194: Joubert to Kruger, 28 January 1881; p. 204: Joubert to Kruger, 30 February 1881.

26 BV 11, pp. 194–6: Joubert to Kruger, 28 February 1881.

27 Colley was very aware of the 'kudos' Wood had clawed back in the Anglo-Zulu War by crushing the Zulu army at the battle of Khambula (29 March 1879) the day immediately after his disastrous rout on Hlobane Mountain. See Laband, *Kingdom in Crisis*, chap. 8.

28 Colley to Wolseley, 30 January 1881, quoted in Butler, *Life of Pomeroy-Colley*, pp. 285–6, 289–90.

29 Emery, *Marching over Africa*, p. 104: Morris in the *Northampton Mercury*, 19 March 1881.

30 Laband, *Kingdom in Crisis*, p. 222; Callwell, *Small Wars*, p. 439.

31 BV 11, p. 204: Joubert to Kruger, 30 January 1881.

32 See Laband and Thompson, *Anglo-Zulu War*, pp. 165–9.

33 *BPP* (C. 2866), enc. in no. 70: Colley to Childers, 1 February 1881.

34 BV 11, p. 194: Joubert to Kruger, 28 February 1881.

35 Carter, *Boer War*, p. 167.

36 Grobler, 'Laingsnek', p. 154. Childers in parliament repudiated the misleading telegrams from South Africa upon which these reports were based.

37 Emery, *Marching over Africa*, p. 106: Sgt Henry Coombes, Army Hospital Corps, in the *Sheffield Daily Telegraph*, 5 April 1881.

38 G.A. Chadwick, 'War Graves Registers, Monuments, Headstones and Crosses with Special Reference to the War of 1880–1881', *Militaria*, 1, 11 (1981), pp. 31, 35.

39 Emery, *Marching over Africa*, p. 104: Morris to his mother, the *Northampton Mercury*, 19 March 1881.

40 Butterfield, *War and Peace*, p. 198: Journal of the Natal Field Force, 28 January 1881. See also WO 32/7810, no. 079/4016: Colley to Childers, 1 February 1881. In the recapitulation to this report made a few days later, Colley gives the final tally as 7 officers and 76 men killed and 2 officers and 109 men wounded with 2 men taken prisoner. However, although he includes 2 support personnel killed and 2 wounded, he leaves out the mounted casualties except those in the King's Dragoons Guards (who were part of the Mounted Squadron) who had 2 men killed and 3 wounded.

41 Commander Romilly estimated that the British lost 83 killed and 100 wounded, slightly lower than Colley's final count. See *BPP* (C. 2866), enc. in no. 73: Romilly to Richards, 29 January 1881.

42 E. Bok to the relatives of J.D. Venables, 2 February 1881, quoted by S. Benson, 'Laing's Nek' in Crouch and Knight, eds, *Forged in Strong Fires*, p. 27. Though left for dead, Trooper Venables survived.

43 Colley to Lady Colley, 28 January 1881, quoted in Butler, *Life of Pomeroy-Colley*, p. 291.

44 Carter, *Boer War*, p. 168.

45 Lt Percival Marling's later comment, quoted in Emery, *Marching over Africa*, p. 106.

46 *Illustrated London News*, 29 January 1881. See Lehmann, *First Boer War*, p. 159 for the response in Britain.

47 Colley to Wolseley, 30 January 1881, quoted in Butler, *Pomeroy-Colley*, p. 289.

48 Joubert to Cronjé, 28 January 1881, quoted in Carter, *Boer War*, p. 172.

chapter 8

Ingogo

In deciding to remain at Mount Prospect, Colley concluded that a strategic withdrawal would have considerable adverse political repercussions both in South Africa and Britain, dishearten the garrisons in the Transvaal, encourage the Boers to take aggressive action and bring waverers onto their side.[1] To stay was to signal that the failure to carry Laing's Nek was only a temporary check.[2] It could not be helped that his camp was at the terminus of a long and fragile line of communications which brought up all the NFF's food, ammunition, correspondence and medical supplies, and which even the most amateur enemy could be counted on to attempt to sever.

Meanwhile, to strengthen their position, the British constructed an entrenchment on a hill about 1,600 yards east of the camp and stationed a company of infantry and the division of 7-pounders there. With the death of Colonel Deane, who had commanded the NFF, Colley assumed personal command. On 1 February, which was the first day without rain since the battle, Colley moved the camp (which had become a sanitary necessity in the wet weather) and the next day built two circular redoubts 60 yards across to help defend it until reinforced. In his report that evening to Childers, Colley apologised that he could not enclose Major Ruscombe Poole's sketch of the camp since all his papers had been lost when he was killed.[3] That night a convoy of empty wagons left for Newcastle, and a convoy of ambulances followed the next morning in rain and dense fog. The weather continued most inclement with a violent thunderstorm breaking over the camp on 6 February.

Childers learned of Colley's 'check with much regret', and immediately on 29 January offered further reinforcements, suggesting a light cavalry regiment from England and another from India, as well as a battery of horse artillery.[4] The crippling effects of the dearth of mounted troops with the NFF were clearly becoming obvious to the War Office. But stung by his defeat, Colley was too proud to admit this, and turned Childers's offer down. He assured the War Secretary that the reinforcements already on the way were quite sufficient, that the effects of his check were 'not serious' and that his men were 'in excellent spirits and eager to attack again'.[5] Gladstone's cabinet were not convinced by these brave words. Kimberley advised his colleagues that the war must either be pursued to a rapid and successful close, or that a peace should be negotiated before the Dutch population in the rest of South Africa was alienated from Britain, and before British weakness resulted in a fresh Zulu outbreak.[6] On 29 January the cabinet, beset by more pressing concerns such as the Irish question, plumped for the second option, and authorised Kimberley to initiate peace feelers.[7]

Unaware that the politicians were planning to pull the rug out from under them, the British at Mount Prospect observed the Boers busying themselves 'erecting schanzes [breastworks]', digging out trenches and otherwise strengthening their defences across Laing's Nek.[8] Indeed, the recent battle had taught the Boers a number of things. They now thoroughly grasped the necessity for breastworks and trenches in defence, especially against artillery, even though this arm had proved not nearly so frighteningly effective as anticipated. At another level, the Boers' victory had enormously boosted their morale. It had swept away all doubts and restored their self-confidence in a successful end to the war. Internationally, it had done much to enhance their reputation as fighters and, more materially, it had encouraged volunteers from the Free State to join their blood-brothers in their righteous struggle.[9]

Joubert, however, was not carried away by this wave of enthusiasm. He fully understood that he had repulsed the British, not defeated them, and was uncertain what steps to take next beyond strengthening his defences on Laing's Nek. The weather was still severe and his men were neither well provided with clothes and blankets nor enjoyed a variety in their diet, everything but meat from slaughtered cattle being very short. Their morale probably would have been worse had Red Cross doctors from Cape Town and other aid not started to come through the Orange Free State.[10] He consequently wrote urgently to Kruger (whose considerable military experience gained fighting Africans he valued) begging him to come to the front with other advisers, and also to Piet Cronjé at Potchefstroom urgently requesting reinforcements.[11]

Immediately after the battle at Laing's Nek, Colley had sent the NMP back to Newcastle to patrol around his base and guard against Boer raids. Though the NMP were fully trained they were relatively few in number and the Boers had little to fear from them. Mounted Boer patrols therefore probed deep into Natal, roaming around and beyond Newcastle as far south as the Biggarsberg, keeping Joubert thoroughly informed of every British move.[12] At the beginning of February Joubert learned from his scouts that large British reinforcements had reached Pietermaritzburg on their way to Mount Prospect. At a council of war Joubert and his officers resolved that every effort must be made to prevent these troops reaching Colley. Accordingly, at 18h00 on 5 February Field Commandant-General Nicolaas Smit (fresh from victory at Bronkhorstspruit and considered to possess the best military qualities among the Boers[13]) led out a patrol of 205 men to intercept the reinforcements. The secrecy of their mission dictated that they advance carefully, out of sight of British patrols. On Sunday, 6 February, Smit's force passed far to the west of the road to Newcastle, rode through Orange Free State territory where some volunteers joined them, and off-saddled for the night in a kloof in the Drakensberg. At midday on 7 February a party of 20 Boers from Smit's bivouac intercepted the mailbags from Mount Prospect south of the Ingogo River[14] as they were being carried by several mounted Africans escorted by six men of the Mounted Squadron.[15] All but one of the British turned and fled back to the safety of Mount Prospect, but one of the escort broke through and hurried on to Newcastle. The next morning Colley received a telegraph from Fort Amiel informing him that it would be unwise to send forward the wagon convoy of supplies he had been expecting because of increased Boer activity in the vicinity.[16] Colley had had enough. He decided he must act at once to remove this growing threat along his lines of communication and supply by making a demonstration in force along the road to Newcastle.

At first light on 8 February some ambulance wagons and mail carts set out from Mount Prospect for Newcastle.[17] Colley planned to give them a good start and then follow with a strong escort to see them safely over the most hazardous points of the route, and then to escort back the stalled convoy from Newcastle. Colley himself took command and at 08h30 led out 6 staff officers including a chaplain and civilian interpreter, 5 companies and the Headquarters (11 officers and 295 men) of the 3/60th Rifles under Colonel Ashburnham, the division of two 7-pounder mountain guns and the division of two 9-pounder field guns of N/5 Brigade, RA under Captain Greer, RA with another officer and 28 artillerymen, a detachment of 3 officers and 40 men of the Mounted Squadron under Major Brownlow to patrol the road, 4 men of the 2/21st Regiment to act as stretcher bearers, and 2 medical personnel. This was an operation ideally suited to mounted troops, but Colley had few available since he had sent the NMP back to Newcastle and the Mounted Infantry had suffered heavily at Laing's Nek. However, he still believed the Boers to be awed by artillery, so did not anticipate that they would attack. No orders were given to issue rations or for a water cart to accompany the column since Colley expected to be back at 15h30 when dinner would be awaiting its return.

About two miles north from where the Harte (Imbezane) River flows into the Ingogo River the wagon road encountered the first of a series of spurs stretching out eastwards from Inkwelo Mountain. It then meandered down a long, stony hill to the double drifts about 100 yards apart, each just above the confluence of the two rivers. Fermistone's rustic inn stood on the north bank. Across the rocky drifts with their fast-flowing waters the road climbed gently to a rocky plateau about a mile and a half away, known as Schuinshoogte. Before marching down the hill to the crossings, his front covered by the mounted troops and infantry on his flanks, Colley detached the two 7-pounders and one company of the 3/60th Rifles to take up position on a lower spur of the high ground on the north bank. There they would command the approaches to the rivers should any Boer move out from behind Inkwelo and dispute his return. Colley sent back orders for a company of the 58th Regiment from the camp about two and a half miles away to relieve them, upon which the company of the 3/60th Rifles was to move down and rejoin its battalion.

Meanwhile, Smit's scouts had reported back to the Boer bivouac under the Drakensberg next to the Ingogo River that Colley's force was on the move southwards. Smit immediately gave his men the order to saddle up and to move east towards Schuinshoogte and there to await the British with the intention of attacking them while strung out on the march. About midday British scouts riding ahead of the column south of the Ingogo noted the presence of Boer patrols. When they reported back the column had just waded across the drifts where the water was only knee-height, and Colley reformed it on the level ground south of the double drift before resuming his march. As the column approached the foot of the plateau, scouts breasting the rise suddenly encountered Smit's force of some 200 mounted men drawn up on a low ridge about 1,000 yards to the west of the road. They were in a strong skirmishing line with several bodies in support. The British vedettes hastily fell back to warn Colley. He responded by pushing forward rapidly with an advanced guard to occupy the edge of the ridge where the road ascended Schuinshoogte. The highest point of the position was a plateau, roughly triangular in shape, covered in short grass with a perimeter of rough outcrops of rock. The ground below the plateau was also dotted with rocks, but the tambookie-grass which grew there was much more luxuriant, four feet high in places and offering excellent cover.

As the British artillery came up onto the heights of the plateau, Smit's men on their ridge seemed to hesitate at the sight of these still dreaded weapons. Then Smit ordered his force to spread out and charge the British, even though many of their horses were too tired and weak from prolonged campaigning to manage even a canter. The guns quickly unlimbered and fired two shells which were only just too high to hit their target and fell behind the Boers. So instead of turning back to seek shelter, the Boers accelerated obliquely down the ridge, and when they reached the foot of the plateau dismounted and scattered for cover, setting up a heavy and accurate fire on the British guns and skirmishers who were beginning to come into action. Butler later wrote that with this intrepid movement the Boers seized the initiative and sealed the fortunes of the day. It showed the Boers were no longer daunted by artillery, and that they were confident in fighting it out with the British in the open. At Bronkhorstspruit they had chosen the ground and laid an ambush; while at Laing's Nek they had fought on the defensive on prepared ground. But the fight at Ingogo came on unexpectedly and the Boers demonstrated that they were sufficiently versatile to take advantage of opportunities when they arose.[18]

When the four British infantry companies came up the hill they were extended in skirmishing order around part of the rocky perimeter on both sides of the guns facing the Boers, the right flank parallel to the road, and returned fire. But the Boers did not disperse under this weight of fire as Colley had presumed they would. Instead, they made practised use of the folds in the ground below the plateau, of the excellent cover afforded by the tambookie-grass and the convenient scattering of large rocks to work closer towards the British. They then rapidly threw out their right to envelope the soldiers. In danger of being outflanked, and with too few horsemen to attempt to roll up the dangerously extended Boer right, the British extended still further in a rough circle around the plateau until the only undefended sector was that on the north-east. The guns were repositioned so that one fired from the south of the perimeter, and the other from the north. By 12h15 firing was heavy all around Schuinshoogte.

The 3/60th Rifles lay prone, taking what advantage they could of the rocky cover while surrounding Boer fire raked them from the front and rear. Being against the skyline on the plateau the British made good targets for the accurate Boer fire. The British found it almost impossible to raise their heads above the rocks to return fire, and all too many British helmets later seen by burial parties had at least two bullet holes in them, and one as many as six. For lack of cover the unfortunate horses proved particularly easy targets. The artillerymen who valiantly continued to service their guns were also vulnerable to the Boer fire which concentrated on picking them off. Captain Greer, serving the southern gun, early became a fatality. Colley, as a means of taking the pressure off Lieutenant Parson's gun, ordered Major Brownlow and the men of the Mounted Squadron to charge the Boers to the north. Brownlow moved his horsemen to the edge of plateau where they became sitting ducks as he tried to steady them in formation. Before they could charge, a Boer volley carefully aimed at their horses from a range of little more than 150 yards hit half of the unfortunate animals and wounded one man. Thoroughly daunted, Brownlow brought his men back and dismounted those who still had horses. His was indeed an unfortunate record, for to his ignominious rout at Laing's Nek was added the aborted charge at Schuinshoogte.

Casualties continued to mount among the artillerymen working their pieces, half of whom were hit, and volunteers from the 3/60th Rifles began to take their places. Colley had at length no choice but to withdraw the guns from the exposed perimeter. With their field of fire against the surrounding Boers consequently limited, they concentrated instead on Boer reinforcements moving late in the afternoon towards the battlefield by a road behind Inkwelo from the laagers at Laing's Nek. However, the approaching Boers made such excellent use of cover that the artillery fire was ineffective. By nightfall Boer numbers had grown by another 100 or so to about 300. Close to sunset Joubert despatched a further 200 reinforcements from Laing's Nek, but they got no further than the foot of Majuba. Limited as Smit's numbers remained, therefore, the rapid and sustained firepower they were able to concentrate on the British position persuaded Colley that he was facing at least 1,000 Boers by evening and not, in reality, a force slightly smaller than his own. Colley, as he later wrote to his wife, found he could not break off the engagement with his small force and want of cavalry, and had no option but to hold the plateau until night, when he hoped to draw off.[19]

At about 14h30 the Boers initiated an attempt to move further around to the north-east in order to enfilade the open flank of the British perimeter. This manoeuvre, if successful, would greatly have increased the casualty-rate within the British position. Colley ordered out the reserve company of the 3/60th rifles, many of them young recruits, to foil it. They were commanded by Captain J.C. MacGregor, RE, Colley's Assistant Military Secretary who had served in both the Anglo-Zulu War and the Sekhukhune campaign. Despite his experience, he miscalculated. He led his men out too far below the brow of the plateau to a position detached from the rest of the British line and within 50 yards of the Boers. This vulnerable position was, more-over, fatally exposed since there were hardly any rocks for cover. The men nevertheless gallantly held on despite appalling casualties. Fifty-six were killed or wounded, and only four riflemen and one officer (the diminutive Lieutenant Francis Beaumont who had coxed the Oxford University Eight for three years[20]) survived unscathed. Their extreme bravery under intense fire succeeded in preventing the Boers from completing their encirclement, but MacGregor, who led his men forward while absurdly still mounted, became the latest of Colley's ill-fated staff to perish. Surely, with few other generals can a staff posting have proven so perilous.

At one stage volunteers, frustrated at being pinned down for hours, suggested they attempt a bayonet charge against the Boers in this same sector, but Colley, having seen the devastating effects of Boer fire against the 58th Regiment at Laing's Nek, would not give permission. Colley later com-mended the coolness and steadiness of the 'comparatively young' soldiers of the 3/60th Rifles who had 'fired steadily, husbanding their ammunition' and holding or changing their ground in good order.[21]

Somewhere about 15h30 there was a lull in the battle, when Colley managed to send off two despatch riders to Mount Prospect. They carried orders to bring up two further companies of the 58th Regiment to join the companies of the 3/60th Rifles and 58th Regiment already stationed overlooking the two drifts with their two 7-pounders. When it became clear that the Boers did not have the forces facing the British left rear to oppose reinforcements, Colley next ordered a company of the 58th Regiment to remain with the 7-pounders, while the two reinforcing companies of the 58th Regiment, with the company of the 3/60th, pack mules carrying ammunition and six pairs of horses for the artillery, were to move down towards the drifts and occupy a position on a ridge overlooking them to the west of the road. This initiative was timely, for during the later afternoon a considerable body of Boers made a move on the double drift with the intention of cutting off Colley's retreat. The arrival of the reinforcements Colley had ordered up, combined with effective firing from the two 7-pounders supported by Parson's battery on Schuinshoogte, sufficiently discouraged the Boer advance. At 18h00 Colley ordered half a company of the advanced force to stay in their position above the drifts while the rest moved in skirmishing order over the Ingogo Drift to a stony hill to the east of the road.

Meanwhile, the situation on the plateau was awful. Wounded horses were tearing about trampling everything in their path. Without a water cart it was impossible to slake the tormenting thirst of the ever-mounting numbers of wounded being tended by the overwhelmed Surgeon McGann and his small staff in their 'hospital', which was sheltered by the bodies of shot artillery horses. Many wounded lay untended as it was impossible to remove them under the heavy fire, and the Boers had already shot up the one ambulance wagon with the column. Throughout the hot afternoon the firing continued to flare up and then die down again for a while. The Boers, like the British, were suffering from exhaustion brought on by lack of water and food, the heat of the day and the terrible strain of skirmishing from behind minimal cover – though they were much better than the British in making effective use of the terrain for shelter, and improvising little breastworks of packed stones with loopholes for firing through. But they were also running short of ammunition.[22]

As is normal in the summer rainfall area of the foothills of the Drakensberg, the sultry afternoon which had been full of heavy thunder was finally relieved soon after 17h00 by a torrential downpour. The men could drink again but, typically, the temperature dropped drastically in the pelting rain and many of the wounded succumbed to the sudden wet and chill. The light at last began to fade, and at 18h00 the Boers raised a white flag. Colley, who had been coolly exposing himself all day to enemy fire, had the ceasefire sounded and sent forward his chaplain to parley. Many Boers used the opportunity to move closer to the British line, while firing continued on the opposite flank where the Boers seemed in ignorance of the parley. In these unsatisfactory circumstances Colley recalled Ritchie and the fight went desultorily on. This was the third time during the war that the Boers had apparently exploited a flag of truce, and the British perception of their ingrained treachery was confirmed. On the Boer side, Smit did his best to encourage his men – now also wet and cold and running out of ammunition – to attack once more and win the battle before complete darkness. However, there was growing danger that they would fire on each other in the dark, and Smit's young men in particular believed the British would not be able to withdraw in a storm across the swollen river, and could not be made to sacrifice themselves in a final push.[23]

All firing on Schuinshoogte ceased by 19h30. The British had expended 40.5 rounds per carbine and 40 per rifle, quadruple the average in a typical 'small war' so heavy had been the engagement, and double the expenditure at Laing's Nek. The artillery had thrown 78 shrapnel shells and 32 common, more than at the pitched battle of Ulundi.[24] Over the next hour and more Colley had the British wounded collected together and tended as well as possible. But what was Colley to do next? There were too few troops available to relieve him, and the camp at Mount Prospect was itself now weakly defended and extremely vulnerable to attack. On the plateau Colley's sodden men were without food or shelter and had only rainwater to drink or the wet grass to chew. There was no way of replenishing their ammunition, and Colley could not see how they could successfully fend off an anticipated Boer attack in the morning. The only alternative to capitulation, therefore, was a hazardous night retreat. And if this were put off too long, the drifts across the Ingogo and Harte, swollen by the storm, would be impassable. That, in turn, would cut off any possible reinforcements. By 21h30, when heavy rain began to fall again, Colley was ready to prepare for his last throw. Out of the 76 horses with the column, 39 had been killed and most of the rest wounded. The few remaining relatively unscathed horses were attached to the two guns and to one of the ammunition limbers. The rest of the limbers were abandoned and the ammunition destroyed or buried. Those men too seriously wounded to move were left on the field under the care of the padre, the Reverend Richie, and Surgeon McGann who had bravely exposed himself throughout the day. All too many of the wounded would die of exposure during the cold, rainy night.

The Boers had made a major miscalculation. Smit mistakenly believed that since all the British horses were either dead or wounded, it would be impossible for the British to withdraw their guns across the Ingogo, flooded by the volume of water that rises in the nearby mountains during a storm. So, calculating that the British could not move in the dark and rain and would still be stranded on Schuinshoogte in the morning, Smit set no guards and ordered his cold, rain-soaked men to find what shelter they could and prepare to resume the battle at first light.

Colley began his march in intense darkness at about 23h00. The men were formed in a hollow square in extended order with the guns in the middle and what was left of the Mounted Squadron in skirmishing order all around. They moved cautiously forward, maintaining a strict silence, though the noise of the guns over the stone could have been easily heard, even through the drumming of the rain. For fear of non-existent Boer patrols they approached the river across the hills rather than by the road, and reached it undetected. Colley halted the column and sent forward a few scouts to make sure that the drift was clear of Boers. After keeping the column anxiously waiting for over an hour, they reported no Boers were holding the drift (the few Boer sentries had taken shelter from the rain), but were also unable in the darkness, teeming rain and noise of the storm to locate the whereabouts of the British forces stationed at the river. These had withdrawn with the fall of darkness to concentrate on the ridge overlooking the drifts from the north. Crossing the drifts was extremely hazardous for the swiftly running river had risen to the height of men's armpits on account of the downpour, and they had to link arms to cross safely. Even so, six of the 3/60th Rifles were drowned. Once across the river the men had to help the exhausted and wounded horses drag the guns and wagon up the long, uphill road, made as slippery as ice by the rain, until they finally reached Mount Prospect at about 04h00 on the morning of 9 February. The depleted garrison was mightily relieved to see them, for they had nervously been anticipating a Boer attack all night.

Very early on that cold, foggy morning, Smit sent urgently to Joubert for more ammunition, and his shivering men prepared to renew the fight. They were astounded when they found nothing on the battlefield but the dead and wounded whom Colley had left behind when he slipped away. The guns, which they had confidently expected to capture, had vanished.[25] Since they presumed they had killed enough artillery horses to prevent Colley from taking the guns with him, they could only imagine that he had somehow succeeded in hiding them. The Boers spent many days afterwards searching the battlefield for them, and the river too. In the course of the morning Joubert arrived on the battlefield with more than 100 men and

9 wagons and loaded up the ammunition and everything else of use which the British had abandoned. Later that morning an unarmed party of NMP brought up ambulance wagons, and the Boers humanely helped load them with the wounded. They permitted the NMP to set off back to Newcastle where the badly shaken townspeople were vainly clamouring to be admitted to the town laager, which the Natal government had constructed in 1877–1878 by connecting all the solid government buildings by a brick wall around an enclosed yard.[26] Later that day a burial party of 40 men of the 3/60th Regiment returned to the battlefield to help bury the dead.

Once again, British casualties had been very heavy indeed. The 3/60th Rifles had lost 2 officers and 56 men killed and 3 officers and 60 wounded with Bugler J. Field taken prisoner, a crushing 40 per cent casualty rate. Lieutenant E.O.H. Wilkinson, Old Etonian, Adjutant of the 3/60th Rifles, and veteran of the Anglo-Zulu War, whom Colley regretfully described as of 'singularly winning disposition and manners' and cool and gallant in battle,[27] drowned late that day while crossing the river for the fourth time as he returned to help the wounded. His body was not recovered until 18 February, wedged between rocks five miles below the drifts. With his death, Colley lamented, he had lost 'every personal friend' he had messed with or he and his wife, Edith, had 'become intimate' with.[28] The Artillery had lost one officer and 2 men killed and an officer and 11 men wounded (or 50 per cent casualties) and 14 of their 27 horses. The ineffective Mounted Squadron had suffered only 3 killed and 2 wounded, but had lost 23 of their 38 horses. Once again Colley's staff had been badly hit. Captain MacGregor, his Assistant Military Secretary, was dead, and his Dutch and Zulu inter-preter, Marthinus Stuart, the Resident Magistrate of the Ixopo Division of southern Natal, had been killed as he tried to bring in a wounded man. 'Lucky' Major Essex survived unscathed yet again. Boer losses are once more unclear, but seem to have been 8 killed and 9 wounded, 2 mortally. This meant the British expended 514 rounds of small arm ammunition and 6 shells for each Boer casualty they inflicted.[29]

Despite their evident success, Commandant Smit and the Boers were left kicking themselves at the opportunity they had let slip. Colley's capit-ulation had seemed a certainty, and they could scarcely believe that he had succeeded in getting back safely to his camp with his guns.[30] For his part, though he had contrived to slip away under the cover of darkness and rain in a very hazardous manoeuvre which he could have presented as a victory of sorts, Colley was under no illusion that the day's fighting represented a dismal reverse. As Lieutenant Marling wryly put it, 'one or two more Pyrrhic victories like this and we shan't have any army left at all'.[31] After two costly defeats the NFF was in no position to take the initiative again, and Colley was left with no option but to remain strictly on the defensive until the arrival of the promised reinforcements. Almost 25 per cent of his men lay dead or wounded, he had lost many close comrades on his staff, and all he wished for now was a quick end to 'this hateful war'[32] in which he had singularly failed to distinguish himself as a field commander. Not only had the Boers thrown him back from their defensive positions on Laing's Nek, but they had thoroughly worsted him on open ground at Ingogo as well. Novices the Boers might have been in 'the business of tactics', but they were 'apt students', and in the effective deployment of mounted rifleman they had shown the outclassed British that 'a new power had been developed in war'.[33] Colley admitted precisely that when he informed Childers on 16 February that none of his troops were nearly as well trained as the Boers in musketry, skirmishing, equitation and the use of cover, that his artillery did not at all compensate for his crucial lack of good mounted troops which 'had told so heavily' against him. As a result of all these deficiencies his unfortunate troops (despite a superficial cheeriness) were acquiring a fatal 'sense of inferiority and want of confidence in themselves'.[34] Boer morale was now as high as that of the British was dangerously low.

Notes and references

1 For operations by the NFF between the engagements at Laing's Nek and Ingogo, see Butterfield, ed., *War and Peace*, pp. 198–201: Journal of the Natal Field Force, 29 January–7 February 1881.

2 Butler, *Pomeroy-Colley*, pp. 293–4.

3 WO 32/7810, no. 079/4016: Colley to Childers, 1 February 1881.

4 *BPP* (C. 2837), no. 4: Childers to Colley, 29 January 1881.

5 *BPP* (C. 2837), no. 6: Colley to Childers, 30 January 1881.

6 A Zulu resurgence had become an entirely unlikely eventuality since Wolseley's fragmentation of the Zulu kingdom at the end of the Anglo-Zulu War, but played on longstanding fears of a general African uprising in southern Africa.

7 Schreuder, *Gladstone and Kruger*, p. 113.

8 *BPP* (C. 2837), no. 8: Colley to Childers, 3 February 1881.

9   Grobler, 'Laingsnek', p. 157. See Norris-Newman, *With the Boers*, p. 170; Bellairs, ed., *Transvaal War*, p. 377; H. Rider Haggard, *Cetywayo and his White Neighbours; or, Remarks on Recent Events in Zululand, Natal and the Transvaal* (London, 1888), p. 228.

10 Norris-Newman, *With the Boers*, pp. 179–81, 190–1.

11 BV 1, p. 195: Joubert to Kruger, 28 January 1881; pp. 204–5: Joubert to Kruger, 30 January 1881; p. 263: Joubert to Kruger, 3 February 1881; *De Staatscourant Gedurenden den Vrijheidsoorlog van 1881*, p. 17: Joubert to P.A. Cronjé, 28 January 1881.

12 Meintjes, *Commandant-General*, p. 79.

13 Meintjes, *Commandant-General*, p. 79.

14 In Zulu, an *ingogo* is a bag made of skin, used for carrying food. Why the river should bear this name is not known.

15 Grobler, 'Die Geveg by Schuinshoogte' in Van Jaarsveld, Van Rensburg and Stals, eds, *Eerste Vryheidsoorlog*, p. 164.

16 Carter, *Boer War*, p. 196.

17 First-hand accounts of the battle of Ingogo (Schuinshoogte) upon which the following descriptions are, unless otherwise indicated: *BPP* (C. 2837), no. 22: Colley to Childers, 9 February 1881; WO 32/7813, no. 079/4184: Colley to Childers, 12 February 1881; Butterfield, ed., *War and Peace*, pp. 201–6: Journal of the Natal Field Force, Tuesday, 8 February and Wednesday, 9 February 1881; Butler, *Pomeroy-Colley*, pp. 297–315; Carter, *Boer War*, pp. 197–226. Carter accompanied Colley's column across the Ingogo and was present at the battle and during the retirement that night. See also Norris-Newman, *With the Boers*, pp. 157–64, 344–9; Lady Bellairs, ed., *Transvaal War*, pp. 377–9; Ransford, *Majuba Hill*, pp. 51–60; Lehmann, *Boer War*, pp. 164–74; Grobler, 'Schuinshoogte' in Van Jaarsveld, Van Rensburg and Stals, eds, *Eerste Vryheidsoorlog*, pp. 164–72.

18 Butler, *Pomeroy-Colley*, p. 300.

19 Colley to Lady Colley, 9–19 February 1881, quoted in Butler, *Pomeroy-Colley*, p. 313.

20 Lt P. Marling and Lt B.M. Hamilton, quoted in Emery, *Marching over Africa*, pp. 107–8.

21 WO 32/7813, no. 079/4184: Colley to Childers, 12 February 1881.

22 JC 26, no. 2455: N.J. Smit to Joubert, 9 February 1881; *De Staatscourant Gedurenden den Vrijheidsoorlog*, 9 February 1881, p. 34: Het gevecht bij Schuinshoogte (Door een Engelsh ooggetuige, 8 February 1881).

23 *De Staatscourant Gedurenden den Vrijheidsoorlog*, 23 February 1881, p. 29: Joubert to H.P. Malan, 11 February 1881; Smit's account to an English officer, quoted in Butler, *Pomeroy-Colley*, p. 307.

24 The British infantry shot away 7,010 rifle rounds, the Mounted Infantry 1,625 carbine rounds, and the officers 110 revolver rounds (Butterfield, ed., *War and Peace*, pp. 204–5: Journal of the Natal Field Force, Tuesday, 8 February 1881).

25 JC 26, no. 2455: N.J. Smit to Joubert, 9 February 1881.

26 Holt, *Mounted Police*, p. 105; Laband and Thompson, *Buffalo Border*, p. 22.

27 WO 32/7813, no. 079/4184: Colley to Childers, 12 February 1881.

28 Colley to Lady Colley, 9 February 1881 and Colley to his sister, 16 February 1881, quoted in Butler, *Pomeroy-Colley*, pp. 308–9, 311.

29 Butterfield, ed., *War and Peace*, pp. 204–5: Journal of the Natal Field Force, Tuesday, 8 February 1881; WO 32/7813, no. 079/4184: Report by Captain E. Essex, 14 February 1881: Natal Field Force, List of Casualties on 8 February 1881; *De Staatscourant Gedurenden den Vrijheidsoorlog*, 16 February 1881, p. 27: note by P.A. Cronjé, 15 February 1881; 11 May 1881, p. 62: Gewond in den slag op Schuinshoogte.

30 Colley to Lady Colley, 9–19 February 1881, quoted in Butler, *Pomeroy-Colley*, p. 314.

31 Lt Marling, quoted in Emery, *Marching over Africa*, p. 110.

32 Colley to his sister, Lily, 16 February 1881, quoted in Butler, *Pomeroy-Colley*, p. 312.

33 Butler, *Pomeroy-Colley*, pp. 313, 316–17.

34 Colley to Childers, 16 February 1881, quoted in Butler, *Pomeroy-Colley*, pp. 317–18.

chapter 9

Seeking a way out of the war

ollowing Colley's reverses at Laing's Nek and Ingogo, it became obvious to General Smyth at the Cape that the war must now be a prolonged one, and that it would be 'mere military prudence' to have a column ready in Cape Town for any 'unforeseen emergency'. He suggested to Sir Hercules Robinson that, conditional on having sufficient reinforcements, a second column operating out of Cape Town should be sent to assist the NFF.[1] Robinson and the Cape government still believed that direct military involvement in the struggle against the Transvaal would bring a hornet's nest of pro-Boer sentiment about their ears, but were reluctantly prepared to yield local political considerations 'to the general interests of the Queen's service'.[2] Fortunately, perhaps, they were never called on to do so because in England the military experts remained at odds over the best course to follow. Sir Garnet Wolseley, with all his South African experience, strongly warned against the logistical, political and military dangers and disadvantages of the mooted second column, but the influential Deputy Quartermaster-General, Sir Archibald Alison, strongly advocated the advance of a powerful column through the Orange Free State as 'the surest means of bringing this unfortunate war to a termination'.[3] However, a political solution imposed by Gladstone's government would bring the war to an end before it was decided whether or not to activate the second, inland column Alison favoured, and its efficacy would never be put to the test. In the interim, the obvious course seemed that of sufficiently reinforcing the NFF to ensure its military success.

Colley, meanwhile, was trying to cope with the immediate aftermath of defeat.[4] He wrote to Joubert on 9 February acknowledging the Commandant-General's 'courtesy' in permitting the removal of the British wounded after the battle of Ingogo and offered in return medical assistance for the Boer wounded.[5] The next day the Boers received Colley's ready permission to permit nine wagons of wounded Boers to pass from Ingogo west of Inkwelo Mountain to Laing's Nek under the protection of a flag showing the Red Cross. This was only as it should be, for Colley's government had instructed him to treat the Boers according to the recognised rules of civilised warfare and to respect ambulances and Red Cross personnel in accordance with the Geneva Convention of 22 August 1864.[6]

At Laing's Nek the bodies of the officers had been carried from the field on the afternoon of the battle for burial at Mount Prospect, but this had not been possible at Ingogo. There the five dead officers had hurriedly been buried with the other ranks and horses in three large pits before Colley withdrew. On 12 February Colley ordered the Reverend Richie with two officers and ten men of the 3/60th Rifles to proceed to Ingogo under flag of truce to exhume the officers' bodies for appropriate reburial. It was a day of pouring rain, vultures scavenged the battlefield, and many of those opening the pits were violently sick at the disgusting work.[7] They returned in the afternoon to bury the corpses with military honours in a third row of graves in the cemetery near the camp. The band accompanied the interment with the doleful strains of the 'Dead March' in *Saul*.[8]

On 14 February the convoy of empty British ambulances returned from Newcastle without any incident. But it was reported that communication by mail cart between Newcastle and the Biggarsberg to its south had been cut since 12 February by a large party of Boers at the Ngagane River, who had also rustled horses and burned and looted passing wagons.[9] The next day they cut the telegraph wire to Ladysmith. Anticipating that they would also cut the line between Mount Prospect and Newcastle, the British attempted to extemporise a heliograph apparatus, but were foiled by the cloudy weather and interminable rain. To keep spirits up Colley ordered athletic sports in the camp on 16 February, and the mule race was apparently 'great fun' and the men 'thoroughly amused'.[10]

Yet Colley had urgently to look beyond his immediate circumstances and take stock of the wider military situation. On 11 February he was forced into the compounded humiliation of requesting Childers to send the reinforcements he had turned down with misplaced confidence a few days before, only for the War Secretary to reply that these were no longer sufficient and that he was sending out more immediately, and that further units were available from India, Ceylon and Bermuda.[11] Meanwhile, reinforcements already on their way began to pour in, and everyone at Mount Prospect was cheered to learn that they were steadily approaching Newcastle. The 15th (King's) Hussars, the 2/60th Regiment (King's Royal Rifle Corps) and F/3 Brigade, RA – all of which had sailed from India on HMS *Euphrates* and disembarked on 25 January in Durban – as well as the 92nd Regiment (Gordon Highlanders), who had likewise sailed from India on HMS *Crocodile* and had landed on 30 January, were now all on their way up-country from the port. The 83rd Regiment (County of Dublin), which had sailed on the *Crocodile* with the 92nd Highlanders, remained just south of Pietermaritzburg in the Lilliefontein camp near the Richmond Road station. The 97th (Earl of Ulster's) Regiment from Halifax and Gibralter, who had arrived in Durban on 4 February on HMS *Tamar*, also remained at the coast. A wing of the 6th (Inniskilling) Dragoons and Barrow's Mounted Infantry,[12] who arrived shortly thereafter on HMS *Hankow*, proceeded up-country, the Mounted Infantry on re-mounts brought around by sea from the Cape. The transports *Ararat*, *Palmyra* and *Queen* followed with the rest of the Inniskilling Dragoons, and drafts for the 97th Regiment and Artillery.[13]

In command of these reinforcements was the popular and energetic Sir Evelyn Wood. He had cooperated well with the Boers of the Utrecht District when he had been in command of No. 4 Column during the Anglo-Zulu War, and he had been almost unique in emerging from that unfortunate war with his reputation enhanced. Though Wood was associated with the Wolseley Ring, he was also a canny political soldier who knew how to keep his options open. The Duke of Cambridge consequently had felt able to approach him as early as 4 January with the intention of sending him out to South Africa to buttress Colley, in whose operational abilities he had limited faith. Wood consented to serve under Colley as his second-in-command – though in fact one senior to him in the Army List – only on condition that he retained the rank and pay he currently enjoyed at his Chatham command. His rank of Brigadier-General on the Staff of the Army in South Africa thus secured,[14] Wood went to see Kimberley, who candidly let him know that he favoured the retrocession of the Transvaal. Wood then did not set sail until the Queen, with whom he was a great personal

into action by other, ingenious means. While out on a mounted picquet, Lieutenant Pigott of the 60th Rifles found a letter on Inkwelo addressed to 'Mr Colley', in which the writer jeered that the Boers were tired of waiting for the 'English' whom they had once believed to be plucky, but now knew to be otherwise, and that meanwhile the English were starving in Pretoria.[20]

Indeed, while Colley was stalled below Laing's Nek and no nearer relieving them, the beleaguered garrisons were hanging grimly on in generally deteriorating circumstances. Since the Boers besieging the British fort at Potchefstroom were not prepared to storm the position, their only option was to keep the noose tight until starvation, disease, exposure or events elsewhere caused the garrison to surrender. To this end they continued to improve their encircling trench system. By 7 March they had added a strong point, with a wall of earth and sandbags some 4 yards high, only 100 yards from the fort which was crammed with soldiers and civilians. From it they commanded the whole British position with accurate rifle fire. The sick and wounded were squeezed into the badly shot-up medical tents and by the end of February numbers of the defenders began to die of enteric fever. Stocks of food were down to maize and sorghum and these were almost entirely depleted by early March when scurvy broke out.[21] Even so, after the war Sir Garnet Wolseley wrote to the War Office stating that Colonel Winslow 'might have done better' with his defence of Potchefstroom.[22] Wood disagreed, and his official opinion was 'that the defence was gallant, well conducted and reflects credit on all concerned'.[23] However, Wood did single out Major Thornhill, RA, for his failure in 'enterprise and resource' in the way he handled the two precious 9-pounder guns during the siege, and tartly reminded him that 'the first duty of an Artillery Officer is to destroy the enemy, and that to improve cover for his men although an essential is but a secondary consideration'.[24]

The situation was somewhat better for the defenders at Lydenburg though, as at Potchefstroom, the Boers kept up a close and active investment. The garrison successfully brought their home-made gun, which fired a 2 lb 6 oz round shot, into action on 1 February. The Boers then moved the less protected of their two guns to the ruins of the levelled laager 150 yards from the fort, where an iron screen gave it good protection. Even carefully placed volleys by the defenders every time the gun was run out did not deter the Boer gunners, and they continued to rain shots on the crumbling buildings within the fort. Yet, since the Boer bombardment and sniping were irregular, the defenders could exploit the moments of respite to repair shot and bullet holes. After dark they replenished supplies by shooting and collecting cattle that strayed close to the fort. Raiding parties also sallied out on several occasions, and tried to dislodge the Boers from outposts they had established close to the fort. In turn, the Boers attempted to tunnel under the fort, but were deterred when the garrison succeeded in exploding a mine. As the siege progressed Lieutenant Long had to cut the garrison's rations, but never to the extent suffered by the defenders of Potchefstroom. The water supply, though, became an increasing problem, and on 3 February Long reduced the water ration to one pint a day. Deepening the existing well and sinking another made little difference, though heavy rains helped the situation. There was no shortage of beer for those who would drink it, and these had their water ration augmented by a pint of beer a day. In early March the siege flared up one last time when the Boers succeeded in setting fire to some of the thatched roofs, followed by heavy rifle and cannon fire lasting several hours which inflicted several casualties.[25]

At Rustenburg Captain Auchinleck conducted an active defence to Wood's subsequent approbation.[26] When on 4 February the Boers opened a new sap some 400 yards to the rear of the fort, he sallied under cover of darkness with nine men and drove the besiegers out of their trench. Alerted, the Boers brought down a heavy fire. Auchinleck was wounded and his party retired. On 3 March the Boers brought their second Ras gun into action, and every few days it fired several rounds. But the investment remained a stalemate and, though under heavy fire from close range, the garrison was never put under serious pressure.[27]

When Colley's relieving force failed to arrive in Standerton by the end of January as promised, Major Montague proclaimed martial law, requisitioned all supplies and placed the townspeople on the ration list. His administration was firm and decisive and the civil population responded well. He too attempted to conduct an active defence, and before dawn on 7 February led out a sally of some 70 men to the north of the town. He was quickly driven in again by the Boers with a few wounded on both sides. Smaller-scale raids continued to be mounted occasionally, but with little effect except some welcome excitement. Otherwise, this siege too settled into a stalemate. Neither the garrison nor townspeople suffered anything like the hardships endured at other posts like Potchefstroom, though they were constantly harassed by long-range rifle fire.[28] Wood was of the opinion that the successful defence of Standerton on the main road between Heildelberg and Laing's Nek had a material influence on the campaign, for 'the position enchained in its front a considerable force of Boers' who otherwise would have rein-forced Joubert's commando.[29]

The occasional brisk skirmish occurred at Wakkerstroom, such as on 22 February when Private Osborne earned the Victoria Cross for rescuing a wounded comrade,[30] but otherwise the investment remained neither an onerous nor a close one, and the garrison was never seriously menaced.[31] At Marabastad, where the Boer investment had got off to a slow start, continu-ous rain and a well kept the garrison well supplied with water, and obtain-ing food was no problem since it was easy enough to pass through the Boer outposts. Fresh meat was available right up to the end of the siege. Firing ceased on most Sundays. Conditions in the fort were naturally unpleasant, but nothing like the deprivations and hardships at Potchefstroom and Lydenburg were suffered, and it was only towards the end, after 17 March, that increased Boer activity forced the garrison to keep within the fort.[32]

After the end of the war the Duke of Cambridge wrote to Wood ordering him to recommend officially a few officers he thought 'worthy of honours in defence of their posts . . . during the uprising', and to recommend several whose conduct for gallantry should not pass unnoticed.[33] Wood secured the Duke's permission to respond privately since 'a frank expression of opin-ions' would be more useful'.[34] Among those deserving promotion he placed Auchinleck at Rustenburg nearly at the top of his list since he had exhibited 'skill and courage, and made no mistakes'. He put Montague next for doing 'well' at Standerton, but added that although '[a]ll his arrangements were excellent . . . they were in part made by Captain Froom'. Captain Saunders, who had eighteen years' service, also did 'very well' at Wakkerstroom, while Brook at Marabastad made 'good' arrangements.[35]

Wood was to be much less complimentary about the conduct of the defence of Pretoria. He told the Duke that although he would have liked to have been able to recommended Bellairs for his leadership (the more so since Cambridge had good reports of him during his long service), he could not 'honestly write that he has done well. Pretoria was invested by a force which never exceeded the strength of *Half* the garrison, and the investing force was scattered on a circle of some 60 miles, and the fact that he never himself went under fire, was not conducive to success.'[36] In Wood's eyes Colonel Gildea proved himself the most able soldier in the Transvaal because he commanded the 2/21st Fusiliers 'very well' and was the 'active agent at Pretoria'.[37] This judgement is borne out by the final weeks of the siege of Pretoria. Lanyon believed with Colley that more offensive operations were both feasible and necessary in order to break through the Boers thinly investing Pretoria. 'Inaction', he decided, 'brought on by dread of responsibility, has had a bad effect'.[38] Lanyon accordingly persuaded Bellairs to attempt one more attack on the Red House Laager. This time Gildea tried a night attack (that most difficult of operations to bring off successfully) in order to gain the advantage of surprise. At 02h00 on 12 February he led out a force of 606 men (273 of whom were mounted) with two 9-pounder guns, a Krupp 4-pounder and a rocket. Far from being caught napping, however, the well-positioned Boers were waiting for him. Despite the advantages of numbers and artillery support, Gildea's men were repulsed, almost outflanked and their disorderly retreat put in real danger of being cut off. Only one of the British was killed outright, but 17 (including Gildea himself) were severely wounded, with 7 or 8 of them subsequently dying. The Boers suffered no casualties at all.[39] Thoroughly chastened, the garrison never again attempted to venture forth. While under Bellairs's sole command as Gildea recovered from his wound, it remained unadventurously on the defensive. No news was any longer reaching Pretoria of the progress of the NFF (though rumours abounded of another disaster), and with no relief in sight, on 14 March Bellairs put male adults on half rations.[40]

Back in Natal, Colley was heartened by the arrival of reinforcements into believing that he would soon break through and relieve the Transvaal garrisons. In Newcastle on 21 February he addressed the newly arrived reinforcements who had been dubbed the 'Indian Column' because the Hussars and Highlanders had come straight from India where they had fought with distinction in the Second Afghan War of 1878–1880. They were accustomed to irregular warfare in difficult terrain against a determined foe, but Colley warned them against underestimating the Boers who fought and shot well.[41] The Indian Column marched out at 02h00 the following morning. Five companies of the 3/60th Rifles with a division of 9-pounders and a company of the 58th Regiment sallied out of Camp Mount Prospect to secure the drifts over the Ingogo for its passage, and the NMP were detailed to protect its left flank from Boer patrols coming over the Drakensberg. Contact was made between the two forces, and on the morning of 23 February Colley and his staff led in two squadrons of the 15th Hussars (103 all ranks), looking 'very odd in their big helmets and Karki jackets', six companies of the 92nd Highlanders (518 all ranks) bronzed and shaved and also in very light khaki tunics and wearing the kilt,[42] the Naval Brigade of 58 officers and men from HMS *Dido* (who had landed in Durban on 7 February) with their two

9-pounder guns, and various other details, making up a total of 727 officers and men, 105 horses, and 81 wagons and 4 carts. The 15th Hussars and 92nd Highlanders camped on the hill to the east of the existing camp. On their way discipline had temporarily broken down among these veterans and they had comprehensively looted a farmer's house on Schuinshoogte before burning it down. The farmer gained considerable compensation after a court of enquiry was held. A small fort was subsequently built on Schuinshoogte and garrisoned by 20 NMP and a few Highlanders under Major Napier.[43]

Having brought in the Indian Column, Wood returned to Pietermaritzburg, officially to accelerate the advance of other reinforcements – such as the 97th Regiment which had been ordered up from Ladysmith, and the Mounted Infantry, drawn from the 83rd Regiment and the Inniskilling Dragoons – though there is more than a hint that Colley wanted his famous subordinate out of the way while he planned his next move.[44]

While Colley was moving forward his reinforcements preparatory to breaking into the Transvaal, negotiations were simultaneously underway which had an entirely contradictory purpose. On 30 December 1880 Kimberley issued Sir Hercules Robinson with a set of 'Instructions' agreed upon by Cabinet to guide him as High Commissioner.[45] As far as the Transvaal was concerned, it was clear from the Instructions that the government was still determined to maintain annexation and was keeping the door open for confederation and its alluring vision of a self-governing and self-supporting South Africa. At that stage it appeared the government was more concerned about the Gun War in Basutoland and the possibility of a major African conflagration on the scale of the recent Anglo-Zulu War than it was about the consequences of a Boer rebellion. Yet, by an extraordinary anomaly, point 9 of the Instructions promised the 'Dutch of the Transvaal' a 'generous peace' once 'the authority of the Crown had been vindicated', and assured them of 'such full control of their local affairs as may be consistent with the general interests of Her Majesty's dominions in South Africa'. What exactly, it may well be asked, was Gladstone's Liberal administration actually trying to achieve in the Transvaal? It clarifies little that Gladstone himself said at the time, 'I have always regarded the South African question as the one great unsolved and perhaps insoluble problem of our colonial system.'[46]

It should be understood that the Transvaal crisis took a long time to reach the boil in Britain, and government was slow to respond, partly because of lack of public concern. Opinion was formed in later nineteenth century Britain by the newspaper media which were normally quick to take advantage of the sensational potential of the wars of empire. War correspondents and special artists had become a standard presence with British armies on active service and were regarded as the glamorous elite among journalists. Military self-advertisers like Wolseley or Wood knew well how to cultivate them to boost their own reputations.[47] However, compared with newspaper coverage of the recent Anglo-Zulu War and the Second Afghan War, the British press gave relatively little attention to the Transvaal campaign, and was slow to do so. After all, this war was taking place in an obscure part of the Empire quite unknown to most readers, and correspondents and artists reached the theatre of operations too late to cover the early stages of the fighting. Besides which, not only was reportage on the Transvaal Rebellion likely held back by the simultaneous but much more news-worthy assassination of Tsar Alexander II and the death of Disraeli, but it was also muted on account of shame at military defeat compounded by uneasy doubts about the propriety of fighting the Boers at all.[48]

T.F. Carter of the *Times of Natal*, who was the first newspaperman to arrive at the front (and who would later write the history of the war), was just too late to report the battle of Laing's Nek,[49] though he was present at Ingogo and would also personally witness Majuba, where the Boers captured him. No war correspondent had been there to describe the battle of Bronkhorstspruit. Charles Norris-Newman, who had been the *Standard* correspondent for the Anglo-Zulu War, was still in South Africa when the Transvaal Rebellion broke out. He was determined to report it from the 'enemy' side,[50] but did not manage to reach the Boer camp until after the fighting had ended, and was a first-hand witness only to the peace negotiations. Even more determined to get the Boer viewpoint across was Arthur Aylward, a Fenian, outspoken republican and sometime editor of the *Natal Witness* in Pietermaritzburg. As he could not secure British permission to join the Boers as a reporter, he simply absconded after the battle of Ingogo and sent in hard-hitting and anti-British reports from the Boer camp, including one of the battle of Majuba which the *Daily Telegraph* did not publish until 15 April (nearly two months afterwards), by which time the public temper in Britain had cooled.[51] Nor was it possible for reporters to put together a coherent story of the sieges for the British public because the Boers had sealed off the garrisons. The campaign was in any case brief, so that by the time the 'specials' did begin to arrive in any numbers the armistice was already in place.[52] Melton Prior, the famous war artist who had also been active in the Anglo-Zulu War, made it to the front, but his sketches did not appear in the *London Illustrated News* until 5 March 1881, by which time the fighting was over. C.E. Fripp, another veteran of the Zululand campaign, only did his drawings of Majuba a month after the battle.

Press criticism of Colley's generalship only became widespread in mid-February after the Ingogo fiasco though, for lack of concrete and authoritative information from the battle front, the media in Britain exploited his setbacks primarily to pursue their domestic political agendas. This was the moment for Conservative organs like the *Army and Navy Gazette* or *Daily Telegraph* to excoriate Liberal policy in South Africa, denounce short service and revel in the humiliation of the brightest star in Wolseley's Ring.[53]

The Transvaal Rebellion was first raised in the Commons only on 22 January 1881. When Cabinet had met on 30 December the pressing Irish issue was its first concern and the decision was taken to apply strong coercion there, as well as in the Transvaal. But behind this stern facade there were deep divisions. The more conservative Whig faction – which included Kimberley – was for militant coercion, while the Gladstonians – who, besides the Prime Minister himself, included Childers at the War Office – were instinctively against it. For a time the Whig faction prevailed because it was assumed by all that Colley would swiftly succeed against the Transvaal rebels. Yet by the end of January the bellicose party in Cabinet and its supporters among the permanent officials of the Colonial Office were in retreat, and the Gladstonians had prevailed with their policy of conciliation in South Africa. This revolution in Cabinet was caused by three factors in particular.

The first was the increasingly alarmed tone of reports from the Cape concerning the growing support among Afrikaners for the Transvaal cause. Throughout South Africa the Afrikaner population was being swept up into a storm of nationalism by news of the unexpected victories of their blood-brothers in the Transvaal, while British loyalists were increasingly dismayed. The press reflected these differences and was sharply divided in its response. *De Zuid-Afrikaan* and *De Patriot* in the Cape were strongly pro-Boer while the *Grahamstown Journal* was pro-British, as was the *Natal Mercury* in Durban. The *Natal Witness*, on the other hand, was much more critical and inclined to sympathise with the Boers. Newspapers were equally divided in the Orange Free State, with *De Vriend* siding against the Transvaal Boers and

De Express being for them.[54] In the Orange Free State President Brand found his neutrality being increasingly assailed; while in the Cape Colony meetings were held in every town and district and resolutions passed expressing sympathy with the Transvaal Boers and urging mediation and the adoption of a lenient settlement. Pro-Boer sentiment was manifest even in loyalist Natal, where the northern districts had a large Dutch-speaking population.[55] As January gave way to February 1881 public opinion became even more vehement, openly regretting the war, condemning the nature of British rule in the Transvaal, deploring Britain's violent methods, and calling for the restoration of the Transvaal's independence. Thousands were signing the blizzard of petitions which were warning of permanent damage to relations between the white races and the alienation of Afrikaner loyalty in the Cape. Deputations of leading Cape Afrikaners beat their way to Robinson's door.[56] The politically sophisticated Kruger was not slow to take advantage of the agitation. He addressed a public appeal to the Cape ministry for its support which was then endorsed by mass meetings and severely embarrassed J.G. Sprigg's predominantly English-speaking administration.[57] Considering the situation from its removed and broader vantage point, the British government was becoming increasingly concerned that with the temper of the country as it was, protracted military operations might well result in open civil war. The difficulty, though, following the humiliating and repeated defeats of British arms, was to find a settlement that was not an affront to British national honour and prestige.[58]

The second cause of cabinet concern was that the Africans in the Transvaal and elsewhere might take advantage of the conflict between the white races. Throughout the war the British government deprecated anything that 'would tend to excite a war of races throughout South Africa'. In particular, it earnestly hoped that Africans would not be drawn into the conflict because, as Kimberley put it, nothing could be 'more lamentably disastrous to the interests of white colonists'.[59] The Boers on various occasions complained that the British were using Africans in the field, but besides Nourse's Horse in Pretoria (a small body of mounted scouts built up on the black police force which pre-dated the rebellion),[60] the British never did so. Of course, as Haggard pointed out, the Transvaal administration 'need only have spoken one word to set an enormous number of armed men in motion against the Boers', but that was entirely against policy.[61] Lanyon definitively expressed the official British position when he turned down any possibility of the Tswana Chief Magato aiding the Rustenburg garrison – a prospect which sufficiently alarmed both Kruger himself and loyalist civilians in the neighbourhood into visiting Magato to browbeat him into neutrality.[62] Not only would it have had a 'baneful effect' upon British prestige to allow the 'natives' to believe that the government depended upon them to put down the rebellion, but it would also have been very difficult to 'restrain . . . a general and indiscriminate attack' from being made 'upon their ancient foes the Boers'.[63] The rebellion did fleetingly present the Africans of the Transvaal with a choice of white masters, and on the whole the British were deemed the lesser of two evils. As the captive Zulu king, Cetshwayo, succinctly put it: 'It will be a happy day for the black people of South Africa when the English are South Africa's sole rulers. The Boers are fond of lawlessness and taking away land from the dark races . . . We always wished to live with the English as our neighbours, but never with these dogs the Boers.'[64] The Boers in the Zoutpansberg District were thus playing with fire then when they tried to incite the Pedi to join them against the British, for the chiefs firmly decided to remain loyal.[65] So did the Tswana chiefs in the western districts, who gave sanctuary to several loyalists, took charge of government property and cattle, and kept safe the recently collected hut tax for the British-appointed commissioner.[66] Similarly, in the Waterberg District the Venda took charge of government property, defied the Boers and offered assistance to the British garrison at Marabastad.[67] The Boers also did their best to entice the Swazi into joining them, but the Special Border Commissioner, Sir Morrison Barlow, dissuaded them and prudently turned down their offers to attack the Boers instead.[68]

The final factor swaying the British government into reassessing its Transvaal policy was a dawning realisation that, for all his assurances, Colley was not actually winning the war in the Transvaal. Since the struggle was proving longer and more expensive than ever imagined, it had to be questioned whether it was worthwhile pursuing it to the bitter end.[69]

President Brand of the Orange Free State therefore made a crucial intervention when, on 10 January 1881, he offered Kimberley his services as mediator in order to reach a negotiated settlement for the Transvaal before his neutral republic was drawn into the war. Yet if Brand's timely overture helped change Kimberley's mind on the wisdom of pursuing a coercive policy in the Transvaal, Colley's defeat at Laing's Nek confirmed it. Fresh and alarmed reports of the rising tempo of Afrikaner agitation and its threats of civil war only served to underscore the need to find a way out of the war. At the Cabinet meeting of 29 January Kimberley presented his arguments in favour of negotiation and the faction favouring them carried the day.[70] For their part, the Transvaal Triumvirate were anything but averse to negotiations. Neither Kruger nor Joubert had ever imagined that they could achieve such a complete victory over the British forces that they could dictate peace terms. Rather, they saw their rebellion as a great demonstration of their determination to regain their independence. Just before the battle of Laing's Nek they issued a proclamation on 27 January stating their readiness to be satisfied with the 'annulment of the Annexation' and 'the restoration of the South African Republic, under the protection of the Queen'.[71] Following their success at Ingogo they again made known their desire for peace, which strongly suggests that they were fearful of the weight of reinforcements being built up against them, and that they wished to use their temporary military advantage to secure a political settlement before they were inevitably overwhelmed.[72]

Thus far Colley had been kept relatively in the dark concerning his government's pursuit of peace, but in early February he was drawn directly into the discussions going on between London, Heidelberg, Bloemfontein and Cape Town. He was clearly disconcerted by the direction these were taking and began to demur.[73] On 8 February Kimberley telegraphed Colley advising him that the British government was willing to treat with the Boers if they would submit and 'cease from armed opposition'.[74] As instructed, Colley informed President Brand of Kimberley's offer, but he was having none of this weak-kneed truck with rebels. In the immediate aftermath of the Ingogo battle he sharply responded on 10 February that he did not believe that any settlement could be permanent unless the Boer leaders were punished sufficiently to deter future malcontents from resorting to arms 'and bringing on the country all the calamities of civil war'.[75] He wrote again two days later, insisting that if any of the leaders of the revolt were allowed to retain positions of influence, 'the loyal and moderate parties [will] be afraid to come forward'.[76] But Colley was not making policy, and his arguments were based on the mistaken assumption that the British government intended to retain the Transvaal. A significant further step towards eventual retrocession was taken when Kruger, who had arrived at Laing's Nek to inspect the Boer positions, wrote Colley a letter on 12 February which he received the next day. Kruger had learned through Brand of Kimberley's conditions of 8 February, and now declared that his government was willing 'to submit to a Royal Commission of Enquiry, who we know will place us in our just rights', and undertaking to permit all British troops 'to retire with all honour' when ordered to be withdrawn. However, warned Kruger, should 'the annexation be persevered in', then 'subject to the will of God' the Boers were prepared to fight to the last man and the responsibility for all the attendant miseries would be on Colley's shoulders.[77]

In London, the Cabinet met again on 15 February in the midst of the mounting and wearying crisis in Parliament over Irish coercion. Kimberley and Gladstone persuaded their colleagues that the rising Boer unrest in South Africa was akin to the troubles sweeping Ireland, and that to avoid being embroiled in a second, comparable rebellion, the Transvaal must be let go.[78] When Colley met Wood in Newcastle on 17 February he was handed Kimberley's telegram of 16 February which followed hard on the Cabinet decision of 15 February. Kimberley announced that he was ready to accept Kruger's terms of 12 February and to call a Royal Commission. He authorised Colley to suspend hostilities if the Boers agreed to end their armed opposition.[79]

At this point Colley jibbed. Many believed this was on account of the urging of his wife Edith, Lady Colley, the daughter of Major-General H. Meade 'Tiger' Hamilton, whom Colley had married in 1878 at the age of 45, much to the surprise of vice-regal society in Simla. Lady Colley was no Victorian shrinking violet and played a very active role in Colley's public life. Wood wrote the Queen that he believed her burning ambition for her husband 'obliterates apparently every thought of the personal danger which he has undergone'.[80] This ungenerous judgement is contradicted by two of her letters to Colley on 15 and 24 February, respectively, in which she regretted that nothing she could do would keep him from performing his soldierly duty, and in which she touchingly declared that she would never again 'care a rush for any such rubbish as work or success' if she could but see him safe home again, and that 'nothing in this world is worth anything to me in comparison with that.'[81] No letter from his wife goading Colley into action has survived, though rumour had it that one such was found on his body. Colley's own desire to retrieve his reputation through a decisive engagement would have been no different from Lord Chelmsford's determination in July 1879 to win a validatory battle before resigning his command in Zululand.[82] As Colley wrote his wife on 18 February about the government's peace plans, 'I would rather resign than carry out the scheme I understand to be contemplated'. However, he then added the significant rider that he would soon have 'broken the back of military resistance, and my words may carry more weight than they would just now'.[83]

Apparently determined, therefore, to proceed with military operations despite the clearly stated wishes of his government, Colley still tried his best with words. On 19 February he caustically telegraphed Kimberley: 'There can be no hostilities if no resistance is made, but am I to leave Lang's Nek [sic], in Natal territory, in Boer occupation, and our garrisons isolated, and short of provisions, or occupy former and relieve latter?'[84] To which Kimberley responded immediately and in unambiguous terms: '. . . we do not mean you should march to the relief of garrisons or occupy Lang's Nek [sic], if arrangement proceeds. Fix reasonable time within which answer must be sent by Boers.'[85] Apparently stymied, Colley vented his anger and frustration with his political masters when he wrote on 21 February to Wolseley, his patron:

I am now getting together a force with which I think I could command success, but the Home Government seems so anxious to terminate the contest, that I am daily expecting to find ourselves negotiating with the 'Triumvirate' as the acknowledged rulers of a victorious people; in which case my failure at Lang's Nek [sic] will have inflicted a deep and permanent injury on the British name and power in South Africa which it is not pleasant to contemplate.[86]

On the same day, and in this frame of mind, Colley wrote to Kruger as instructed informing him that if the Boers ceased their 'armed opposition' the British government was prepared to appoint a Commission 'with large powers' to 'develop' Kimberley's proposal of 8 February. Colley ended: 'I am to add that upon this proposal being accepted within forty-eight hours, I have authority to agree to a suspension of hostilities on our part.'[87] This limited deadline of 48 hours was Colley's unauthorised intervention and would have fatal consequences. It seems Colley carried this letter written on 21 February with him back to Mount Prospect, and it was received by Commandant Smit on Laing's Nek only on 24 February. In Bok's official acknowledgement of the letter on 25 February he informed Colley that since Kruger had already returned to Heidelberg he had despatched the letter there by horseman, and that an answer could not be expected in less than four days. On 26 February Lieutenant-Colonel Herbert Stewart, 3rd Dragoon Guards, Colley's senior staff-officer and military secretary, learned from Smit that Kruger had gone on to Rustenburg, so any reply to the letter must be even further delayed.[88] Forty-eight hours had now passed, and Colley could convince himself that, as Butler put it, 'by the rules of war and of honour he was free to move'.[89] The Boers, on the other hand, could rest in their belief

certain is that he did not inform Cabinet of his intentions. With a renewed offensive clearly in mind, very early on the morning of the 24 February Colley and his staff, escorted by the 15th Hussars and the Mounted Squadron, crossed the Buffalo River at Van der Merwe's Drift and proceeded to a hill below Phogwane Mountain from which they obtained a full view of the Boers' position. What they saw alarmed them, for the Boers were throwing up fresh entrenchments either side of the nek and on the lower slopes of Majuba. They looked much more daunting against the skyline than they were in fact, but it was obvious that they would make any frontal attack on Laing's Nek more hazardous than before. Colonel Stewart, who had just joined Colley's staff, pondered alternative options with him. He later affirmed that it seemed a good idea to seize Majuba which commanded the right of the Boer position, and that since it was only guarded by day-time picquet, it was quite feasible to do so in a night attack. No documentation survives to explain precisely what were Colley's intentions in occupying Majuba, but Stewart believed he intended to seize the summit, build redoubts to secure the position, and remain there for at least three days, his line of approach kept open by two entrenched posts supported by artillery fire from Mount Prospect. Within a day or so the reinforcements marching from Newcastle would be able to join him, when they and the troops on Mount Prospect would be in a position to turn the flank of the Boers on Laing's Nek. Either that, or the sight of the British occupation of Majuba would make the Boers believe that their position had been turned so that they withdrew, opening the road to the Transvaal without further fighting.[93] Subsequently, critics have questioned Colley's state of mind at this juncture, citing his exhaustion and anguished determination to retrieve his military reputation as reasons for contemplating an absurd *coup de main*. Again, it has been suggested that Colley was taking advantage of Wood's temporary absence to gain all the credit for a stunning success, very much as Lord Chelmsford had seized his opportunity at Ulundi before Wolseley arrived to take over his command.[94] Yet it is clear that Colley and his staff did not embark on the venture impetuously. They spent the next days gaining what intelligence they could about Majuba, while keeping their plans as secret as possible. As a diversion on the opposite flank, Colley sent a company of the 92nd Highlanders with a Gatling gun down on the morning of the 25 February to secure a farmhouse on the banks of the Buffalo report-edly used as a base by Boer patrols.[95] The next morning, 26 February, the Mounted Squadron left camp at 01h30 with a convoy of empty wagons for

Newcastle, their routine departure disguising covert preparations for that night. Colley was about to stake the campaign and his reputation on a single throw. In a quiet moment before fall-in Colley wrote a last, prescient and fatalistic letter to his wife:

I am going out tonight to try and seize the Majuba Hill . . . and leave this behind, in case I should not return, to tell you how very dearly I love you, and what a happiness you have been to me . . . It is a strange world of chances; one can only do what seems right to one in matters of morals, and do what seems best in matters of judgment, as a card-player calculates the chances, and the wrong card may turn up and everything turn out to be done for the worst instead of the best.[96]

Notes and references

1 WO 32/7811, no. 079/4018: Smyth to Robinson, 7 February 1881.

2 WO 32/7812, no. 079/3821: Robinson to Smyth, 14 February 1881.

3 WO 32/7806, no. 079/3930: memorandum by Wolseley, 18 February 1881; memorandum by Alison, 14 February 1881.

4 For the operations of the NFF between the battles of Ingogo and Majuba, see Butterfield, ed., *War and Peace*, pp. 205–13: Journal of the Natal Field Force, 9–26 February 1881.

5 WC III/4/2: Colley to Joubert, 9 February 1881.

6 *BPP* (C. 2866), enc. in no. 28: Earl Granville to Count de Bylandt, 7 February 1881; no. 38: Herbert to Thompson, 12 February 1881. Red Cross societies were formed in Cape Town, Bloemfontein and Durban to work in association with similar societies in Britain and the Netherlands engaged in helping both Boer and British wounded. See Norris-Newman, *With the Boers*, pp. 164–5.

7 Carter, *Boer War*, p. 223; Lt Marling quoted in Emery, *Marching over Africa*, p. 110.

8 Carter, *Boer War*, p. 226.

9 Norris-Newman, *With the Boers*, p. 165.

10 WO 32/7817: Journal of Naval Brigade, 16 February 1881.

11 *BPP* (C. 2837), no. 23: Childers to Colley, 10 February; no. 27: Colley to Childers, 11 February 1881; no. 28: Childers to Colley, 12 February 1881.

12 Major Percy Barrow had raised and commanded mounted infantry with distinction during the Anglo-Zulu War. See Laband, ed., *Chelmsford's Zululand Campaign*, p. 272.

13 Norris-Newman, *With the Boers*, pp. 154–5, 163–4.

14 WC III/1/2: Childers to Wood, 13 January 1881.

15 Sir E. Wood, *From Midshipman to Field Marshal* (London, 2nd edn, 1906), vol. II, pp. 107–9. On Queen Victoria's insistence, Wood had accompanied the Empress Eugénie to Zululand in 1880 to visit the grave of her son, the Prince Imperial of France, who had been killed in action during the Anglo-Zulu War. See J. Laband, 'An Empress in Zululand', *Natalia*, 30 (December 2000), pp. 45–57.

16 Colley to Wood, 4 February 1881, quoted in Butler, *Pomeroy-Colley*, pp. 294–6.

17 Norris-Newman, *With the Boers*, p. 199.

18 Meintjes, *Commandant-General*, p. 80.

19 *BPP* (C. 2837), no. 31: Colley to Childers, 15 February 1881; Holt, *Mounted Police*, p. 106.

20 WO 32/7817: Journal of Naval Brigade, 22 February 1881.

21 See in particular WO 32/7831, no. 079/4720: Winsloe's report, 23 March 1881 and Bennett, *Rain of Lead*, pp. 175–201.

22 WO 32/7831, no. 079/4812: Memorandum by Sir G. Wolseley on the Defence of Potchefstroom, 28 June 1881.

23 WO 32/7832, no. 079/5184: Wood to AG to the Forces, 3 October 1881.

24 WC III/3/8: By order, Maj-Gen Buller, 7 May 1881.

25 See especially WO 32/7820, no. 079/4665: Lt Long's report, n.d. and Mrs Long, *Fort Mary*, chaps IX–XIII.

26 WO 32/7833, no. 079/4724: Wood to AG to the Forces, 9 May 1881.

27 See especially WO 32/7833, no. 079/4722: Auchinleck's report, 7 April 1881.

28 See especially WO 32/7833, no. 079/4715: Montague's report, 29 March 1881.

29 WO 32/7833, no. 079/4715: Wood to the Military Secretary, Horse Guards, 26 April 1881.

30 WO 32/7816, sub-enc. 3 in enc. 1 in no. 079/4356: Capt H.M. Saunders to Colley, 23 February 1881.

31 WO 32/7833, no. 079/4814: Wood to AG to the Forces, 22 May 1881. See also WO 32/7833, no. 079/4814: Saunder's report, [?] April 1881.

32 WO 32/7833, no. 079/4722: Wood to AG to the Forces, 7 May 1881. See also WO 32/7833, no. 079/4724: Brook's report, 7 April 1881.

33 WC III/2/9: Cambridge to Wood, 9 August 1881.

34 WC III/3/3: Wood to Cambridge, 3 October 1881.

35 WC III/3/3: Wood to Cambridge, 3 October 1881.

36 WC III/3/3: Wood to Cambridge, 3 October 1881.

37 WC III/3/3: Wood to Cambridge, 13 November 1881.

38 WO 32/7816, sub-enc. 2 in enc. 1 in no. 079/4356: Lanyon to Colley, 10 February 1881.

39 WO 32/7816: enc. 2 in no. 079/4457: Lt-Col F. Gildea to the DAAG, 12 February 1881; Davey, 'Siege of Pretoria', p. 287.

40 See especially Bellairs, ed., *Transvaal War*, pp. 171–225.

41 Norris-Newman, *With the Boers*, p. 199.

42 WO 32/7817: Journal of Naval Brigade, 22 February 1881.

43 Holt, *Mounted Police*, pp. 107–8.

44 Norris-Newman, *With the Boers*, p. 199.

45 *BPP* (C. 2754): Kimberley to Robinson, 'Instructions Addressed to Governor H. Robinson, G.C.M.G.', 30 December 1880. See especially points 5, 8–23.

46 J. Morley, *The Life of William Ewart Gladstone* (London, 1906), vol. II, p. 262.

47 For a discussion on British war correspondents and special artists in the 1870s and 1880s, see J. Laband and I. Knight, *The War Correspondents: The Anglo-Zulu War* (Stroud, 1996), pp. v–xx.

48 Emery, *Marching over Africa*, pp. 100–2.

49 Carter, *Boer War*, pp. 158–9.

50 Norris-Newman, *With the Boers*, pp. xiv–xv.

51 Norris-Newman, *With the Boers*, pp. 170–3.

52 Norris-Newman, *With the Boers*, pp. 195–6.

53 Lehmann, *Boer War*, pp. 181–3.

54 Lt A.M. Adlam, 'Die Pers as Bron oor die Geskiedenis van die Eerste Vryheidsoorlog', *Militaria*, 1, 11 (1981), pp. 62–8.

55 See *BPP* (C. 2783), no. 33: Strahan to Kimberley, 16 January 1881; no. 38: Strahan to Kimberly, 22 December 1880 and encs 1–3; no. 39: Strahan to Kimberley, 27 December 1880 and encs 1–4; no. 45: Strahan to Kimberley, 4 January 1881; *BPP* (C. 2866), no. 21: Strahan to Kimberley, 11 January 1881 and enc.; no. 22: Strahan to Kimberley, 18 January and enc.; no. 23: Strahan to Kimberley, 18 January 1881 and enc.; no. 25: Strahan to Kimberley, 18 January 1881 and encs 1–3.

56 *BPP* (C. 2950), no. 13: Robinson to Kimberley, 25 February 1881 and enc. of resolutions adopted at 34 meetings in the Cape.

57 *BPP* (C. 2794), enc. 1 in no. 1: Kruger, Pretorius, Joubert and Bok to the Colonial Secretary of the Cape Colony, December 1880. See no. 1: Strahan to Kimberley, 11 January 1881.

58 Butler, *Pomeroy-Colley*, pp. 319–20, 324–5, 335–6.

59 *BPP* (C. 2866), no. 64: Kimberley to Sir F. Roberts, 4 March 1881.

60 Davey, 'Siege of Pretoria', pp. 299–300.

61 Haggard, *Last Boer War*, pp. 136–7.

62 Kruger, *Memoirs*, pp. 175–8; Dennison, *Fight to the Finish*, pp. 12–13; Carter, *Boer War*, pp. 439–41. Bellairs had strongly been pressing Lanyon 'to raise the natives on the Boers'. See TS 46: Haggard to Sir T. Shepstone, 30 March 1881.

63 WO 32/7822: Lanyon to Bellairs, 14 March 1881. See also SS 8651, no. R139/81: G. Hudson, Colonial Secretary, Transvaal, to Landdrost Rustinburg [sic], 14 March 1881 for identical sentiments.

64 *BPP* (C. 2866), enc. 2 in no. 95: Cetwayo M'pande's son, written by the interpreter, J. Storr Lister, to the Governor of South Africa, 1 March 1881.

65 Theron-Bushell, 'Lanyon', p. 274. In the neighbouring Waterberg District there were instances of Africans attacking Boers on their farms. See Carter, *Boer War*, p. 442.

66 Haggard, *Last Boer War*, p. 136.

67 *BPP* (C. 2950), enc. 1 in no. 60: A. Woolls-Sampson, Native Commissioner, Waterberg, to H. Shepstone, 18 April 1881.

68 WC III/1/4: Sir M. Barlow to Lanyon, December 1880; CTAR, GH 11/27, pp. 457–62: Sworn statement by L. Spring, Clerk to the Special Commissioner, Swazi Border, 21 July 1881.

69 Schreuder, *Gladstone and Kruger*, pp. 100–6.

70 Schreuder, *Gladstone and Kruger*, pp. 107–14.

71 The Transvaal Proclamation, 27 January 1881, quoted in Schreuder, *Gladstone and Kruger*, p. 116, n. 2.

72 Schreuder, *Gladstone and Kruger*, pp. 115–17.

73 Butler, *Pomeroy-Colley*, pp. 322–9.

74 Kimberley to Colley, 8 February 1881, quoted in Butler, *Pomeroy-Colley*, p. 329.

75 *BPP* (C. 2866), no. 74: Colley to Kimberley, 10 February 1881.

76 Colley to Kimberley, telegram, 12 February 1881, quoted in Butler, *Pomeroy-Colley*, pp. 329–30.

77 Kruger and Bok to Colley, 12 February 1881, quoted in Butler, *Pomeroy-Colley*, pp. 330–1.

78 Schreuder, *Gladstone and Kruger*, pp. 118–22.

79 *BPP* (C. 2837), no. 34: Kimberley to Colley, telegram, 16 February 1881. Kimberley also telegraphed Wood and Brand to ensure that his message got through to the Boers and was not smothered by Colley.

80 Wood to Queen Victoria, 27 February 1881, quoted in Beckett, *Victorians at War*, p. 27.

81 Lady Colley to Colley, 15 and 24 February 1881, quoted in Butler, *Pomeroy-Colley*, pp. 347–8.

82 See Laband, ed., *Chelmsford's Zululand Campaign*, pp. xlii–xliv.

83 Colley to Lady Colley, 18 February 1881, quoted in Butler, *Pomeroy-Colley*, p. 339.

84 *BPP* (C. 2837), no. 49: Colley to Kimberley, telegram, 19 February 1881.

85 *BPP* (C. 2837), no. 50: Kimberley to Colley, telegram, 19 February 1881.

86 Colley to Wolseley, 21 February 1881, quoted in Butler, *Pomeroy-Colley*, p. 343.

87 Colley to Kruger, 21 February 1881, quoted in Butler, *Pomeroy-Colley*, p. 344.

88 Schreuder, *Gladstone and Kruger*, p. 132.

89 Butler, *Pomeroy-Colley*, pp. 357–60.

90 Schreuder, *Gladstone and Kruger*, pp. 127–9.

91 *BPP* (C. 2837), no. 58: Brand to the OFS Consul, London, 24 February 1881. The resolution passed the Orange Free State Volksraad by 36 votes to 3. See also Norris-Newman, *With the Boers*, p. 167.

92 Norris-Newman, *With the Boers*, pp. 178–9; Lehmann, *Boer War*, pp. 177–8. A voluntary Free State commando under Cornelis de Villiers served with Joubert.

93 WO 32/7827, enc. 2 in no. 079/4617: Lt-Col H. Stewart to Wood, 4 April 1881; Butler, *Pomeroy-Colley*, pp. 352, 361–2, 364.

94 Ransford, *Majuba Hill*, pp. 66, 71–2.

95 WO 32/7817: Journal of Naval Brigade, 25 February 1881.

96 Colley to Lady Colley, 26 February 1881, quoted in Butler, *Pomeroy-Colley*, pp. 367–8.

chapter 10

Majuba

Surprise was essential if Majuba were to be seized without Boer opposition, and Colley divulged his intentions to no one besides Colonel Stewart and another recently arrived staff officer, Major T. Fraser, RE. Only after lights out had been routinely sounded at 20h30 on 26 February did staff officers issue orders for two companies of the 58th Regiment, two companies of the 3/60th Rifles, three companies of the 92nd Highlanders and a company-strength Naval Brigade drawn from the *Boadicea* and *Dido*, as well as small detachments from other units and the Army Medical Department, to be ready to march at 22h00 in that order. Commentators have wondered ever since why Colley chose to lead out a mixed force when a single regiment, with its developed *corps d'esprit*, would have been more cohesive and reliable. It has been surmised that Colley wished to give representatives of the 58th Regiment and the 3/60th Rifles an opportunity to redeem their poor showings at Laing's Nek and Ingogo. It is also not unlikely that Colley – as an army reformer and member of Wolseley's ring – hoped that by performing well these two short-service regiments would undercut the criticisms by the Duke and his cronies of short-service and their declared preference for old long-service regiments like the 92nd Highlanders.[1]

Colley and two staff officers (Colonel Stewart and Major Fraser) led out the force of 27 officers and 568 men, three newspaper correspondents and an unrecorded number of African guides and servants who carried three days' rations for the troops. Each soldier was ordered to carry the regulation

70 rounds of ammunition, a greatcoat, waterproof sheet and a full water bottle. Four picks and six shovels for entrenching were issued to each company. The men were not told of their destination. No artillery or Gatling guns accompanied the task force because Colley considered the mountain too steep and there was in any case no proper tackle available to strap the guns onto draft animals.[2]

It was a moonless night, no lights were carried and strict silence was observed. The spirits of the men were reported high, though there is evidence too of grumbling and an expressed lack of faith in Colley's generalship – not altogether surprising with his dismal record of two defeats in a row. The column moved out west from Mount Prospect, crossed the Laing's Nek road, and climbed the lower eastern slopes of Inkwelo. After an hour's march it reached a plateau halfway up the mountain, where it reformed. The column then turned north-west and followed a track traversing the mountain which came out on another plateau on the northern slopes of Inkwelo. Here Colley detached two companies of the 3/60th Rifles to secure his line of march, giving Captains C. Smith and R. Henley no orders other than to entrench and hold their position. From this plateau Colley marched northwards along the wide ridge which connects Inkwelo to Majuba. At about midnight the column halted for about an hour at the far end of the ridge to allow part of the rear of the column, which had lost its way, to be brought in. Colley then detached a company of the 92nd Highlanders under Captain P. Robertson with orders to take charge of the officers' horses and reserve ammunition. At 12h30 a further 3 officers and 77 men of the 3/60th Rifles with 10 mules carrying 16 boxes of ammunition moved up from Fort Prospect to reinforce them, and by 06h00 had completed a small earthwork redoubt and shelter trench.

The diminished column began to move up Majuba's steep slopes in the early hours of 27 February. The men found the going ever more difficult, and it became necessary to make regular halts every hundred yards to keep the column together. Scouts temporarily lost the path that gained the south-western summit and the men had to scramble up the final slope on hands and knees. Scouts sent ahead reported the mountaintop deserted and the presence of the column undetected. It was 03h40 and still dark when the first men breasted the summit, and the rear of the column was not finally up much before 05h30, just as dawn began to break. Since order and formation had been lost in the climb, the men milled about looking for their units while staff officers tried to get them into position. Exhausted stragglers were pushed into the nearest gap in the perimeter regardless of which unit they belonged to. Much was later made of the difficulty of the climb, yet Majuba was nothing as formidable a mountain as many previously encountered by the 92nd Highlanders in Afghanistan.[3]

The summit of Majuba is roughly triangular in shape. It has a rocky perimeter of about three-quarters of a mile which slopes inwards to form a basin, in some places nearly 40 feet below the outer line of boulders. It is bisected from east to west by a low rocky ridge which in the darkness Colley mistakenly believed to mark the northern perimeter of the summit. On the western side of the mountain top the rocky ridge runs to the foot of a rounded rocky outcrop, or koppie, later known as Macdonald's Knoll (or Koppie) after Lieutenant Hector Macdonald. To the east the ridge terminates in another, less well defined feature later called Hay's Koppie after Major H.C. Hay.

Colley was pleased with the apparent strength of the position, but his confidence was misplaced. After detaching three companies to secure his lines of communication, he only had 19 officers and 383 men to hold the position, or about half a battalion. As we have seen, they were jumbled up somewhat, but in effect the two companies of the 92nd Highlanders (141 officers and men) held the perimeter along the rocky ridge from Macdonald's Koppie to Hay's Koppie. The two companies of the 58th Regiment (171 officers and men) continued the line on their right along the south-eastern perimeter to the south-western point where the force had reached the summit. The 65 officers and men of the Naval Brigade then completed the line along the western side of the mountain up to a steep grass gully which extends down the mountainside below Macdonald's Koppie. The men were in extended skirmishing order with fifteen-pace intervals between files and reserves in support. A further mixed reserve, drawn from all the units, was formed up in the hollow behind the rocky ridge close by Colley's headquarters and the hospital and commissariat. Water was found at only three feet, and Colley was assured that his men could maintain their position on top of Majuba as long as was necessary. With their objective attained and apparently secured, the mood of the men became relaxed and optimistic.

The first streaks of light on 27 February destroyed this complacency. The rocky ridge held by the 92nd Highlanders proved not to be the true northern perimeter of the summit since the ground slopes away gently from it before dropping abruptly to a wide, flat grassy terrace beyond which the ground sloped sharply downwards. At about 04h30 Colley ordered the 92nd Highlanders to move forward from the ridge and occupy the true brow of the mountain. A handful of Highlanders took up exposed position on an isolated, featureless knoll which juts out from the north-western angle of the mountain like a bastion from a curtain wall. Gordons' Knoll, as it later became known in honour of the 92nd Regiment (Gordon Highlanders), would prove the key to Majuba, though its significance was not at first appreciated. Yet if lost to the Boers the northern perimeter would be exposed to flanking fire and be made untenable.

Extending the perimeter even further to the north had dispersed the widely spaced Highlanders even more, yet Colley made no concerted effort to fortify his vulnerable position. He had initially intended to construct small square redoubts on Macdonald's Koppie, Hay's Koppie and a third knoll overlooking the path to the summit, but the hurried extension north of the defensive perimeter rendered this plan redundant. However, he did not order alternative perimeter entrenchments because he considered the men too fatigued from their climb to begin work immediately. This decision has been considered fatal to Colley's situation. Yet it is not as if he was unaware of the necessity to construct defences; nor were his men without entrenching tools. As the *Field Exercise* puts it with great clarity:

Taking into consideration the long range, extreme accuracy and great rapidity of fire of the rifled guns and small arms now in use, it may be desirable to shelter the troops as much as possible from unnecessary exposure . . . It is self-evident that troops behind cover must have a considerable advantage over an enemy advancing, unprotected, against them.[4]

It was well understood that a very slight earthen parapet 1 ft 6 in high was sufficient to protect men from rifle bullets, and that for a kneeling man the trench behind it had only to be 1 ft 6 in deep and 2 ft 6 in wide. A soldier was expected to complete 5 feet of such a trench and parapet in only 30 minutes, so it made for the best form of passive defence when time of preparation was short.[5] Some of Colley's junior officers therefore took the initiative and encouraged the men under their immediate command to improvise defences and pile rocks and stones in front of their positions, rather as the Boers had done at Ingogo. The Naval Brigade also went its own way and doggedly erected some strong stone breastworks.

It seems it was Colley's intention, once his men were firmly established on Majuba, to hand over command to Commander Romilly of the Naval

Brigade and return to Mount Prospect to take command of joint operations. Yet the viability of this plan depended on firmly holding Majuba to threaten (however imperfectly) the Boer flank. But it was far from secure. Not only was it thinly held and lacking entrenchments, but the angle and nature of the north and north-eastern slopes of the mountain turned them into dead ground for the defenders, making it possible for assailants to scale two-thirds up them without being seen. Besides, eroded dongas and kloofs running down the mountain, choked in thick bush, provided excellent cover. By a fatal dereliction no serious reconnaissance was carried out to ascertain the extent to which the mountain slopes were dead ground, so the British were not on heightened alert against an assault taking advantage of the favourable terrain.

Unconscious, therefore, of the precariousness of their situation, and pumped up rather by their successful seizure of Majuba and the command-ing position it gave them over the Boer positions, the British advertised their presence at first light. Highlanders standing on the skyline shook their fists and yelled at the three Boer laagers far below where, on that Sabbath morning, some Boers were being mustered to take up their positions on the nek while the rest were preparing for divine service. The Boers were astounded at the unexpected and unwelcome sight of the British above them.[6] Many, including Commandant-General Joubert himself, were gripped by an initial panic. Some saddled up and inspanned their wagons to escape the anticipated bombardment by the guns they imagined the British must have dragged up to the summit of Majuba, and others rushed to man the defences across the nek. But no shells fell, for Colley had no artillery, and there were no signs either of a coordinated assault from Mount Prospect. Joubert, spurred on by his indomitable wife, Hendrina, who had accompanied him to war,[7] rode through the laager calling for volunteers to drive the British off Spitskop, as the Boers called Majuba. While about a hundred volunteers began gathering at his headquarters, Joubert called a council of war. According to some, pointless recriminations flew between Nicolaas Smit and Frans Joubert over whose responsibility it had been to station a night-time picquet on Majuba to give due warning of a British attack. But all agreed that now the British were unfortunately in possession of the mountain and had succeeded in turning their flank, that they must be promptly evicted. So while Joubert rode off to encourage the burghers holding the Laing's Nek defences against an anticipated British attack, Smit led the volunteers, among whom morale was high, to the lower slopes of

Majuba. More men would gradually follow as the Boers in the laagers behind Laing's Nek realised that there was to be no British attack that day, until about 450 joined in the assault. Busily coordinating strategy, and confirming his reputation (as Butler generously expressed it) 'as one of the ablest leaders of mounted infantry that have appeared in modern war',[8] Smit organised a second group of about 150 horsemen to ride around the western side of the mountain to prevent any British reinforcements reaching Colley and to cut off a British withdrawal. So Colley, rather than intimidating the Boers into a precipitate withdrawal through his bold stroke in seizing Majuba, now found the knife turning in his hand and his little force in imminent danger of being isolated and attacked.

The first group of Boers coming up to the base of Majuba dismounted under cover and formed into two assault groups under Assistant Field Cornet Stephanus J. Roos from Pretoria and Commandant Joachim J. Ferreira from Utrecht. With Roos on the left and Ferreira 100 yards away on the right, the two parties began to move unchallenged up the lower slopes of the mountain because Colley had set no picquets or sent out any patrols. The British on the summit had little sight of them as they worked up the mountain taking every advantage of the dead ground and the natural cover provided by the sparse scrub (the heavy growth of trees and bushes today were not present then), the rocky outcrops and a large gully. Meanwhile, a second group of Boers joined the assault under Field Cornet D.J.K. Malan and Field Cornet Stephanus Trichard and advanced on Roos's left. Throughout the morning more volunteers continued to trickle up the mountain to join the assault parties. Smit deployed a cordon of older and less physically active Boers at the foot of the mountain who from about 06h00 hours opened a heavy covering fire which ensured that the British did not care to expose themselves along the skyline to fire down at the Boer assault groups. These demonstrated their mastery of fire and movement techniques as the rear line of skirmishers provided covering fire for the advance line until it had come to a halt behind suitable cover when the second line moved up and the process was repeated.[9]

At first, the British on the summit felt no alarm since they believed their position to be unassailable. The reserve in the hollow behind the rocky ridge breakfasted, and many fell asleep, tired out by the difficult climb and sleepless night. Colley still did not divulge his intentions, but at 08h00 he sent a signal to Mount Prospect ordering them to telegraph Childers at the War Office that he had occupied Majuba 'immediately overlooking Boer position', and that the Boers were firing from below. Three-quarters of an hour later he again signalled the camp by flag. He ordered forward the 2/60th Rifles and three troops of the 15th Hussars stationed at Newcastle, urging them to arrive by the next morning, and also ordered up the scattered detachments of the NMP. It is not known precisely how Colley intended to use these reinforcements, but it must be presumed they were intended to strengthen an assault on Laing's Nek combined with a flank movement from Majuba. Meanwhile, the situation on the mountain seemed under control, and two signals followed concerning the bringing up of rations. That of 09h30 confidently ended: 'All very comfortable. Boers wasting ammunition. One man wounded in foot.'[10]

It was not until a little after 10h30 that increasing Boer fire induced Colley to consider the construction of defences. While standing on the exposed south-western point of the summit discussing the possibility with his staff, a Boer marksman 900 yards below shot Commander Romilly through the body and he fell mortally wounded at Colley's side. Colley was deeply shocked at the loss of his second-in-command, and his demeanour became markedly gloomy. Even so, his situation still seemed favourable. The size of the Boer assault groups were underestimated because so few of the burghers were visible to the defenders, and at about 11h00 a few Boer wagons were seen driving off from the Boer laagers. Colley could consequently reassure himself that all was well, and at 11h00 signalled Fort Prospect to inform Childers that 'Boers still firing heavily on hill, but have broken up laager and begin to move away. I regret to say Commander Romilly dangerously wounded; other casualties, three men slightly wounded.'[11] Nothing in this final signal from Majuba gave any indication that Colley had any cause for alarm.

The most northerly sector of the British defensive perimeter was occupied by some 18 men of the 92nd Regiment under Lieutenant Ian Hamilton (who was Lady Colley's brother), and he had stationed about five of them on the isolated Gordons' Knoll and the spur that connected it to the summit. The Boers' commanders realised that the knoll commanded the northern perimeter and that it was tactically imperative to gain possession of it. A group under Ferreira concentrated under the protection of the edge of the rocky-sided terrace directly below, but to storm the knoll required a 20-yard dash across the flat, grassy terrace, fully exposed to British fire. A successful assault therefore hinged on the effective use of fire and movement. Roos's men extended to the left of Ferreira along the edge of the terrace and opened a heavy fire on the Highlanders, pinning them down under cover. With British fire suppressed, small groups of Boers took it in turn to rush across the terrace and take shelter in the dead ground immediately under the rocky face of the knoll itself, where about 100 of them finally congregated. Hamilton, who was an efficient officer, well understood the threat this posed to his position. Risking the Boer fire he reported in person to Colley, whom he found in the hollow behind the rocky ridge where the reserve was comfortably eating, sleeping or smoking. No Boer threat was apparent in this safe haven, and Colley politely sent his young brother-in-law back to his post. When Hamilton saw that the Boer strength along the edge of the terrace had increased to about 200, he went back to Colley urgently to request reinforcements to help suppress the Boer fire. Colley remained unconvinced, and only gave Hamilton five men and an officer of the 58th Regiment.

Shortly after midday Hamilton made his hazardous way back to headquarters for a third time to report that he was sure some 400 Boers (which was a great over-estimation) were grouped directly below his position and that they were on the verge of an attack. But Colley, exhausted with the mental strain and physical exertion, was asleep, and Stewart would not wake him. So all Hamilton could do was report to Major Hay, his senior officer, before going back to his imperilled post.

When Ferreira had collected between 60 and 80 men directly below Gordons' Knoll, they suddenly emerged from their cover somewhere between 12h30 and 12h45 and opened fire on the Highlanders, killing three on the knoll and causing the two survivors to flee back to the British perimeter. Ferreira's men thereupon took possession of Gordons' Knoll and opened a heavy fire on the thinly extended Highlanders from only 70 yards away. With the British along their northern perimeter pinned down, Roos next led his men in a dash across the open terrace to the dead ground directly below them. Continuing covering fire from the knoll made it impossible for the British to lean over the brow of the mountain to shoot at Roos's men 100 yards below.

The outbreak of heavy firing at the knoll literally caught Colley and his staff napping. All was confusion and disarray at headquarters where the reserve was ordered out to reinforce the threatened northern perimeter. But the men, unprepared, half awake and half dressed, and with their units all jumbled together, only reluctantly breasted the security of the rocky ridge to the north of them. Once over it they flung themselves down in the grass and

opened a heavy but ineffectually random fire on the knoll which nevertheless caused the Boers to fall back for cover behind its crest. A lull in the firing
ensued as both sides regrouped. An intense outburst of firing then broke the
uneasy spell as the burghers on the knoll covered Roos and about 50 of his
men who were scrambling up the steep approach to just below the brow of
the hill within only yards of the British perimeter. Roos encouraged his men
by falsely telling them that the British were already in flight, and they
climbed over the brow to join in the fire-fight. This proved too much for
the British reserve which had already suffered about 16 casualties. They
stampeded back towards the shelter of the rocky ridge, and were joined in
their flight by the Highlanders from the northern perimeter. They did not
stop when they made the rocky ridge but carried on running in panicked
disarray, making for the southern-western side of the summit and the path
back to Mount Prospect. Their officers succeeded in rallying most of them,
and brought them back to the rocky ridge where they clustered towards the
higher ground of Macdonald's Koppie at its western end. Officers did their
best to shift the mob back into their own units and to extend them along
the full length of the ridge. Colley, who was undoubtedly courageous, kept
a cool head and did much to calm his men. The British were given a brief
respite in which to regroup while Boers reduced their firing as they consolidated their new positions preparatory to renewing the attack.

The British now occupied the perimeter they had originally held during
the night before pushing forward to occupy the brow of the mountain.
Their situation was not yet disastrous, however. Macdonald's Koppie was
analogous to Gordons' Knoll in that it commanded the new northern
perimeter. The men posted on it could provide effective covering fire for the
soldiers behind the rocky ridge, and also dominate the ground between it
and the brow of the mountain. The troops on Hay's Koppie on the eastern
side of the mountain could protect the rear of the rocky ridge and headquarters in the bowl. The men in the more southerly sectors of the perimeter had not yet been attacked and their morale should have remained
unshaken. Yet morale in combat is a volatile thing. Primary group motiva-
tion is considered essential in battle, yet the troops were widely spaced
along the perimeter and sometimes separated from their units. This meant
they did not have the support and encouragement of their familiar comrades. Troops often fail in combat because of poor leadership, and on
Majuba they were often isolated from their officers' words of encouragement and had no real sense of what they were expected to achieve, or what

the enemy were up to.[12] Earlier confidence was being overtaken by perplexity and anxiety, and troops along the untested southern perimeter, unnerved by the sounds of firing and the obvious confusion to the north of them, began to quit their posts and move in towards the apparent security of the rocky ridge, thus weakening the outer defences.

Meanwhile, on the northern side of the mountain, some Boers were working their way forward to within 40 yards of the rocky ridge, taking advantage of every fold in the ground, while those in support pinned the British down with a heavy fire. The troops on Macdonald's Kop were ineffective in enfilading the Boers on the open ground north of the ridge because they in turn were pinned down by Boer fire from Gordons' Knoll. Their flank was in any case about to be turned because a party of Ferreira's men was moving around the western slopes of the mountain below them with the intention of moving up the gully south of Macdonald's Kop. On the eastern side of Majuba Malan's men, who were working their way round behind the rocky ridge, opened fire at the men of the 58th Regiment holding Hay's Kop. These were already taking casualties from high fire from the Boers attacking the ridge. The Boers were closing in on Colley in the classic pincer movement so favoured by their old enemy, the Zulu, with their bull's horns formation.

The British officers succeeded in restoring some order among the troops behind the ridge, and the command was given to fix bayonets. Yet Colley never gave the order for the standard volley followed by a bayonet charge. Some of his officers were keen to try the bayonet, and it is one of the abiding debates about the battle whether or not it would have succeeded. Given the faltering morale of the men, and the fact that the Boers were scattered, under cover and out of sight, it is most unlikely. British casualties were slowly mounting, meanwhile, though return fire against the Boers was extremely ineffective. The Boers later claimed that many of the captured British firearms were sighted at 400 yards – far too high for the increasingly close-range fire-fight. It was for officers to order their men to change their sights, and their inability to make them do so speaks for the increasing breakdown of cohesion on the mountain-top.

The Naval Brigade positioned along the south-west perimeter reported that Ferreira's men were moving up the large gully on the west of the mountain below Macdonald's Kop and that the British along the rocky ridge were in danger of being enfiladed. Colley responded by ordering his men nearest to the gully – a medley of the 92nd Highlanders, 58th Regiment and some sailors – to extend their line about 20 yards to their left to block the gap. But discipline was breaking down with morale, and the men were unwilling to leave the cover of the rocky ridge or to follow officers who were not their own. Stewart and Fraser of the staff joined the regimental officers in exhorting them, and a few small groups finally pulled themselves forwards on their stomachs. More men were now slipping away from their posts on the perimeter and making for the apparent security of the rocky ridge despite the efforts of their officers to stop them. Amidst these growing signs of breakdown Major Hay reported to Colley that Malan's men were threatening Hay's Kop which, if lost, would expose the rear of the rocky ridge to Boer fire. Colley, who now had his revolver drawn, ordered the 92nd Highlanders to hold Hay's Kop at all costs, and directed his men to extend further to the right in support.

At that moment the left of the British position collapsed. Soldiers at the head of the gulley broke and rushed with cries of terror towards the southern side of the mountain and the path back to Mount Prospect. With their flank turned, the men behind the ridge faltered in their firing, and small groups began to break away and make for the rear despite threats from their officers to shoot them. General panic then set in, and the whole line along the ridge collapsed as the men sprinted to the rear. Colley was seen standing with his revolver held above his head, yelling at the men to make a stand at the higher ground that commanded the way down the southern side of the mountain. But the day was lost. The triumphant Boers seized the abandoned rocky ridge and Hay's Kop, and opened a devastating fire on the fleeing British. The hospital was left completely exposed with the collapse of the British line. Lance Corporal J.J. Farmer of the Army Hospital Corps was wounded twice while trying to indicate its presence to the Boers with a white bandage waved above his head and was later awarded the Victoria Cross for his determined courage.

With the ridge and two koppies lost the British made no further attempt at a stand. They simply threw themselves over the edge of the southern side of the mountain in a desperate *sauve qui peut*, bounding and tumbling down the steep, boulder-strewn slopes, many losing their rifles. Lieutenant Macdonald concentrated a group of about 20 men on Macdonald's Kop, presuming that the rest of the force would rally to the south of him. But when he saw that no stand was being attempted and that his men were taking heavy casualties, he ordered them to retire as well. All were killed or wounded except for Macdonald and one other man. Their surrender ended organised resistance on the mountain-top. It had taken only 30 minutes from the Boer assault on Gordons' Kop to sweep the British from the summit of Majuba.

Colley's end is not clear, except that he was fatally shot in the head, the bullet entering through the helmet above the right eye and exiting behind the left ear. Accounts have him dying as he tried to rally his men, as he was retiring or as he walked towards the Boers in an attempt to surrender with a white handkerchief tied to his sword. One report has him shot at short range by a 12-year-old boy, and others say that he was shot at longer range by a group consisting of Ferreira, Roos and Gideon Erasmus. Rumours also abounded that the wound was self-inflicted. Wood later obtained the helmet Colley had been wearing, and sent it to Lady Colley as a relic. In Wood's opinion the damaged helmet showed without doubt that Colley had died 'with his face to the foe'.[13] Colley's widow tartly responded that the precise position of Colley's head when he was shot was an accident of no interest to her because she had 'never heard him charged with any fault in regard of personal courage except having it in excess'.[14]

The victorious Boers who had stormed Majuba seized the abandoned British ammunition and looted the dead and wounded before opening a heavy fire on the fleeing British from the southern side of the mountain.[15] Later that day the Boers rounded up many fugitives from their hiding-places behind bushes and rocks from which they had hoped to make their way back to camp under cover of darkness. The company of the 92nd Highlanders under Captain Robertson whom Colley had posted on the ridge between Majuba and Inkwelo had been reinforced earlier by a company of the 3/60th Rifles and a troop of the 15th Hussars. They prepared to hold their redoubt to cover the troops scrambling down the mountain, but they soon came under attack from the mounted Boers who had ridden around the western flank of Majuba at the onset of the battle, and from a fresh group on foot, under Commandant J. Uys, who hurried up from the nek. Almost surrounded, their position became increasingly untenable. Under heliographed orders from Mount Prospect they withdrew with difficulty while dismounted troopers of the 15th Hussars on their left flank gave them covering fire. Their losses were heavy with an officer and 6 men killed, and 12 wounded. An officer and 23 men were taken prisoner. However, no ammunition boxes were lost and the wounded were all evacuated. The two companies of the 3/60th Rifles left on the shoulder of Inkwelo were not engaged and put up a poor show by withdrawing to Mount Prospect without making any attempt to support the troops falling back from Majuba. The two 9-pounder guns of N/5 Brigade, RA, two Gatling guns RN and two companies of the 92nd Highlanders were advanced from Fort Prospect to below the ridge connecting Inkwelo and Majuba, and their fire (30 shells were expended) helped deter the Boers from advancing any further and cutting off the retreating British. The NMP were sent out of camp to carry fugitives in on their horses. Preparations were made in the Mount Prospect camp for meeting an attack which seemed imminent, but the Boer did not press on and firing ceased by 15h30. Some Boer leaders saw the sudden descent of a thick mist as God's way of telling them to go thus far and no further, but Joubert also believed the British defences to be too strong to risk an assault.[16]

Once the survivors from Majuba itself finally straggled in, and the men on the summit had been buried, the scale of the British reverse became clear. Five officers were dead, 8 wounded and 7 prisoner, a total of 71 per cent of those engaged. Eighty-seven men were killed, 123 wounded and 50 taken prisoner with 2 more missing. This was 46 per cent of the men engaged. The 92nd Highlanders suffered the worst with a loss of 58 per cent of those in action. Casualty figures such as these attended only the most crushing of defeats, and were made to seem even worse when contrasted with the Boer losses which included only 1 man killed and 6 wounded (one mortally).[17] The battle was a devastating vindication of Boer fire and movement tactics and brought British marksmanship and discipline into considerable question. Ironically, untrained irregulars had demonstrated a better grasp of modern fighting techniques than their professional opponents. The total collapse of British morale on Majuba was perhaps the most troubling aspect of the whole miserable debacle. It was later attributed by the embarrassed military authorities to the unwise lack of cohesion and familiar command structure in Colley's mixed task force. But the NMP (who were used to being looked down upon by British professional soldiers) noted with wry colonial amusement that there was 'much heartburning that night amongst the troops, for each regiment accused the other of having been the first to run'.[18]

In the Boer camp where British and Boer wounded alike were being tended, Commandant Joachim Ferreira declared: 'I do acknowledge that it was not *us* who defeated them, but the Lord our God. It was utterly impossible for humans alone.'[19] Indeed, the Boers, like the Israelites of old, saw their victory over impossible odds as nothing less than God's support in their fight for freedom against oppression.[20] Kruger, in his response to

Joubert's report on the evening of the battle of his God-given victory,[21] declared in an Order of the Day:

We glory not in human power, it is God the Lord who has helped us – the God of our fathers, to whom for the last five years, we have addressed our prayers and supplications. He has done great things to us, and hearkened to our prayers. And you, noble and valiant brothers, have been in His hands the means of saving us.[22]

Notes and references

1 Butler, *Pomeroy-Colley*, p. 370; Ransford, *Majuba Hill*, p. 78; Lehmann, *Boer War*, p. 236.

2 Unless otherwise indicted, the following account of the battle of Majuba is based upon WO 32/7817, enc. in no. 079/4389 [also printed in *BPP* (C. 2950), enc. 2 in no. 27]: Maj Fraser to the GOC Natal, 5 March 1881; *BPP* (C. 2950), enc. in no. 31 [see annotated proofs in WO 32/7817]: Commodore F.W. Richards to the Secretary of the Admiralty, 14 March 1881; Report by Sub-Lt A.L. Scott, 1 March 1881; Report by Surgeon E.H. Mahon, 4 March 1881; WO 32/7827, enc. 1 in no. 079/4617: Memorandum by Wood, 20 April 1881; enc. 2: Lt-Col H. Stewart to Wood, 4 April 1881; enc. 5: Lt H.A. Macdonald to Chief of the Staff, 13 April 1881; enc. 6: Maj H.C. Hay to the Chief of the Staff, 2 March 1881; enc. 7: Capt E.H. Thurlow to Officer Commanding 3/60th Rifles, 28 February 1881; enc. 8: Capt F.M.E. Vibart, RA to the Chief of the Staff, 28 February 1881; enc. 9: Capt C.H. Smith to the Chief of the Staff, 28 February 1881; enc. 11: Lt H. Morgan to the Chief of the Staff, 28 February 1881; enc. 12: Report by Capt G. Sulivan, 27 February 1881; see encs 14–18 for clarifications of the above statements; see encs 19–27 for courts of enquiry held at Fort Amiel on 3 April 1881 to enquire into the circumstances under which officers and men became prisoners of war; Butterfield, ed., *War and Peace*, pp. 213–15: Journal of the Natal Field Force, 26–27 February 1881; *De Staatscourant Gedurenden den Vrijheidsoorlog*, 16 March 1881: 'Het Gevecht bij Amajuba, door een ooggetuig, 5 March 1881'; Carter, *Boer War*, pp. 253–303; Butler, *Pomeroy-Colley*, pp. 368–406; Bellairs, ed., *Transvaal War*, pp. 379–83; Norris-Newman, *With the Boers*, pp. 201–6, 350–1; J. Cromb, ed., *The Majuba Disaster: A Story of Highland Heroism, Told by Officers of the 92nd Regiment* (Dundee, 1891), 44 pp.; B. Bond, 'The Disaster at Majuba Hill 1881', *History Today* (July 1965), pp. 491–5; Ransford, *Majuba Hill*, pp. 72–123; Lehmann, *Boer War*, pp. 236–60; C.M. Bakkes, 'Die Slag van Majuba, 27 Februarie 1881' in Van Jaarsveld, Van Rensburg and Stals, eds, *Eerste Vryheidsoorlog*, pp. 179–97; J.E.H. Grobler, 'Die Eerste Vryheidsoorlog, 1880–1881: 'n Militêr-Historiese Benadering' (unpublished PhD thesis, University of Pretoria, 1981), chapter 11; Castle, *Majuba*, pp. 60–85.

3 Vaughan, *My Service*, p. 248.

4 War Office, *Field Exercise*, p. 382.

5 War Office, *Field Exercise*, pp. 382–40; War Office, *Fortification and Military Engineering*, p. 51.

6 BV 13, p. 454: Joubert to Kruger, 27 February 1881.

7 Meintjes, *Commandant-General*, p. 82.

8 Butler, *Pomeroy-Colley*, p. 390.

9 D.N. Pitout, 'Die Slag van Amajuba, 27 Februarie 1881' (unpublished MA thesis, University of Pretoria, 1980), p. 60.

10 All four of these messages are quoted in Butler, *Pomeroy-Colley*, pp. 386–7.

11 At the same time Colley signalled the Commodore concerning Romilly's dangerous wound. Both signals quoted in Butler, *Pomeroy-Colley*, pp. 391–2.

12 See Lynn, *Combat and Culture*, pp. 241, 251–4.

13 WC III/3/6: Wood to Lady Colley, 17 September 1881.

14 WC III/2/6: Lady Colley to Wood, 26 October 1881.

15 BV 13, p. 454: Joubert to Kruger, 27 February 1881.

16 BV 13, p. 473: Joubert to Kruger, 1 March 1881.

17 BV 16, p. 82: List of killed and wounded at the taking of Colley's Mountain on 27 February 1881.

18 Holt, *Mounted Police*, p. 109.

19 Meintjes, *Commandant-General*, pp. 83–4.

20 JC 26, no. 2457: Kruger to Joubert, 5 March 1881.

21 BV 13, p. 454: Joubert to Kruger, 27 February 1881.

22 Order of the Day by Vice-President Kruger: To the Commandant-General, Commanders, Officers, and Burghers in the Transvaal Army at the Drakensberg, 7 March 1881, quoted in Carter, *Boer War*, p. 301. For the original, see *De Staatscourant Gedurende den Vrijheidsoorlog*, 9 March 1881: Dagorder, 7 March 1881.

chapter 11

Peace and betrayal

At daylight on the wet and foggy morning of 28 February an unarmed British burying party of 3 officers and 100 men left for the battlefield where (with some Boers assisting them) they laid the 59 British dead to rest three deep in a communal grave on the mountain top. Fourteen more bodies were gathered on the mountainside and buried 200 yards below the summit.[1] Another party was sent to assist in bringing down the wounded. A small house at the foot of Majuba about two miles from camp, known as O'Neill's cottage, was used as a temporary halting place.[2] The cottage could accommodate about twenty men at a time, and from there they were gradually brought into camp. The Boers at the nek sent down a list of prisoners, and blankets and medical supplies were forwarded up to them. Colley's body, which the Boers had removed from the battlefield to Joubert's laager at Laing's Nek lay in a tent watched over by captured Highlanders. It had, as Joubert complained, begun to smell,[3] and was brought into the British camp early on the rainy morning of 1 March. That afternoon the bodies of Colley and the other officers who had died on Majuba were interred, Colley's grave next to Deane's. During March Sappers Halliday and O'Brien were detailed to put up tombstones.[4] Colley's wife and friends petitioned Joubert to return Colley's personal belongings,[5] but he sent back only Colley's patrol jacket without the private letters and other papers believed to have been in its pockets. Wood later obtained his helmet, as we have seen.

The rest was looted, and today his revolver can be seen in the Fort Skanskop Museum outside Pretoria, while his sword is reported to be in a private collection.

The Boers sent Colonel Stewart and 7 other officers and 49 men held prisoner to Heidelberg. According to Stewart, they belied their bogey-man reputation by treating them throughout their captivity with 'exceptional kindness' and issuing them the very best of rations.[6] The Boers also held Colley's African guides prisoner and Joubert was uncertain what to do with them since he regarded them as spies.[7] Their fate is uncertain. The weather improved on 2 March and a convoy of ambulances with 49 British wounded set out for Newcastle, where the hospital rapidly became overcrowded.

Since the rout on Majuba had thrown the British entirely onto the defensive, Lieutenant-Colonel William Bond of the 58th Regiment, who was now the senior office of the NFF, ordered the fortifications around the Mount Prospect camp improved with the construction of earthwork entrenchments and additional redoubts. Because of the heavy rains the sodwork parapets had to be constantly repaired.[8] The system of picquets was strengthened and a countersign was introduced. The two naval 9-pounder guns were placed in a redoubt on the hill and a detachment of 20 men of the Naval Brigade encamped nearby. The Boers, however, made no attempt to attack the demoralised NFF, but remained ensconced on Laing's Nek.

Colonel Bond immediately telegraphed the news of Colley's defeat and death, and Wood at once assumed the civil government of Natal in Colley's place. Early on 28 February, the morning after the battle, he left Pietermaritzburg to take command of the troops in the field. In the pouring rain he arrived at Mount Prospect on the afternoon of 3 March escorted by a troop of the 15th Hussars and promptly inspected the camp and its defences. He and his staff returned very early the next morning to Newcastle where the 2/60th Rifles and one-and-a-half squadrons of the 15th Hussars were stationed. Such was the despondency at this latest disaster to befall British arms that the Hussars' horses were not allowed out of camp to graze for fear of Boer patrols, while there was only enough food in Fort Amiel to last the men for twelve more days. Reinforcements in the form of the 6th (Inniskilling) Dragoons, one-and-a half batteries RA, the 58th Regiment and the 83rd Regiment were marching for Newcastle, but the distances and the heavy rain which completely flooded the roads meant that they did not reach Newcastle until 25 March – by which stage the Dragoons had not a hundred horses still fit for work.[9]

On 4 March 1881 Kimberley appointed Sir Frederick Sleigh Roberts to succeed Colley in South East Africa. Roberts had made his reputation in the Second Afghan War while in command of the Kurram and Kabul Field Forces and was celebrated for his relief of Kandahar.[10] He was precisely the sort of high-profile commander required to assure the public that the government was now seriously prosecuting the disastrous war in the Transvaal. Childers therefore made it clear to Wood that it was for Roberts to clear up the mess left by Colley, and that although Wood was to remain in command until he arrived, he was to 'exercise military discretion'.[11] Yet at the same time Kimberley expressed the Cabinet's deep ambivalence when he informed Roberts that while the government 'will not relax their determination to carry on the military operations with the utmost vigour, they would rejoice should any opportunity present itself for an honourable and satisfactory settlement of the affairs of the Transvaal without further bloodshed.'[12] Roberts and his staff boarded the SS *Balmoral* on 5 March for South Africa, but at Madeira they learned to their consternation and disgust that Wood had arranged an armistice which Viscount Melgund, Roberts's private secretary, believed would be 'ruinous' for British policy in South Africa. When they arrived in Cape Town harbour on the evening of 28 March a boat came out with people crying 'Peace'. A furiously disappointed Roberts, who deeply felt the government's shabby and fumbling treatment, would not stay in South Africa a moment longer than he had to lest it seemed that he was soliciting employment, and he and his staff took the very first ship home they could, leaving Cape Town on SS *Trojan* on 30 March.[13]

Years later, in 1892, George Pretyman, who had been Roberts's AMS in 1881 and was thus highly partisan, wrote that Wood was 'a shifty chap – too much of a Political Soldier' and that he could never be forgiven for his 'abject surrender' to the Boers.[14] At the time, Melgund damned Wood as a 'talking swaggering man' who had been playing his own game and who had settled with the Boers to gain all the kudos and to thwart any chance Roberts might have had of garnering success.[15] Such paranoia was a feature of the bitter rivalry between the Wolseley and Roberts 'rings'. Yet Wood, as he stated unequivocally in a memorandum written in late March, did not in any way approve of negotiations with the Transvaal rebels, and did not believe they would secure a lasting peace. In a series of telegrams from the middle of March addressed to Kimberley and Childers he insisted that with the number of troops soon reaching the front – which would give him an available force of some 14,000 men – he could guarantee the entire success of a renewed offensive and 'enforce dispersion' of the Boer forces. Nevertheless, although he was sorely tempted 'to use a force which is ready to hand and eager to strike', he also conceded that it was the first duty of the 'honourable soldier' to carry out the instructions of his superiors. In any case, while his military position did begin to improve later in March, it was still poor when he first took up his command. He was only too aware that in early March the 1,400 men holding Mount Prospect were badly demoralised and that their situation would become critical if they were not swiftly reinforced.[16] With food also in short supply and the wretched roads impassable because of the rains, Wood understood that in the immediate aftermath of Majuba he had no option but to suspend hostilities if he could, for it actually would have been impossible for him to take the offensive against a well posted enemy believed to be in superior numbers.[17] This was the counsel of reason and duty; yet, as he later admitted in his memoirs, he still believed that 'a majority of the Nation . . . would have been better satisfied if I could have consulted my own wishes, and driven the Boers from the Nek before the Transvaal was given back.'[18]

However, in March 1881 Wood acted as a realist, so that at the same time he was expressing his genuine desire to renew the offensive, he was also exchanging letters with Joubert concerning an armistice. Through the determined mediation of President Brand arrangements were at length made for a meeting between the two commanders. Wood, who had now been appointed to the local rank of Major-General, suggested O'Neill's cottage half-way between the British camp and the Boer positions on Laing's Nek. On Sunday, 6 March, he and his staff arrived back at Mount Prospect from Newcastle and met Joubert at O'Neill's cottage. The two commanders agreed to an armistice up to midnight on 14 March which would allow Kruger time to respond to Colley's ill-fated letter of 21 February. In addition, the British were to be permitted to send eight days' supplies to their besieged garrisons in the Transvaal. The commencement of the armistice at each fort was to date from the receipt of the provision convoy.[19]

While negotiations proceeded, convoys of wagons carrying supplies were sent up from Newcastle to Mount Prospect. The men were kept busy cutting wood, clearing the camp (which had become foul during all the rain which had at last let up), enlarging and neatening up the officers' cemetery, improving the road, maintaining mounted picquets and guarding the entrenchments against possible attack. On 11 March Colonel Redvers Buller, VC, a hero of the Anglo-Zulu War, dashing leader of irregular horse and refused to concede either Boer representation on the Commission or the withdrawal of garrisons. Since Joubert had not the authority either to accept or reject these terms in the absence of his colleagues, it was agreed to prolong the armistice until midnight of 21 March for consideration of the other Boer leaders, and of President Brand whose arrival was expected. Meanwhile, the British were to be allowed to send the besieged garrisons provisions and medical comforts.[28] On 21 and 23 March Wood held further meetings with the Boer leaders, facilitated by President Brand who arrived on 20 March as 'a friend of both parties'. After protracted discussions, due chiefly to the Boers' lack of confidence in the British government, they finally agreed to accept the final terms offered them, which were the acknowledgement of the right of the Transvaal people to complete independence subject to British suzerain rights. In return, the Boers agreed to disperse in order to await the final settlement of the Royal Commission.[29]

At daylight on 24 March the Boers fulfilled their side of the bargain and quitted their position at Laing's Nek, the long chain of their ox-wagons threading its way over the undulating plain towards the Transvaal. The younger Boers were reportedly dissatisfied with the terms of the armistice, but the older men, though doubting the good intentions of the British, placed their confidence in President Brand and Wood.[30] For his part, Wood believed the situation still to be so volatile that he did not believe that there should be any immediate reduction of British forces in South Africa lest the Boers not abide by the terms of the armistice. He felt it necessary, while the Royal Commission was sitting, to concentrate the scattered detachments in Natal at Newcastle to be immediately available as a striking force to suppress any possible outbreak in the Transvaal, and in addition to maintain a reduced garrison at Mount Prospect. The need for the services of Naval Brigade had gone, however, and it was released and rejoined the Squadron.[31]

It remained to carry out the terms of the armistice affecting the besieged British garrisons. On 12 March Cronjé at Potchefstroom received a letter from Kruger informing him that an armistice had been arranged and instructing him to notify Colonel Winsloe as soon as the supplies despatched in terms of the agreement arrived. Until such time he was free to continue the war. On 7 March a supply convoy of four mule-wagons for Potchefstroom had left Mount Prospect. The rain and bad roads meant it took it much longer to arrive at its destination than the negotiators had anticipated, and it was unable to cross the flooded Vaal until 26 March. Meanwhile, the Landdrost of Kroonstad in the Orange Free State arrived in with the terms of the agreement, which were published on 29 March. The civilians were immediately authorised to move back into town after a siege lasting 97 days.[35] A very dispirited Lanyon wrote to Sir Theophilus Shepstone, his predecessor as Administrator: 'I know that I would far rather have remained in captivity for another six years even, & living on cats & dogs, than that broken faith & promises should have set us free . . . so many sad and heartbroken faces.'[36] The next day, 31 March, Lanyon revoked martial law. He quietly left Pretoria on 8 April having been recalled in semi-disgrace, and was never again employed in the colonial service.[37] Word of the armistice reached Rustenburg on 14 March but, pending the arrival of rations provided for in the agreement, the Boers insisted on maintaining their investment. News arrived on 30 March that peace had been negotiated, so after 93 days of extreme privation the gallant garrison marched out with all the honours of war.[38] Peace came last of all to Marabastad where, following a brisk exchange of rifle-fire on 2 April, the Boers approached under flag of truce with the news that a British officer had arrived with despatches. Commandant Vorster was not convinced that the war was at an end, but his own orders arrived the next day and the Boers dispersed.[39]

Once set in motion it was not easy to reverse the momentum of reinforcements being despatched to Natal, so despite the armistice Wood found himself in command of a considerable force much too large for its current mission. On 10 April the dispositions of the NFF were as follows: a company of the 58th Regiment, the depot of the 94th Regiment and a squadron of Mounted Infantry at Newcastle; at Signal Hill, three miles north of Newcastle, were the 6th Dragoons, the 15th Hussars, C/1 RA and a division of F/3 RA, the 2/60th Rifles, the 83rd Regiment, 92nd Highlanders and the 97th Regiment; a company of the 2/21st Fusiliers held the small fort on Schuinshoogte; Mount Prospect was garrisoned by divisions of N/5 RA and 10/7 RA, the HQ and five companies of the 3/60th Rifles and a squadron of Mounted Infantry; the 14th (The King's) Hussars were concentrated at Estcourt; at Pietermaritzburg were the HQ of the 58th Regiment and a half battery of F/3 RA; the 7th (The Queen's Own) Regiment of Hussars and the 41st and 85th Regiments were encamped at Pinetown in the healthy hills north-west of Durban.[40] Wood noted that the regiments which had served in India clung together and treated the others as 'griffins', or new boys.[41] Wood withdrew the Potchefstroom garrison from the Transvaal (it arrived in Ladysmith in Natal on 2 May), concentrated the Rustenburg and Marabastad garrisons in Pretoria by mid-April, and left the others temporarily in place. However, events in Lydenburg required the retention of a British presence. Released suddenly from a state of privation and close confinement in their tiny fort, the garrison entirely escaped the control of Lieutenant Long and went on a drunken spree, breaking into stores and committing many other acts of insubordination. On 3 May (once the news of the near-mutiny had eventually filtered through) Wood sent two companies of the 2/21st Fusiliers to relieve the garrison and re-establish order in the town. Long, whom Wood had initially commended for his staunch defence of Lydenburg, had his career blighted instead.[42]

As a show of force, and to retrieve the honour of the Potchefstroom garrison and cancel out a capitulation achieved by dishonourable means, Wood ordered a column consisting of the 6th Dragoons, 15th Hussars and the 94th Regiment under the command of Lieutenant-Colonel Curtis symbolically to reoccupy Potchefstroom and hoist the British flag. Major-General Buller accompanied the column since Wood believed that his experience of South African warfare would be invaluable should there be any opposition, though Buller objected to being made 'a puppet-show'.[43] The column left Laing's Nek on 30 May and, by way of Standerton and Heidelberg, reached Potchefstroom on 14 May. It left the town again on 17 June, and was back in Newcastle by 4 July.[44] With its return, operations in the Transvaal finally ended, though there were moments in the coming months when Wood believed the Boers would leave the conference table, and quietly bought up oxen and grain against the possibility of a renewed campaign.[45]

From a purely military point of view, and with the future security of Natal in mind, Wood pushed very hard during the negotiations to annex about 6,000 square miles of the south-eastern Transvaal to Natal in order to gain control of the passes into the highveld, eliminate the Utrecht salient which flanked the road to the north, and cut the Boers off from their destabilising meddling in the affairs of Swaziland and Zululand. There is no doubt at all that Wood, supported by Buller and Alison in the War Office, were entirely correct in strategic terms, and that retention of this territory would have prevented the subsequent Boer intervention in the Zulu civil wars and the annexation of a third of Zululand in 1886,[46] as well as the imposition of a protectorate over Swaziland in 1895.[47] Certainly, if the British had held on to this portion of the Transvaal it would have given a quite different cast to the opening stages of the South African War in 1899, and perhaps have dissuaded the Boers from a Natal offensive, or even from risking war at all. But in 1881 these events were unforeseen. Supported by

President Brand, Sir Hercules Robinson and Sir Henry de Villiers (the Chief Justice of the Cape) – who, with Wood, were the three Royal Commissioners appointed by Kimberley – argued that for Britain to retain any Transvaal territory against the will of the Boers would be political folly. Kimberley concurred and Wood's plan was dropped (despite his protests) in return for the Transvaal's disingenuous recognition of the Swazi and Zululand frontiers.[48] The boundary line adopted in the south-western Transvaal, which the Commissioners conceived of as no better than a compromise between competing Boer and Tswana land claims, proved no solution to future conflict either. Continuing unrest over the Transvaal's western borders during the 1880s would eventually lead to Britain setting up the Bechuanaland Protectorate to curb Boer expansion and keep open the 'road to the north'.[49]

Despite his government's eventual extreme satisfaction with his handling of negotiations and the winding down of the war,[50] Wood, overworked and querulous, confided in Buller that the latter would have been better suited to the uncongenial task.[51] The Duke of Cambridge, who certainly did not support handing the Transvaal back to the Boers, wrote when the transfer was complete to commiserate with Wood: 'I can well imagine that the duties you have been engaged upon are not agreeable ones to you, and that you are glad they are over.'[52]

After prolonged bargaining, the Pretoria Convention was agreed upon and signed on 3 August 1881.[53] The Republican flag was hoisted at Pretoria on 8 August 1881 when the transfer of power ceremonially took place.[54] The Convention was a complex document which conceded the substance of Transvaal independence while appearing to retain ultimate imperial control. It defined the Transvaal's frontiers and the extent of its debt, and placed a British Resident in Pretoria to represent the Queen's 'suzerainty' – a nebulous term and typical Gladstonian obfuscation that primarily referred to restrictions on the Transvaal's right to make treaties and offered some protection of African rights. The Convention, though subsequently ratified by the Volksraad, was thus not so much a treaty as a prerogative act conferring rights on the Transvalers. On 12 April Kimberly had done away with the dual authority of two High Commissioners in southern Africa when he vested Robinson with the powers of High Commissioner for all South Africa and eliminated the High Commission for South East Africa held by Colley, and for a short time intended for Sir F. Roberts. Thus a shadowy British presence was retained north of the Vaal through the British Resident reporting to the High Commissioner. Yet even though British policy was now essentially to abstain from interfering north of the Orange River, most Transvalers did not read the Pretoria Convention to mean this. They only accepted it with reluctance and distaste, and the intention was always to revise its terms as soon as feasible.[55]

Trouble was thus being stored up for the future, but in 1881 the prime objective of Gladstone and Kimberley had been achieved, namely, the reassurance of the South African Afrikaners. During the course of the war Kimberley came more and more to fear a pan-Afrikaner uprising throughout southern Africa which might be the signal for a general African revolt, and ultimately create another version of the intractable Irish problem which was bedevilling the Liberal administration. The Convention, by placating the Transvaal Boers and conciliating the Cape and Free State Afrikaners, defused the grim possibility of a united Afrikaner front challenging British dominance in South Africa. It also heralded a new approach to solving the South African problem. The Tory policy of formal confederation was to be replaced with the idea of informal paramountcy, the making of friends and the winning of influence – which meant courting the Boers and creating stronger and more amiable ties for the future. What this amounted to in practical terms was that English colonists, who formed the settler minority in South Africa, were to be sacrificed on the altar of improved Anglo-Boer relations.[56]

When Kimberley wrote on 31 March 1881 to Sir Hercules Robinson appointing him to the Royal Commission for the settlement of the Transvaal, he declared that 'Her Majesty's Government are bound to take care that those who have been faithful to the British cause during the late war shall not suffer any detriment in consequence of their loyalty.' It was to be the three Commissioners' duty to lay down conditions securing for loyalists 'full liberty to reside in the country, with enjoyment of all civil rights and protection for their persons and property.'[57]

It soon became apparent, however, that the category of 'loyalist' applied solely to white settlers. The Aborigines Protection Society wrote with little practical effect to Kimberley on 31 March gravely concerned at the potential plight of Africans abandoned to harsh Boer republican rule.[58] White loyalists also raised the spectre of loyal Africans suffering under restored Boer administration, but did so less out of altruism than as a ploy to prick the conscience of a Liberal administration into retaining British rule.[59] Yet the special pleading of British philanthropists and Transvaal loyalists aside, there is no doubt that Africans themselves in the Transvaal were appalled at the prospect of a return to Boer rule. They made their feelings abundantly clear to British officials still in positions of authority in the Zoutpansberg, Waterberg, Rustenburg, Marico and Bloemhof Districts.[60] Henrique Shepstone, while still the Transvaal Secretary for Native Affairs, wrote to his father, Sir Theophilus, that 'nearly every chief in the country has sent to me begging not to be handed back to the Boers & alluding to their loyalty during the late war in obeying orders'.[61] African chiefs had made the decision to support the British during the rebellion and, as Chief Masibi of the Ndebele expressed it, could no more have believed their defeat possible than if they had witnessed 'a wolf [hyena] beat a lion'.[62] Their consternation was coupled with dismay at the British betrayal of a loyalty which was about to bring Boer retribution down upon their heads, and some fleetingly considered armed resistance. Lanyon, for one, considered it 'a cruel and crying shame' that the British were so ready to desert the Africans who had stuck by them,[63] but the prime concern of the British government remained its working relationship with white settler society.

As for the Transvaal English, cabinet ministers' glib assurances of their continued well-being under Boer rule did nothing to dissuade them from their conclusion that Gladstone had sold them down the river. On 7 April representatives of the Central Committee of the Loyal Inhabitants of the Transvaal, which had been formed in Pretoria on 29 March with branches in Wakkerstroom, Newcastle and elsewhere to coordinate the protests of loyal subjects across South Africa,[64] sent their petition to the home government. Gladstone was reminded that the repeated promises that the Transvaal would ever remain British had induced large investments in land and property which were now jeopardised since 'the banks are leaving, capitalists are endeavouring to withdraw, and all enterprise . . . is paralysed'. Thus valuable property had become unsaleable, and certainly 'extremely depreciated in value'. Besides which, active collaboration with the British forces during the war had placed the loyalists in a position where it would be unsafe to remain in the Transvaal under Boer rule. As it was, since the armistice many had suffered 'in person and in property' from the Boers. The petitioners declared themselves 'cruelly deceived by the mother country', and claimed the right 'for the fullest material compensation' from the imperial government for their losses.[65]

Not content with memorialising Gladstone, the Central Committee of the Loyal Inhabitants also had printed a Humble Petition to the House of Commons, in which the points made in the letter to Gladstone were

Nor did protests against the 'humiliation and shame' of the Transvaal peace limply end with genteel petitions and resolutions by orderly – if excited – public meetings in English-speaking towns of the Cape such as Cape Town, King William's Town, Port Elizabeth and East London.[76] Popular anglophone anger against Gladstone and his administration increasingly took on the time-hallowed form of the 'authorised transgression' of carnivalesque rites, expressed as an immediately recognisable inversion of the patriotic songs, representations of public personalities and nationalistic flag waving of the distinctive British music hall culture of the time.[77] On 26 March in Pietermaritzburg a flag-staff was set up in the middle of Market Square flying the British Ensign reversed with the Transvaal *Vierkleur* above it. The Saturday market crowd reportedly relished the symbolism, and when the insulted Ensign was ripped down by an indignant 'Jingo' the anti-government mob dragged it through the mud and trod it under foot.[78]

An even more satisfying act of symbolism was already establishing the pattern of protest, one that projected familiar and easily recognisable cultural resonances that went back to the seventeenth century: the ritual burning in a bonfire each fifth of November of the effigy of the arch-traitor and foe of British liberty and established Protestant religion, Guy Fawkes, who in 1605 had plotted to blow up parliament. On 3 April a large cartoon of the British lion being blindfolded by Gladstone was paraded on a cart around Cape Town accompanied by a loud band. That evening a crowd estimated to be nearly 6,000 strong gathered on the Grand Parade to burn Gladstone's effigy in a huge bonfire.[79] This satisfying immolation was emulated in Newcastle on 28 March by the loyal townspeople and refugees (with the prudent exception of a few merchants in the 'Boer trade'). In the Market Square the Union Jack, draped in mourning, was hoisted at half-mast. An effigy of Gladstone was tried and found guilty of high treason and then hanged and burnt by the tumultuous crowd.[80] In Kimberley Gladstone's effigy met a similar fate on the Market Square to the jeers of a large crowd and the appropriate accompanying strains of the 'Dead March' from *Saul* and raucous jingo songs. However, the serious intent of the carnival was emphasised by newspapers which were at pains to report how 'well conducted' was the crowd and that it was not out simply for a 'lark'.[81] Nor was that the end of the public burnings. In Wakkerstroom, where the loyalists had suffered severely from Boer depredations, Gladstone's effigy was burned on 5 April 'in the presence of the whole town'.[82] On Saturday 9 April in Pietermaritzburg a well-advertised demonstration took the form of another effigy of Gladstone – this time in full evening-dress with a rope around his neck – being paraded through the streets on a funeral car accompanied by a coffin labelled 'Liberal Ministry' and an inverted Ensign with a mourning fringe, and then being hanged and burnt on the Market Square to the accompaniment of many patriotic speeches.[83] The last of this rash of public burnings, whose intended implications Gladstone (when he learned of them) could hardly have failed to miss, took place in Pretoria on 17 April.[84]

Nevertheless, none of the wide-ranging pleas for comprehensive restitution or compensation could signify – let alone the cries for the continuation of British rule – if the Liberal government refused to entertain them. Queen Victoria might fret that 'the interests of our loyal friends' in the Transvaal were being sacrificed 'for the sake of a few discontented Boers',[85] but Gladstone (though already burnt six times in effigy) was not to be deflected. It is true that the skilful petition from the Loyal Inhabitants of the Transvaal, despatched in April, caused Gladstone the maximum of embarrassment. Nevertheless, with Kimberley's help, he was up to concocting what he considered a fitting response. Gladstone's letter of 1 June to the Loyal Inhabitants left them in no doubt as to where the Transvaal British stood. After glibly justifying his termination of the war, the abandonment of the South African confederation policy and the retrocession of the Transvaal, Gladstone turned to the situation of the English settlers. He first 'willingly and thankfully' acknowledged their 'loyal co-operation', and assured them that in the settlement being hammered out, care would be taken to secure them 'the full enjoyment of their property and of all civil rights'. The sting, however, was in the tail. Gladstone declared that whilst his government 'cannot recognise any general claim for compensation in respect of depreciation of property arising from the change of policy involved in the new arrangement, the question of compensation to either side for acts committed during the late troubles, not justified by the necessities of war, has been remitted to the Commission.'[86] This was certainly not what Loyal Inhabitants wanted to hear, and from that moment they knew Gladstone had resolved to throw them over. But before they could decide on further action, they had to learn what the Royal Commission was to decide.

The Commissioners certainly had all the evidence before them necessary to make a ruling over compensation, beside the known wishes of the British government. Considerable discussion ensued among them, and Kimberley was also consulted and his approval sought, as was that of the Boer leaders. In their official Report to the Queen, Robinson and de Villiers (Wood submitted a dissenting report) devoted paragraphs 119 to 133 to the question of 'compensation for losses through war', and paragraph 149 to 'protection of trade and interest of loyals'.[87] Their decisions were incorporated into the Convention signed in Pretoria with the Boer representatives on 3 August 1881. While direct losses as a result of war were recognised, claims for indirect losses were not entertained, thus dashing many loyalists' hopes.[88] Nevertheless, Article 12 met another of their greatest concerns when it stipulated that they would 'suffer no molestation' on account of supporting the British forces.[89] Furthermore, Articles 16, 26, 27, 30 and 31 guaranteed their freedom of religion, movement and commercial activity, residential and property rights, and protection by the courts. By Article 28 all persons who came to live in the Transvaal after British annexation were to be exempt from compulsory military service in the Boer state, thus avoiding a conflict of loyalties. At first glance, the terms of the Convention seemed to have favoured the Transvaal English. But, as Haggard pointed out, most of the losses they believed they had sustained were indirect and thus not compensated for; while many of them believed that – the paper guarantees notwithstanding – a Transvaal no longer under British rule was 'a country that could no longer be their home'.[90] Loyalist leaders predicted that, unless their requests for proper compensation and protection under renewed Boer rule were heeded, 'serious and grave' disturbances must ensue.[91] When it was learned on 2 August that the Convention was to be signed in Pretoria the following day – and in the very same room in which, four years before, Sir Theophilus Shepstone had signed the Annexation Proclamation – the threatened disturbances broke out. They were not as unruly as predicted, but were a carefully orchestrated symbolic pantomime which took the form of the ceremonious burial of the Union Jack. The flag was followed to the grave by a crowd of about 2,000 loyalists. On its coffin was written:

In loving memory of the British flag in the Transvaal, who departed this life on the 2nd August 1881, in his fifth year. 'In other climes none knew thee but to love thee.' Resurgam [may I rise again].[92]

Notes and references

1 JC 26, no. 2465: Maj Essex to Joubert, 27 February 1881. For operations of the NFF between the battle of Majuba and 12 March 1881, see Butterfield, ed., *War and Peace*, pp. 216–220: Journal of the Natal Field Force, 28 February–12 March 1881.

2 The cottage was on the farm Stonewall, and had been built by P.A.H. de Barry who had acquired the farm in 1870. He sold it to an O'Neill of Graaff-Reinet in the Cape, who presented it to his brother, R.C. O'Neill (Ou Gert) in 1878.

3 Meintjes, *Commandant-General*, p. 83.

4 WO 32/7833, no. 079/4743: Report by Lt Brotherton, 19 April 1881.

5 BV 16, p. 89: Bond to Joubert, 1 March 1881; BV 16, p. 100: Lady Colley to Joubert, n.d.; Joubert to Lady Colley, n.d.

6 WC III/2/18: Stewart to Wood, 10 March 1881. Stewart was later held at Heidelberg, where Wood sent him 'articles of apparel and kit'. See JC 26, no. 2467: Wood to Joubert, 8 March 1881.

7 BV 13, p. 473: Joubert to Kruger, 1 March 1881.

8 WO 32/7833, no. 079/4743: Report by Lt Brotherton, 19 April 1881.

9 WC III/1/3: Memorandum by Sir E. Wood showing the state of affairs at and about Newcastle in the first week, March 1881; Wood, *Midshipman to Field Marshal*, vol. II, p. 111.

10 P. Mason, *A Matter of Honour: An Account of the Indian Army, its Officers and Men* (Great Britain: Harmondsworth: 1976), pp. 345, 381; Haythornthwaite, *Colonial Wars*, pp. 322–4.

11 WC III/5/2: Childers to Wood, 2 March 1881.

12 *BPP* (C. 2866): no. 64: Kimberley to Sir F. Roberts, 4 March 1881.

13 Minto Papers, MS 12506: Viscount Melgund's diary, 5, 11, 13, 31 March 1881.

14 Minto Papers, MS 12380: G. Pretyman to Melgund, 18 January 1892.

15 Minto Papers, MS 12531: Melgund's diary, 31 March 1881.

16 WC III/1/3: Memorandum by Sir E. Wood showing the state of affairs at and about Newcastle in the first week, March 1881. On 19 March the state of troops showed 1,438 at Mount Prospect, 48 at Schuinshoogte, 2,833 at Newcastle, 52 at the Ingagane, 42 on the Biggarsberg, 55 at Ladysmith and 37 at Ladysmith; a total of 4,511 officers and men, of whom 1,138 were mounted. There were also 15 9-pounder guns, 2 7-pounder guns and 2 Gatlings. See WO 32/7818, no. 079/4455: Wood to Childers, 19 March 1881: State of Troops.

17 WC III/6/2: Wood to Childers, cypher telegram, 6 March 1881.

18 Wood, *Midshipman to Field Marshal*, vol. II, p. 115.

19 JC 26, no. 2529: Heads of Conditions of an Armistice Proposed to be Agreed between the British and Boer Forces, 6 March 1881. See *BPP* (C. 2950), enc. 11 in no. 30.

20 Colonel C.H. Melville, *Life of General the Right Hon. Sir Redvers Buller V.C., G.C.B., G.C.M.G.* (London, 1923), vol. 1, p. 147. Buller had come out as DAQG in South Africa on Lt-Gen Smyth's staff. On 29 March he was promoted Brigadier-General with the local rank of Major-General.

21 WO 32/7818, no. 079/4455: Wood to Childers, 19 March 1881.

22 For Wood's spirited account of the negotiations at O'Neill's cottage, see Wood, *Midshipman to Field Marshal*, vol. II, pp. 118–21.

23 JC 26, no. 2537: Wood to Joubert, 14 March 1881; no. 2538: Terms of Four Days Prolongation of Armistice, 14 March 1881. See *BPP* (C. 2950), enc. 12 in no. 30.

24 JC 26, no. 2541: Wood to Joubert, 15 March 1881; *BPP* (C. 2950), enc. 13 in no. 30: Wood's Account of Meeting with Boers, 15 March 1881.

25 Letter by Buller, 20 March 1881, quoted in Melville, *Life of Buller*, vol. I, p. 149.

26 Wood, *Midshipman to Field Marshal*, vol. II, p. 121.

27 Kruger, *Memoirs*, pp. 178–82.

28 JC 26, no. 2548: Schedule of agreement between Wood and Joubert, 18 March 1881; WO 32/7818, no. 079/4455: Wood to Childers, 19 March 1881; *BPP* (C. 2950), enc. 1 in no. 40: Account of Meeting with Boers, 18 March 1881.

29 *BPP* (C. 2950), enc. 2 in no. 40: Minutes of Proceedings of Meeting, 21 March 1881; enc. 3 in no. 40: Result of a Meeting, 21 March 1881; enc. 6 in no. 40: Wood, Krüger, Pretorius and Joubert to Kimberley, telegram, 21 March 1881; enc. 7 in no. 40: Minutes of the Proceedings at the Meeting of March 23, 1881; enc. 8 in no. 40: Ratification of Provisional Agreement of 21 March 1881, 23 March 1881.

30 *Natal Advertiser*, 26 March 1881: special war correspondent, Mount Prospect, 24 March 1881.

31 WO 32/7818, no. 079/4532: Wood to Childers, 30 March 1881; WO 32/7824, no. 079/4767: Wood to Childers, 8 May 1881.

32 Bennett, *Rain of Lead*, pp. 202–12.

33 Mrs Long, *Fort Mary*, pp. 91–108.

34 Bellairs, ed., *Transvaal War*, pp. 366–8.

35 Bellairs, ed., *Transvaal War*, pp. 225–35.

36 TS 46: Lanyon to Sir T. Shepstone, 30 March 1881.

37 Theron-Bushell, 'Lanyon', pp. 285–6, 290–5.

38 Bellairs, ed., *Transvaal War*, pp. 283–4.

39 Bellairs, ed., *Transvaal War*, pp. 297–9.

40 WO 32/7818, no. 079/4565: GOC, Natal to the AG to the Forces, 10 April 1881.

41 WC III/3/3: Wood to Cambridge, 21 November 1881. The 'Indian' regiments were the 15th Hussars, 2/60th Rifles and 92nd Highlanders.

42 WO 32/7823, no. 079/4682: The GOC South East Africa to the AG of the Forces, 5 May 1881; WC III/2/9: Cambridge to Wood, n.d.

43 Letter by Buller, 16 May 1881, quoted in Melville, *Life of Buller*, vol. I, p. 150.

44 WO 32/7828, enc. in no. 079/4965: Maj-Gen R. Buller to GOC, Natal and Transvaal, 4 July 1881.

45 WC III/3/5: Wood to Childers, 4 December 1881.

46 Laband, *Later Zulu Wars*, pp. 78–80.

47 Maylam, *African People*, pp. 94–5.

48 WO 32/7826, p. 9173: Wood to Kimberley, 23 May 1881; p. 9174: Robinson to Kimberley, 23 May 1881; WO 32/7826, no. 079/4895: Herbert to Thompson, 30 July 1881; memorandum by Alison, 5 August 1881.

49 WO 32/7826, pp. 11, 750: Robinson to Kimberley, 4 July 1881; Davenport, *South Africa*, pp. 209–12.

50 WC III/3/9: Robinson to Wood, 26 September 1881.

51 WC III/3/2: Wood to Buller, 23 June 1881.

52 WC III/2/9: Cambridge to Wood, 9 August 1881.

53 *BPP* (C. 3098), enc. 1 in no. 23: Pretoria Convention, 3 August 1881. See also *BPP* (C. 3114), Appendix no. 1: Convention.

54 SS 8834: Vice President Pretorius to Kimberley, telegram, 15 August 1881.

55 Benyon, *Proconsul and Paramountcy*, pp. 176–8, 192, 323; Davenport, *South Africa*, pp. 209–11. By the London Convention, signed on 27 February 1884, Kruger would succeed in removing the British Resident and any reference to suzerainty, though its substance remained. See C. Headlam, 'The Race for the Interior, 1881–1895', in Walker, ed., *Cambridge History of the British Empire*, vol. VIII, pp. 520–1.

56 Schreuder, *Gladstone and Kruger*, pp. 212–14, 222–4, 465–9.

57 *BPP* (C. 2892), no. 1: Kimberley to Robinson, 31 March 1881.

58 *BPP* (C. 2950), no. 17: S. Gurney, T. Fowell Buxton and F.W. Chesson to Kimberley, 31 March 1881.

59 See, for example, the argument in *BPP* (C. 2950), enc. in no. 66: The Humble Petition of the Loyal Inhabitants of the Transvaal to the Commons of the United Kingdom of Great Britain and Ireland, n.d. [1 May 1881], that the 'Natives' were 'without exception in favour of English rule'.

60 See BV 21: Jacobus More (Mamagali), chief of the Bakwena, to H.C. Shepstone, 30 March 1881; Memorandum of interview between Sir E. Wood and Chiefs Jan Kekana, Lebolo and Matibi Swaartboois, 9 April 1881; *BPP* (C. 2950), enc. in no. 56: statement by Mghotshi, sent by Chief Umkhanla, made to H.C. Sheptsone, 14 April 1881; statement by Bizwa, sent by Chief Kuruman, made to H. Shepstone, 13 April 1881; J.S. Moffat, Native Commissioner, Western Border, to H. Shepstone, 15 April 1881; enc. 1 in no. 60: A. Woolls-Sampson, Native Commissioner, Waterberg, to H.C. Shepstone, 18 April 1881; Chief Fred Maghali to H. Shepstone, 20 April 1881; enc. in no. 61: statement by Chief Sjambok to

A. Woolls-Sampson, Native Commissioner, Waterberg, 24 April 1881; *Natal Advertiser*, 29 April and 2 May 1881.

61 TS 46: H.C. Shepstone to Sir T. Shepstone, 14 May 1881.

62 *BPP* (C. 2950), enc. in no. 60: statement by Tai, Stemmer and Manele, sent by the Indebele chief Masibi, made to H.C. Shepstone, 24 April 1881.

63 Lanyon Papers, vol. 16: Lanyon to C. Lanyon, 25 April 1881.

64 *The Transvaal War, 1881. Reprinted from the 'Natal Mercury'* (Durban, n.d. [1881]), pp. 308–9: Newcastle correspondent, 30 March 1881; p. 344: special commissioner, Pretoria, 7 April 1881; p. 358: leader, 30 April 1881; p. 364: special correspondent, Newcastle, 1 May 1881. The chairman of the committee was C.K. White, a former member of the Transvaal Legislative Assembly, and its secretary was Martin J. Farrell, a surveyor engaged in working on the proposed Delagoa Railway.

65 *BPP* (C. 2950), enc. 1 in no. 49: C.K. White and M.J. Farrell to Gladstone, n.d. [c. 7 April 1881].

66 *BPP* (C. 2950), enc. in no. 66: The Humble Petition of the Loyal Inhabitants of the Transvaal to the Commons of the United Kingdom of Great Britain and Ireland, n.d. [1 May 1881]. See *Transvaal War*, pp. 379, 385, for reports from Pretoria on 17 and 23 April 1881 describing the flight of artisans.

67 *BPP* (C. 2950), enc. in no. 65: Jas. C. Murray and 34 others to Kimberley, n.d. [4 May 1881].

68 Haggard, *Last Boer War*, p. 178.

69 See, as one example among dozens, *BPP* (C. 2959), enc. 2 in no. 8: Memorandum of money, goods, &c. commandeered and taken away by force from the British subjects residing in the Ward Hex River, in the District of Rustenburg, 5 April 1881.

70 See, for example, *BPP* (C. 2950), enc. 2 in no. 60: report of Capt Brook, 5 April 1881; *BPP* (C. 3098), no. 17: Wood to Kimberley, 17 July 1881.

71 Haggard, *Last Boer War*, p. 167. See *Transvaal War*, p. 363, for report of 29 April 1881 describing loyal Europeans arriving in Newcastle.

72 *BPP* (C. 3114), sub-enc. 8 in no. 14 in Appendix: papers laid before the Royal Commission by the Deputation of Loyal Inhabitants of the Transvaal, 16 May 1881; sub-enc. 11 in no. 14 in Appendix: John Nixon to the Royal Commissioners, 20 May 1881; sub-enc. 16 in no. 14 in Appendix: Papers laid before Royal Commission by Deputation of Loyal Inhabitants, 27 May 1881; sub-enc. 17 in Appendix: Interview given to Deputation of Loyal Inhabitants, 27 May 1881; sub-enc. 18 in Appendix: Interview of Deputation with the Royal Commission, 28 May 1881.

73 *BPP* (C. 3114), sub-enc. 20 in no. 14 in Appendix: Report of the meeting of the Transvaal Sufferers' Protection Association, 1 June 1881.

74 *BPP* (C. 3114), sub-enc. 21 in no. 14 in Appendix: Fred. S Whiting to the Royal Commissioners, 20 June 1881; sub-enc. 22 in no. 14 in Appendix: Deputation from the Standard Bank of British South Africa, 21 June 1881.

75 See *BPP* (C. 3114), sub-encs 23–31 in no. 14 in Appendix.

76 *Transvaal War*, p. 299: resolution at public meeting in Cape Town, 8 April 1881; p. 321: resolution at public meeting in East London, 14 April 1881. *Natal Advertiser*, 13 April 1881; *Times of Natal*, 11 April 1881.

77 J. Burke, *An Intimate History of Killing: Face-to-Face Killing in Twentieth Century Warfare* (London, 2000), pp. 41–2; Mackenzie, 'Empire and Metropolitan Cultures' in Porter, ed., *Oxford History of the British Empire*, vol. III, pp. 277–8.

78 *Times of Natal*, 28 March 1881.

79 *Natal Advertiser*, 5 April 1881.

80 *Transvaal War*, p. 308: Newcastle correspondent, 28 March 1881.

81 *Times of Natal*, 18 April 1881.

82 *Transvaal War*, p. 328: Wakkerstroom correspondent, 5 April 1881.

83 *Transvaal War*, p. 299: Maritzburg correspondent, 10 April 1881; *Times of Natal*, 11 April 1881.

84 *Transvaal War*, p. 361: special commissioner in Newcastle, 24 April 1881.

85 Queen Victoria to Kimberley, 26 May 1881, quoted in Schreuder, *Gladstone and Kruger*, p. 196

86 *BPP* (C. 2950), no. 57: Gladstone to White, 1 June 1881.

87 *BPP* (C. 3114), Report of the Commissioners Appointed to Inquire into and Report upon All Matters Relating to the Settlement of the Transvaal Territory, n.d. [August 1881], Part I; no. 11a in Appendix: Robinson to Kimberley, 29 June 1881; no. 11b in Appendix: Kimberley to Robinson, 5 July 1881. See also *BPP* (C. 3219), Report of the Commissioners, Part II: Report of a Conference with the Boer Leaders, 19 July 1881, items 2433–6.

88 *BPP* (C. 3098), enc. 1 in no. 23: Convention, 3 August 1881: Article 8. See Mrs Heckford, *Lady Trader*, p. 412.

89 *BPP* (C. 3098), enc. 1 in no. 23: Convention, 3 August 1881: Article 12.

90 Haggard, *Last Boer War*, pp. 178–80.

91 *BPP* (C. 3114), Report of the Commissioners, Part I; no. 14 in Appendix: Martin Farrell to St Leger Herbert, Secretary, Royal Commission, 28 May 1881.

92 *BPP* (C. 3098), no. 25: Wood to Kimberley, 17 August 1881; Haggard, *Last Boer War*, pp. 182–3; *Times of Natal*, 3 August 1881; Lehmann, *Boer War*, p. 301. During the night the coffin was exhumed and hoisted at the post office nearby. Lt-Col Gildea rescued the flag and took it back with him to England.

Conclusion

'Remember Majuba!'

Shortly before leaving Pretoria on 5 August 1881, Wood received an address from 60 English inhabitants of the town who 'most solemnly' protested against any loyal British subjects 'being handed over to the mercy of the Boers'. Their fears were real, but the Convention was signed and the case closed, and Wood sent them a dusty reply firmly telling them so.[1] The Transvaal loyalists were left with no choice but to buckle down under Boer rule, or leave the country.

Considered dispassionately, the Transvaal British emerged relatively unscathed from the Transvaal Rebellion. Those who stayed suffered no ethnic cleansing or any other meaningful form of persecution; while their direct material losses were recompensed to the tune of £110,000 defrayed by the Imperial Government when the Boers defaulted from paying their share.[2] Besides, it would seem that losses by traders had not been as great as at first claimed, for many of those who had 'kept quiet and held their tongues' during the war had 'done a good business'.[3] As for the indirect losses about which the loyalists had been so extremely concerned, any of the British who remained in the Transvaal, or continued to invest in the country, were rewarded tenfold when, only a few years later, the discovery in 1886 of gold in huge paying quantities on the Witwatersrand heralded boom economic conditions.

Even so, where the Transvaal British considered themselves most hurt was in their sense of 'Englishness', in their ingrained belief that, as loyal subjects, they ought to have been able to rely absolutely on the protection of the Crown, both politically and economically. It was the perceived betrayal by Gladstone's administration which rankled most, the conviction that they had been cravenly and unnecessarily abandoned to the humiliation and inconvenience of rule by the despised and retrograde Boers. As Rider Haggard expressed it, 'such an act of treachery to those to whom we were bound . . . stands, I believe, without parallel in our records, and marks a new departure in our history.'[4] The Uitlanders (or non-Boer outsiders) who continued to make their homes and fortunes in the Transvaal would never be reconciled to Kruger's republic and looked to future Tory administrations under Lord Salisbury to safeguard their interests.

The circumstances of Africans in the Transvaal deteriorated, as so many had feared they would, once the British withdrew and the Boer state resumed control. The Native Location Commission, set up in terms of Article 21 of the Pretoria Convention,[5] and under the chairmanship of Vice-President Kruger, assumed the role of trustee for all tribal lands. It set about delimiting locations for all the large African chiefdoms where they would be under closer administrative surveillance.[6] In retrospect, British rule seemed far easier to bear.

Colonel Gildea, who had distinguished himself during the siege of Pretoria, was reported in October 1881 to be energetically training his men of the Royal Scots Fusiliers at shelter breastworks (what were called 'schanzes' in South Africa), and then to be pulling them down in order to instruct them in forming 'hasty entrenchments'.[7] In other words, as an intelligent and active officer Gildea had taken the military lessons of the recent rebellion to heart. He had seen that even if the necessity for shelter trenches in the new age of accurate, long-range, high velocity and rapid firing rifles was already acknowledged in the British manuals of military practice, British soldiers were not being sufficiently drilled in their effective use. Likewise, in the aftermath of the Transvaal Rebellion where the record of British marksmanship had been nothing short of dismal, the Report of the Committee on Musketry Instruction in the Army recommended radical improvements in musketry instruction, and suggested that firing be regularly practised at extreme ranges over broken country against moving targets.[8] Yet all that practice in using shelter trenches and the greater emphasis on musketry instruction actually amounted to was better training in methods already set down in the regulations. The disastrous campaign against mobile Boer irregulars had, it seemed, shown that British shortcomings lay with poor leadership and execution, rather than with faulty military doctrine. It was with this mind-set that the British would go to war again with the Boers in 1899, determined to restore their bruised military honour. At the battle of Elandslaagte on 21 October 1899, Colonel Ian Hamilton, a survivor of Colley's ultimate defeat, would urge on his men with the cry 'Remember Majuba!'.[9]

Yet more than the straightforward issue of military effectiveness was at stake. A Boer apologist like W.E. Garrett Fisher could write in 1900 that

. . . the tactics of untrained volunteers like the Boers can scarcely be judged by the same standard that we apply to professional soldiers, who have a definite code of military honour which they are rightly punished and reprobated for transgressing in the smallest particular. The Boers had learned their savage fighting from more than a hundred years of savage warfare . . . and in such a warfare none of the rules which govern civilized campaigns were likely to be developed. The various doubtful acts which were proved against them during the war [of 1880–1881], beginning with Bronkhurst Spruit, must be judged, with this in mind, more tolerantly than any similar acts committed by a regular army.[10]

Yet, in the context of the time, it is irrelevant to engage in Garrett Fisher's relativism, or to debate whether the action at Bronkhorstspruit was a perfidious ambush or the legitimate exploitation of the advantages of position and surprise. In terms of prevailing British military culture, dishonourable Boer actions such as the Bronkhorstspruit ambush, the murder of Captain Elliott, the treacherous raising of white flags at Venter's Farm Laager and Ingogo, or the dishonestly induced capitulation of Potchefstroom only confirmed that the Boers had despicably placed themselves outside the norms of 'civilized warfare' as defined in British military discourse. Consequently, defeat in the Transvaal Rebellion could comfortably be attributed not simply to shortcomings in British military technique, but to unacceptable Boer strategisms and deceptions that fell outside the accepted rules of the game. Thus success in the next war against the Boers would hinge in part on being forewarned against their duplicitous and dishonourable ways, just as hegemony in post-Mutiny India was maintained through a true appreciation (according to Creswicke writing in 1900) of inherent Indian treachery.[11]

Paradoxically, the very extent of Boer success in the war of 1880–1881 would lie at the root of their military failure in the conventional stage of the South African War. In 1899 the Boers realistically assessed that, since time was not on their side, they must achieve such striking early military successes that, as in the previous war, the Cape Afrikaners would be encouraged to flock to their cause and that the British would again lose heart and negotiate a settlement.[12] When relations with Britain reached breaking-point in 1899 the Boers were encouraged (so Rider Haggard believed) by the British capitulation eighteen years before to presume 'that England, wearying of an unpopular struggle, [would] soon cede to them all they ask'.[13]

G.C. Gardyne, in his history of the Gordon Highlanders written at the time of the South African War, sensibly commented of the battle of Majuba that its importance was derived not from the defeat of a small British detachment of soldiers and sailors, 'but from the disastrous and abject political surrender which immediately followed'.[14] Writing in 1881 from his farm, Hill Drop, near Newcastle, Rider Haggard confided to Sir Theophilus Shepstone that he did not know what to say about 'this Transvaal business' except that it 'seems to be the result of a most wonderful combination of political dishonesty, cowardice & personal ambition'. He could only suppose that 'Providence is working out some unforeseen end'.[15] By 1899, on the eve of the South African War, Rider Haggard believed he understood what Providence had intended in 1881: Britain was being called upon to 'pay the bill' by either being driven out of South Africa or being forced 'to assert its dominion even at the price of war'.[16]

Imperial agents who had been closely involved in Transvaal affairs – men such as Shepstone, Frere, Wolseley and Lanyon – held the retrocession of the Transvaal to be both an humiliation and a critical blow to Britain's position in southern Africa. Wolseley was concerned that because the British were widely believed in South Africa to have made peace with the Boers because they 'feared to continue the war', that British military power would no longer act as a deterrent, either upon 'the bellicose instincts and proclivities' of the Africans, or upon the Boers who would be 'once more in a position to act as they like' towards the African polities along their borders. The result, Wolseley warned, would be serious future wars.[17] None agreed with him more wholeheartedly than Lord Carnarvon, the now discredited architect of confederation. But in 1881 confederation was dead. The dream of a white-ruled dominion as an addition to the Empire's strategic strength had proved a chimera for which a 'wretched conflict' had been fought which had brought 'neither profit nor honour', and for which the authorities could not bring themselves even to award the usual campaign medal.[18]

F. Reginald Statham wrote in 1897 that the successful Transvaal Rebellion and the collapse of confederation had the unintended benefit of awakening the 'Dutch population' of South Africa, 'whose national feelings had been so deeply touched by the manifest injustices committed against their kinsfolk beyond the Vaal River', to a 'sense of its political import-ance'.[19] Certainly, their military success against Britain and the imperial power's capitulation encouraged Afrikaners to believe that they had the potential to assert their power more generally in South Africa and to fill the vacuum left by the evaporation of Britain's forward confederation policy.[20] A typical pamphlet published in Dutch in the Cape in the early part of 1882 rejoiced in the Boers' 'marvellous victory' over England and her 'policy of robbery and murder', and confidently projected the emergence of an Afrikaner 'nation' as a manifestation of God's will.[21] Yet, as Rodney Davenport has shown, while the Transvaal Rebellion undoubtedly fired up strong feelings of Afrikaner group unity based on an already vigorous cul-tural nationalism grounded on a sense of common history, language and religion, it failed to gain real momentum. During the later 1880s and the early 1890s commercial and political rivalries between and within South African states, sensible concessions to Afrikaner sentiment in the Cape and restraints on British interference north of the Orange meant that the climate was not inducive to pan-Afrikaner nationalist ferment. In that sense, the direct influence of the Transvaal Rebellion on the creation of a heightened Afrikaner national consciousness was probably less than F.A. van Jaarsveld has suggested. It required the new circumstances in the late 1890s of Cecil Rhodes's reckless ambitions, Uitlander unrest in the Transvaal and resusci-tated imperial interest in South African confederation to revive the call for Afrikaner national unity.[22]

The farm on which Majuba stands became in 1981 the property of the Potchefstroom University for Christian National Education and was admin-istered until 2000 by the Voortrekker Museum in Pietermaritzburg. Under their joint administration Majuba long remained a site of fervent pilgrimage and nationalist commemoration for many Afrikaners. Here the victory of the *Volk* over British imperialism could be joyously celebrated, unlike the South African War which was remembered with bitter tears. In a post-apartheid South Africa, however, there has been a realignment of museum and university policies and functions so that Majuba is now in the hands of a private foundation, and the state no longer plays any part in keeping the memory of the war of 1880–1881 alive. The South African War Graves

Board, first appointed in 1956, had charge of the monuments and graves of the Transvaal Rebellion, along with those of other South African wars. One can still visit the military cemeteries at Bronkhorstspruit, Laing's Nek, Schuinshoogte, Mount Prospect and on the summit of Majuba; while the graves of those who died in the various sieges are generally to be found in the town cemeteries. Natural deterioration and vandalism are the foes of such memorials, and in recent years these inimical processes have much accelerated for lack of funds for restoration and custodianship.[23] Besides, the new South Africa celebrates the recent heroes of the freedom struggle against apartheid. It does not remember those Afrikaners who, in a strange and distant age, pitted themselves like David against the British Goliath, nor those British soldiers who died in performance of their duty so far from home. Yet, for all its diminished contemporary resonance, the Transvaal Rebellion marked a critical stage towards the great war of 1899–1902 which cast the shape of South Africa for the century to come.

Notes and references

1 *BPP* (C. 3098), enc. 1 in no. 25: Herbert Lewis and 59 others to Wood, n.d. [4 August 1881]; enc. 2 in no. 25: Maj T. Fraser, Private Secretary for Transvaal Affairs, to C.J. Kidwell, 4 August 1881.

2 Rider Haggard, *Last Boer War*, p. 178.

3 *Transvaal War*, p. 276: *Natal Mercury* leader, 2 April 1881.

4 Rider Haggard, *Last Boer War*, p. 201.

5 *BPP* (C. 3098), enc. 1 in no. 23: Convention, 3 August 1881: Article 21.

6 T.R.H. Davenport and K.S. Hunt, eds, *The Right to the Land* (Claremont, 1974), pp. 31, 40.

7 WC III/3/3: Wood to Cambridge, 25 October 1881. The 2/21st Regiment had been re-designated the Royal Scots Fusiliers.

8 WO 33/37: Report of the Committee on Musketry Instruction in the Army, 1881.

9 Judd and Surridge, *Boer War*, p. 110.

10 Garrett Fisher, *Transvaal and the Boers*, pp. 206–7.

11 Creswicke, *Transvaal War*, vol. I, p. 76.

12 Judd and Surridge, *Boer War*, p. 106.

13 Rider Haggard, *Last Boer War*, p. xix.

14 C.G. Gardyne, *The Life of a Regiment: The History of the Gordon Highlanders* (Edinburgh, 1901–1903), vol. 2, p. 210.

15 TS 47: Rider Haggard to Sir T. Shepstone, 3 June 1881.

16 Rider Haggard, *Last Boer War*, p. xxiii.

17 WO 32/7835, no. 079/5282: Confidential Memorandum by Wolseley, 31 October 1881. Kimberley discussed this memorandum at the War Office with Childers and queried Wolseley's more prescient conclusions.

18 *Illustrated London News*, 19 February 1881; Goodfellow, *Confederation*, pp. 202–3; Bennett, *Rain of Lead*, p. 239.

19 F.R. Statham, *South Africa as It Is* (London, 1897), pp. 132, 135–6.

20 Nasson, *South African War*, p. 23.

21 *The Birth of the Bond. A Translation from a Dutch Pamphlet Issued in 1882, Entitled 'De Transvaalse Oorlog'* (Grahamstown, 1900), pp. 1–3.

22 T.R.H. Davenport, *The Afrikaner Bond. The History of a South African Political Party, 1880–1911* (Cape Town, 1966), pp. 322–4; Van Jaarsveld, *Afrikaner Nationalism*, pp. 220–1.

23 Chadwick, 'War Graves', pp. 34–8 and personal observation by the author while serving on various museum and heritage committees in South Africa.

Select bibliography

Manuscript sources

Private papers

KwaZulu-Natal Archives
A96: Sir Theophilus Shepstone Papers (TS): 46, 47, 72
A598: Sir Evelyn Wood Collection (WC): III

National Archives of South Africa: Pretoria Depot
A 14: P.J. Joubert Collection (JC): 2, 3, 25–27
A 596: Sir Owen Lanyon Papers: 1, 3, 5a, 5b, 8, 16

National Library of Scotland
Minto Papers: MS 12380, 12506, 12531

Unpublished official papers

Cape Town Archives Repository (CTAR)
Department of Defence, Cape Colony: DD 1
Government House, Cape Colony: GH 11, 15, 30, 36

KwaZulu-Natal Archives

Government House, Natal: GH 602, 603, 792

The National Archives: Public Record Office

War Office 32, Papers Relating to the Transvaal Rebellion: WO 32/7797–7803, 7805–7, 7809–33, 7835

WO 33/37: Report of the Committee on Musketry Instruction in the Army, 1881

WO 33/39: Report of the Colour Committee, 1883

Maps: MFQ 1/295 (2), (3); MFQ 1/297 (1), (2), (3), (4); MFQ 1/311; FQ 1/1187

National Archives of South Africa: Pretoria Depot

Archives of the Administrator of the Transvaal Colony: ATC 3, 5

Argief Boeren Voormannen: BV 1, 3, 5, 7–9, 11–30

Staatsekretaris Z.A.R.: SS 473–565, 8651–3, 8834

Transvaal Volunteer Forces: Order Book and Muster Roll of Transvaal Horse, 1878–1881, 1880–1881: TVO 57

Official printed sources

Blue Book for the Transvaal Province 1879 (Pretoria, 1879)

British Parliamentary Papers: C. 2128, C. 2482, C. 2505, C. 2584, C. 2586, C. 2601, C. 2676, C. 2695, C. 2740, C. 2754, C. 2783, C. 2794, C. 2837, C. 2838, C. 2858, C. 2866, C. 2891, C. 2892, C. 2950, C. 2959, C. 2961, C. 2962, C. 2998, C. 3098, C. 3114, C. 3219, C. 3419

By Authority, *The Army List: Containing the Names of Officers of the Army, Royal Marines, Militia, Yeomanry, Volunteers, and Colonial Militia and Volunteers* (London, July 1879 to September 1881); 27 volumes

Callwell, Col C.E., *Small Wars. Their Principles and Practice* (London, 3rd edn, 1906)

De Staatscourant Gedurenden den Vrijheidsoorlog van 1881

Great Britain, War Office, *Field Exercise and Evolution of Infantry* (London, pocket edn, 1877)

Great Britain, War Office, *The Mountain and River Barriers between Natal and the Transvaal* (London, 1881)

Great Britain, War Office, *Text Book of Fortification and Military Engineering, For Use at The Royal Military Academy, Woolwich, Part I* (London, 2nd edn, 1884)

Great Britain, War Office Intelligence Department, *Narrative of Field Operations Connected with the Zulu War of 1879* (London, 1881)

Great Britain, War Office Intelligence Department, *Précis of Information Concerning South Africa. The Transvaal Territory* (London, 1878)

The Lieutenant-General Commanding [Lord Chelmsford], *Special Instructions regarding the Management of Ox Transport on the Line of March and for Conducting the Line of March when Troops March with Ox Wagon Transport and for Forming Wagon Laagers* (Durban, n.d. [1879])

Notes on Transport. Revised 1897 (Ferozepore, 1897)

The Transvaal Government Gazette, 1880–1881 (Pretoria, 1880, 1881)

Unofficial contemporary printed sources

Newspapers and periodicals

Graphic, 1881

Illustrated London News, 1881

Natal Advertiser, 1880–1881

Natal Mercury, 1880–1881

Natal Witness, 1880–1881

Times of Natal, 1880–1881

Transvaal Argus and Commercial Gazette, 1881

De Volksstem, 1881

Articles

Barrett, H.J., 'Social and Domestic Life of the Dutch Boers of South Africa', Ordinary General Meeting of the Society, 14 June 1869, *Proceedings of the Royal Colonial Institute 1869* (London, 1870), vol. I

Montague, W.E., 'Besieged in the Transvaal (the Siege of Standerton)', *Blackwood's Magazine*, 140 (July–August 1881)

Portlock, Maj-Gen J.E. and Nugent, Col Sir C., KCB, RE, 'Fortification', *The Encyclopaedia Britannica* (Edinburgh, 9th edn, 1879)

Winsloe, R.W.C., 'Siege of Potchefstroom', *Macmillan's Magazine*, 47 (1882)

Books and pamphlets: general accounts; autobiographies; memoirs; reminiscences

Bellairs, Lady, ed., *The Transvaal War 1880–81* (Edinburgh and London, 1885)

Benjamin, D., *The Surrender of the Transvaal Territory and the Rights of British Subjects* (Cape Town, 1881)

The Birth of the Bond. A Translation from a Dutch Pamphlet Issued in 1882, Entitled 'De Transvaalse Oorlog', Which Proves Beyond a Doubt How Deep-Laid and Well-Played Has Been the Plotting of the Africander Party to Overthrow British Supremacy in South Africa (Grahamstown, 1900)

Brown, D.B., *Surgical Experiences in the Zulu and Transvaal Wars, 1879 and 1881* (Edinburgh and London, 1883)

Butler, E., Lady, *An Autobiography* (London, 1922)

Butler, Lt-Gen Sir W.F., *The Life of Sir George Pomeroy-Colley, KCSI, CB, CMG Including Services in Kaffraria – in China – in Ashanti – in India and in Natal* (London, 2nd impression, 1899)

Butler, Lt-Gen Sir W., *Sir William Butler: An Autobiography* (London, 1911)

Cachet, F.L., *De Worstelstrijd der Transvalers aan het Volk van Nederland Verhaald* (Amsterdam, 1883)

Carter, T.F., *A Narrative of the Boer War: Its Causes and Results* (Cape Town, Port Elizabeth, Johannesburg and London, 1882; new edn, 1896)

Clark, G.B., *British Policy towards the Boers: An Historical Sketch* (London, 1881)

Clark, G.B., *Our Future Policy in the Transvaal: A Defence of the Boers* (London, 1881)

Creswicke, L., *South Africa and the Transvaal War* (Edinburgh, 1900), vol. I

Cromb, J., ed., *The Majuba Disaster: A Story of Highland Heroism, Told by Officers of the 92nd Regiment* (Dundee, 1891)

Davison, C.F., *The Case of the Boers in the Transvaal* (London, 1881)

Dennison, Major C.G., *A Fight to the Finish* (London, 1904)

Dixie, Lady Florence, *In the Land of Misfortune* (London, 1882)

Du Val, C., *With a Show through Southern Africa* (London, 1881), 2 vols.

Du Val, C. and Deecker, L.W., eds, *The News of the Camp. A Journal of Fancies, Notifications, Gossip, and General Chit Chat* (Pretoria, 1880–1)

Gardyne, C.G., *The Life of a Regiment: The History of the Gordon Highlanders* (Edinburgh, 1901–1903), vol. 2

Garrett Fisher, W.E., *The Transvaal and the Boers: A Short History of the South African Republic, with a Chapter on the Orange Free State* (London, 1900)

Haggard, H. Rider, *Cetywayo and his White Neighbours; or, Remarks on Recent Events in Zululand, Natal and the Transvaal* (London, 1888)

Haggard, Sir H. Rider, *The Last Boer War* (London, 1899)

Heckford, S., *A Lady Trader in the Transvaal* (London, 1882)

Holt, H.P., *The Mounted Police of Natal* (London, 1913)

Kruger, P., *The Memoirs of Paul Kruger, Four Times President of the South African Republic, Told by Himself* (London, 1902)

Lambart, F., *A Few Hints, Facts etc Gathered from Life among the Boers* (Pietermaritzburg, 1881)

Long, Mrs W.H.C., *Peace and War in the Transvaal: An Account of the Defence of Fort Mary, Lydenburg* (London, 1882)

Martineau, J., *The Life and Correspondence of the Right Hon. Sir Bartle Frere, Bart.* (London, 1895)

Montague, W.E., *Besieged in the Transvaal* (Edinburgh and London, 1881)

Moodie, G.P., *Annexation of the Transvaal* (London, 1881)

Nixon, J., *The Complete Story of the Transvaal* (London, 1885)

Norris-Newman, C.L., *With the Boers in the Transvaal and Orange Free State in 1880–1* (London, 1882)

Richards, W., *Her Majesty's Army: A Descriptive Account of the Various Regiments Now Comprising the Queen's Forces, from their First Establishment to the Present* (London, n.d., c. 1888), 3 vols

Statham, F.R., *South Africa as It Is* (London, 1897)

Tomasson, W.H., *With the Irregulars in the Transvaal and Zululand* (London, 1881)

Transvaal Independence Committee, *Deputation to Lord Kimberley and Mr. Grant Duff* (London, 1881)

The Transvaal War, 1881. Reprinted from the 'Natal Mercury' (Durban, n.d. [1881])

Vaughan, Sir J.L., *My Service in the Indian Army – and After* (London, 1904)

Verney, Capt E.H., *Four Years of Protest in the Transvaal* (London, 1881)

White, C.K., *To the Right Hon W.E. Gladstone MP* (London, 1881)

Winsloe, R.W.C., *Siege of Potchefstroom* (Dover, 1896)

Wood, Sir E., *From Midshipman to Field Marshal* (London, 2nd edn, 1906), vol. II

Later edited, annotated and printed contemporary sources

Butterfield, P.H., ed., *War and Peace in South Africa 1879–1881: The Writings of Philip Anstruther and Edward Essex* (Melville, 1987)

Emery, F., *Marching over Africa: Letters from Victorian Soldiers* (London, 1986)

Eybers, G.W., ed., *Select Constitutional Documents Illustrating South African History 1795–1910* (London, 1918)

Laband, J., ed., *Lord Chelmsford's Zululand Campaign 1878–1879* (Stroud, 1994)

Preston, A., ed., *Sir Garnet Wolseley's South African Journal 1879–80: Zululand/Transvaal: Military Campaigns/Cetywayo/Sekukhuni/Negotiations with Boer Committee* (Cape Town, 1973)

Trollope, A., *South Africa* (1878; reprint with introduction and notes by Davidson, J.H., Cape Town, 1973)

Tylden, G., trans., 'Majuba. A contemporary Boer account (Stephanus Roos)', *Journal for the Society for Army Historical Research*, 17 (1938)

Later printed sources

Articles and conference papers

Adlam, Lt A.M., 'Die Pers as Bron oor die Geskiedenis van die Eerste Vryheidsoorlog', *Militaria*, 1, 11 (1981)

Bond, B., 'The Disaster at Majuba Hill, 1881', *History Today* (July 1965)

Book feature, 'Norman Etherington's *The Great Trek*', *South African Historical Journal*, 46 (May 2002)

Chadwick, G.A., 'War Graves Registers, Monuments, Headstones and Crosses with Special Reference to the War of 1880–1881', *Militaria*, 1, 11 (1981)

Conradie, D., 'The Vierkleur and the Union Jack in the 1880–1881 War between the Zuid-Afrikaansche Republiek and Britain', *Militaria*, 1, 11 (1981)

Cuthbertson, G. and Jeeves, A., 'The Many-Sided Struggle for Southern Africa, 1899–1902', *South African Historical Journal*, 41 (Nov. 1999)

Cox, E., 'The First King's Dragoon Guards in South Africa, 1879–1881', *Military History Journal*, 6, 5 (June 1985)

Friend, D., 'Training Doctrines of the Staatsartillerie of the Zuid-Afrikaansche Republiek', *Military History Journal*, 11, 5 (June 2000)

Gough Palmer, M., 'The Besieged Towns of the First Boer War, 1880–1881', *Military History Journal*, 5, 2 (December 1980)

Hall, Maj D.D., 'The Artillery of the First Anglo-Boer War 1880–1881', *Military History Journal*, 5, 2 (December 1980)

Huisamen, Lt J.M., 'Afrikaans en die Eerste Vryheidsoorlog', *Militaria*, 1, 11 (1981)

Jordan, R., comp., 'The Battle of Majuba: Telegrams of 27 February 1881', *Military History Journal*, 5, 2 (December 1980)

Jordan, R., 'The Siege of Pretoria, 1880–1881', *Military History Journal*, 5, 2 (December 1980)

Kinsey, H.W., 'Nourse's Horse at Elandsfontein Ridge, 16 January 1881', *Military History Journal*, 5, 2 (December 1980)

Laband, J., 'An Empress in Zululand', *Natalia*, 30 (December 2000)

Laband, J., ' "The Danger of Divided Command": British Civil and Military Disputes over the Conduct of the Zululand Campaigns of 1879 and 1888', *Journal of the Society for Army Historical Research*, 81, 328 (Winter 2003)

Lambert, J., 'South African British? Or Dominion South Africans? The Evolution of an Identity in the 1910s and 1920s', *South African Historical Journal*, 43 (November 2000)

Machanik, F., 'Firearms and Firepower: First War of Independence, 1880–1881', *Military History Journal*, 5, 2 (December 1980)

Nasson, B., 'The War One Hundred Years On' (paper delivered at the Rethinking the South African War Conference, UNISA, August 1998)

Nöthling, Cmdt C.J., 'Military Commanders of the War (1880–1881)', *Militaria*, 1, 11 (1981)

Orford, J., 'The Siege of Potchefstroom, 16 December 1880–21 March 1881', *Military History Journal*, 5, 2 (December 1980)

Otto, Brig W., 'Die Slag van Majuba, 27 Februarie 1881', *Militaria*, 1, 11 (1981)

Theron, B., 'Theophilus Shepstone and the Transvaal Colony, 1877–1879', *Kleio*, 34 (2002)

Tomlinson, R., 'Fort Tullichewan, Pretoria: An Exercise in Site Excavation and Historical Research', *Military History Journal*, 6, 5 (June 1985)

Trapido, S., 'Aspects in the Transition from Slavery to Serfdom: the South African Republic 1842–1902', *University of London Institute of Commonwealth Studies Collected Seminar Papers No. 20: The Societies of Southern Africa in the 19th and 20th Centuries, Volume 6* (London, 1976)

Tylden, G., 'The British Army and the Transvaal, 1875 to 1885', *Journal of the Society of Army Historical Research*, 40 (1952)

Tylden, G., 'The Development of the Commando System in South Africa, 1715 to 1922', *Africana Notes and News*, 13 (March 1958–December 1959)

Van Heyningen, E., 'The Voices of Women in the South African War', *South African Historical Journal*, 41 (November 1999)

Van Jaarsveldt, Capt A.E., 'Pretoria gedurende die Eerste Vryheidsoorlog', *Militaria*, 1, 11 (1981)

Van Zyl, M.C., 'Die Stryd tussen Boer en Brit in Transvaal 1877–1881', *Military History Journal*, 5, 2 (December 1980)

Visser, Capt G.E., 'Die Eerste Vryheidsoorlog: Enkele Aspekte met die Britse Sening van die Boere en die Verskille tussen Boer en Brit', *Militaria*, 1, 11 (1981)

Von Moltke, Capt R., 'Wapentuig van die Eerste Vryheidsoorlog', *Militaria*, 1, 11 (1981)

Books and pamphlets

Barthorp, M., *The Anglo-Boer Wars: The British and the Afrikaners 1815–1902* (London, 1987)

Beckett, I., *The Victorians at War* (Hambledon, London and New York, 2003)

Bennett, I., *A Rain of Lead. The Siege and Surrender of the British at Potchefstroom 1880–1881* (London, 2001)

Benyon, J., *Proconsul and Paramountcy in South Africa: The High Commission, British Supremacy and the Sub-Continent 1806–1910* (Pietermaritzburg, 1980)

Bond, B., ed., *Victorian Military Campaigns* (London, 1967)

Bonner, P., *Kings, Commoners and Concessionaires: The Evolution and Dissolution of the Nineteenth-Century Swazi State* (Johannesburg, 1983)

Boyden, P.B., Guy, A.J. and Harding, M., eds, *'Ashes and Blood': The British Army in South Africa 1795–1914* (London, 1999)

Burke, J., *An Intimate History of Killing: Face-to-Face Killing in Twentieth Century Warfare* (London, 2000)

Cameron, T. and Spies, S.B., eds, *An Illustrated History of South Africa* (Johannesburg, 1986)

Carrington, C.E., *The British Overseas. Exploits of a Nation of Shopkeepers* (Cambridge, 1950)

Carver, Field Marshal Lord, *The National Army Museum Book of the Boer War* (London, 1999)

Castle, I., *Majuba 1881: The Hill of Destiny* (London, 1996)

Chandler, D.G. and Becket, I., eds, *The Oxford History of the British Army* (Oxford, 2003)

Cock, J., *Colonels and Cadres: War and Gender in South Africa* (Cape Town, 1991)

Cope, R., *Ploughshare of War: The Origins of the Anglo-Zulu War of 1879* (Pietermaritzburg, 1999)

Crouch, J. and Knight, I.J., eds, *Forged in Strong Fires: The Transvaal War 1881. A V.M.S. Centenary Publication* (Chippenham, 1981)

Davenport, T.R.H., *The Afrikaner Bond. The History of a South African Political Party, 1880–1911* (Cape Town, 1966)

Davenport, T.R.H., *South Africa: A Modern History* (Toronto and Buffalo, 4th edn, 1991)

Davenport, T.R.H. and Hunt, K.S., eds, *The Right to the Land* (Claremont, 1974)

Davenport, T.R.H. and Saunders, C., *South Africa: A Modern History* (Basingstoke and New York, 5th edn, 2000)

De Kock, W.J., ed., *Dictionary of South African Biography* (Cape Town, 1968, 1972), vols I, II

Delius, P., *The Land Belongs to Us: The Pedi Polity, the Boers and the British in the Nineteenth-Century Transvaal* (Johannesburg, 1983)

Dennis, P. and Grey, J., eds, *The Boer War: Army, Nation and Empire* (Canberra, 2000)

Duxbury, G.R., *David and Goliath: The First War of Independence, 1880–1881* (Johannesburg, 1981)

Eldredge, E.A. and Morton, F., eds, *Slavery in South Africa: Captive Labour on the Dutch Frontier* (Boulder, CO, San Francisco, CA, Oxford and Pietermaritzburg, 1994)

Etherington, N., *The Great Treks: The Transformation of Southern Africa, 1815–1854* (Great Britain: Harlow, 2001)

Fuller, J.F.C., *The Last of the Gentlemen's Wars* (London, 1937)

Glendinning, V., *Trollope* (London, 1993)

Gooch, J., ed., *The Boer War: Direction, Experience and Image* (London and Portland, OR, 2000)

Goodfellow, C.F., *Great Britain and South African Confederation 1870–1881* (Cape Town, 1966)

Hall, C., ed., *Cultures of Empire: Colonizers in Britain and the Empire in the Nineteenth and Twentieth Centuries: A Reader* (New York, 2000)

Hattersley, A.F., *An Illustrated Social History of South Africa* (Cape Town, 1973)

Haycock, R. and Neilson, K., eds, *Men, Machines and War* (Waterloo, 1988)

Haythornthwaite, P.J., *The Colonial Wars Source Book* (London, 2000)

Holmes, R., ed., *The Oxford Companion to Military History* (Oxford, 2001)

Hutchinson, Walter, ed., *Hutchinson's Story of the British Nation. A Connected, Pictorial & Authoritative History of the British Peoples from the Earliest Times to the Present Day* (London, 1923)

Judd, D. and Surridge, K., *The Boer War* (London, 2002)

Keegan, T.J., *Colonial South Africa and the Origins of the Racial Order* (Cape Town, Charlottesville, VA and London, 1996)

Knight, I., *Boer Wars (1) 1836–1898* (London, 1996)

Knight, I., *Go to Your God like a Soldier: The British Soldier Fighting for Empire, 1837–1902* (London, 1996)

Laband, J., *Kingdom in Crisis: The Zulu Response to the British Invasion of 1879* (Manchester, 1992)

Laband, J., *The Rise and Fall of the Zulu Nation* (London, 1997)

Laband, J., *The Atlas of the Later Zulu Wars 1883–1888* (Pietermaritzburg, 2001)

Laband, J. and Haswell, R., eds, *Pietermaritzburg 1838–1988: A New Portrait of an African City* (Pietermaritzburg, 1988)

Laband, J. and Knight, I., *The War Correspondents: The Anglo-Zulu War* (Stroud, 1996)

Laband, J. and Thompson, P., *The Illustrated Guide to the Anglo-Zulu War* (Pietermaritzburg, 2nd edn 2004)

Laband, J. and Thompson, P. with Henderson, S., *The Buffalo Border 1879: The Anglo-Zulu War in Northern Natal* (Durban, 1983)

Labuschange, P., *Ghostriders of the Anglo-Boer War (1899–1902): The Role and Contribution of Agterryers* (Pretoria, 1999)

Lamar, H. and Thompson, L., eds, *The Frontier in History: North America and Southern Africa Compared* (New Haven, CT and London, 1981)

Lehmann, J.H., *The First Boer War* (London, 1972)

Le May, G.H.L., *The Afrikaners: An Historical Interpretation* (Oxford, 1995)

Lowry, D., ed., *The South African War Reappraised* (Manchester, 2000)

Lynn, J.A., *Battle. A History of Combat and Culture from Ancient Greece to Modern America* (Boulder, CO and Oxford, 2003)

MacKinnon, A.S., *The Making of South Africa: Culture and Politics* (Upper Saddle River, NJ, 2004)

Marks, S. and Atmore, A., eds, *Economy and Society in Pre-Industrial South Africa* (London, 1980)

Mason, P., *A Matter of Honour: An Account of the Indian Army, its Officers and Men* (Great Britain: Harmondsworth, 1976)

Matthew, H.C.G., *Gladstone 1875–1898* (Oxford, 1995)

Maylam, P., *A History of the African People of South Africa: From the Early Iron Age to the 1970s* (Claremont, 1986)

Morley, J., *The Life of William Ewart Gladstone* (London, 1906), vol. II

Meintjes, J., *The Commandant-General: The Life and Times of Petrus Jacobus Joubert of the South African Republic 1831–1900* (Cape Town, 1971)

Melville, Col C.H., *Life of General the Rt Hon. Sir Redvers Buller V.C., G.C.B., G.C.M.G.* (London, 1923), vol II

Morrell, R., ed., *Changing Men in Southern Africa* (Pietermaritzburg, 2001)

Morris, J., *Heaven's Command: An Imperial Progress* (Harmondsworth, 1979)

Nasson B., *The South African War 1899–1902* (London, 1999)

Newbolt, Sir H., *Collected Poems 1897–1907* (London, Edinburgh and New York, n.d.)

Orford, J., *95 Days: The Siege of the Fort at Potchefstroom 16th December, 1880–21st March, 1881* (Potchefstroom, 1973)

Packenham, T., *The Boer War* (Johannesburg and London, 1979)

Porter, A., ed., *The Oxford History of the British Empire. Volume III: The Nineteenth Century* (Oxford, 2001)

Ransford, O.N., *The Battle of Majuba Hill: The First Boer War* (London, 1967)

Robbins, K., *Great Britain: Identities, Institutions and the Idea of Britishness* (London and New York, 1998)

Roussouw, F., comp., *A South African Bibliography to the Year 1925. Volume 6: Subject and Title Indexes* (Cape Town, 1997)

Roussouw, F. and Vockerodt, comps, *A South African Bibliography to the Year 1925. Volume 5: Supplement* (Cape Town, 1991)

Saunders, C., ed., *Reader's Digest Illustrated History of South Africa: The Real Story* (Cape Town, 3rd edn, 1994)

Schreuder, D.M., *Gladstone and Kruger. Liberal Government and Colonial 'Home Rule' 1880–85* (London and Toronto, 1969)

Smith, I.R., *The Origins of the South African War 1899–1902* (Harlow, 1996)

South African Library, eds, *A South African Bibliography to the Year 1925. Being a Revision and Continuation of Sidney Mendelssohn's* South African Bibliography *(1910)* (Cape Town and London, 1979), 4 vols

Spiers, E.M., *The Army and Society 1815–1914* (London, 1980)

Spiers, E.M., *The Late Victorian Army, 1868–1902* (Manchester and New York, 1992)

Strachan, H., *European Armies and the Conduct of War* (London, 1983)

Templin, J. Alton, *Ideology on a Frontier: The Theological Foundation of Afrikaner Nationalism, 1652–1910* (Westport, CT and London, 1984)

Thompson, L., *A History of South Africa* (New Haven, CT and London, 1990)

Usherwood, P. and Spencer-Smith, J., *Lady Butler: Battle Artist 1846–1933* (London, 1989)

Vandervort, B., *Wars of Imperial Conquest in Africa 1830–1914* (London, 1998)

Van Jaarsveld, F.A., tr. Metrowich, F.R., *The Awakening of Afrikaner Nationalism 1868–1881* (Cape Town, 1961)

Van Jaarsveld, F.A., Van Rensburg, A.P.J. and Stals, W.A., eds, *Die Eerste Vryheidsoorlog: Van Verset en Geweld tot Skikking deur Onderhanderling 1877–1884* (Pretoria and Cape Town, 1980)

Walker, E.A., *The Great Trek* (London, 3rd edn, 1948)

Walker, E.A., ed., *The Cambridge History of the British Empire, Volume VIII: South Africa, Rhodesia and the High Commission Territories* (Cambridge, 1963)

Walker, E.A., *A History of Southern Africa* (London, 1969)

Warwick, P., *Black People and the South African War 1899–1902* (Cambridge, 1983)

Wilson, M. and Thompson, L., eds. *The Oxford History of South Africa* (Oxford, 1969 and 1971), vols I and II

Woodward, Sir L., *The Age of Reform 1815–1870* (Oxford, 2nd edn, 1962)

Worden, N., *The Making of Modern South Africa* (Oxford, 3rd edn, 2000)

Worsfold, B., *Sir Bartle Frere. A Footnote to the History of the British Empire* (London, 1923)

Wulfsohn, L., *Rustenburg at War: The Story of Rustenburg and its Citizens in the First and Second Anglo-Boer Wars* (Rustenburg, 1987)

Theses

Coghlan, M., 'The Natal Volunteers in the Anglo-Boer War, September 1899 to July 1902: Reality and Perception' (unpublished PhD thesis, University of Natal, 2002)

Davey, A.M., 'The Siege of Pretoria 1880–1881', *Archives Year Book for South African History, Nineteenth Year, Volume 1* (Parow, 1956)

Dominy, G., 'The Imperial Garrison in Natal with Special Reference to Fort Napier 1843–1914: Its Social, Cultural and Economic Impact' (unpublished PhD thesis, University of London, 1995)

Grobler, J.E.H., 'Die Eerste Vryheidsoorlog, 1880–1881: 'n Militêr-Historiese Benadering' (unpublished PhD thesis, University of Pretoria, 1981)

Paterson, H., 'The Military Organisation of the Colony of Natal, 1881–1910' (unpublished MA thesis, University of Natal, 1985)

Pitout, D.N., 'Die Slag van Amajuba, 27 Februarie 1881' (unpublished MA thesis, University of Pretoria, 1980)

Theron-Bushell, B.M., 'Puppet on an Imperial String: Owen Lanyon in South Africa, 1875–1881' (unpublished D. Litt et Phil. thesis, University of South Africa, 2002)

Index